Retirement Issues, Plans and Lifestyles

snova
New York

Retirement Issues, Plans and Lifestyles

Retirement Security: IRAs, Savings and Financial Risks
Sofia E. Paulsen (Editor)
ISBN: 978-1-53616-506-7
eBook ISBN: 978-1-53616-507-4

Retirement Savings and Security
Trevor Barton (Editor)
ISBN: 978-1-53615-647-8
eBook ISBN: 978-1-53615-648-5

Social Security Disability: Background, Benefits and Programs
Michael Dimitriadis (Editor)
ISBN: 978-1-53615-747-5
eBook ISBN: 978-1-53615-748-2

Retirement: Issues, Benefits and Developments
Thomas M. Osborne (Editor)
ISBN: 978-1-53615-703-1
eBook ISBN: 978-1-53615-704-8

More information about this series can be found at
https://novapublishers.com/product-category/series/retirement-issues-plans-and-lifestyles/

Ryan M. Powell
Editor

Retirement Strategies

Analysis of Policies, Investments, and Security

snova
New York

Library of Congress Cataloging-in-Publication Data

ISBN: 979-8-89530-366-5 (Softcover)\
ISBN: 979-8-89530-400-6 (eBook)

Published by Nova Science Publishers, Inc. † New York

Contents

Preface

One of the main ways Americans prepare for retirement is by investing in various financial assets. Their investment options include directly investing in stocks, bonds, and investment funds through individual brokerage accounts and indirectly investing through pension funds that invest on behalf of employees. Employer-sponsored pensions and individual retirement accounts (IRAs) are crucial sources of income security in retirement for American households.

This book examines the various investment options related to retirement and provides an overview of employer-sponsored pensions, IRAs, and state-facilitated retirement savings programs. By exploring these topics, we aim to offer a comprehensive understanding of the tools available for securing a financially stable retirement.

Chapter 1

Pensions and Individual Retirement Accounts (IRAs): An Overview*

Elizabeth A. Myers
John J. Topoleski
Paul S. Davies
and Katelin P. Isaacs

Summary

A pension is a voluntary benefit that employers can offer to assist employees in providing for their financial security in retirement. Pension plans receive a number of tax advantages and vary along a number of characteristics, such as whether the employer that sponsors the plan is in the public or private sector and whether the benefit is paid according to a specified formula (a defined benefit [DB] plan) or is based on funds that accumulate in a worker's account (a defined contribution [DC] plan). In 2021, nearly three-quarters (71%) of the U.S. civilian workforce had access to, and more than half (56%) participated in, pension plans at their workplaces.

The earliest pensions in what later became the United States were provided by several of the colonies or by the Continental Congress for disabled members of the military. The first private- sector pension plan appears to have been created by the American Express Company in 1875. In the public sector, the earliest pensions were provided by some cities for disabled police and firefighters. The first pension plan to cover general state employees began in Massachusetts in 1911. During this

* This is an edited, reformatted and augmented version of Congressional Research Service Publication No. R47119, dated June 1, 2022.

In: Retirement Strategies: Analysis of Policies, Investments, and Security
Editor: Ryan M. Powell
ISBN: 979-8-89530-366-5

time, pension plans had limited oversight or benefit protections at the federal or state level. In 1963, the bankruptcy of the Studebaker automobile company resulted in a number of plan participants receiving either a fraction of their promised benefits or losing their benefits entirely. The incident became the catalyst for the reform of legislation covering private-sector pensions, leading to the passage of the Employee Retirement Income Security Act of 1974 (ERISA, P.L. 93-406).

Since ERISA, an increasing number of private-sector workers have been covered by DC plans rather than DB plans. In 1984,the number of active participants in the private sector in DC plans surpassed the number of active participants in DB plans and, by 2019, was six times as large. In contrast, state and local government employees continue to be covered mostly by DBplans. More than 97% of current civilian federal employees participate in both a DB and a DC plan.

While pension plans are sponsored by employers, Individual Retirement Accounts (IRAs) are retirement savings accounts workers may establish independently at financial institutions. IRAs serve multiple purposes. Workers, including those without access to pension plans through their employers, may be eligible to save for retirement outside of the workplace through IRAs. Also, a worker can deposit DC savings, or a lump sum payment from a DB pension (if available), into an IRAat job change in a process called a *rollover*. Rollovers preserve the tax advantages of workers' DC savings. IRA-based retirement plans also allow employers to offer their employees a retirement savings option with minimal employer involvement.

In recent years, some states have authorized or implemented state-facilitated retirement savings programs for workers who donot have access to employer-sponsored plans. Most of the state-facilitated programs are IRA-based plans; others include retirement marketplaces and multiple-employer plans.

This report provides an overview of employer-sponsored pensions: both DB and DC plans sponsored by the federal, state, and local governments and employers in the private sector; IRAs (including IRA-based retirement plans); and state-facilitated retirement savings programs. The report provides context for understanding current legislative efforts to improve retirement security.

Introduction

A pension is a voluntary benefit offered by employers to assist employees in providing for their financial security in retirement. Savings in employer-sponsored pensions are one of three possible income sources in retirement, along with Social Security (a federal program that provides monthly cash benefits to most retired or disabled workers and their family members) and private savings.[1] Private savings include Individual Retirement Accounts (IRAs), state-facilitated retirement savings programs, and other non-IRA savings, such as annuities (see *Figure 1*).[2]

Source: CRS.

Figure 1. U.S. Retirement Income.

This report provides an overview of employer-sponsored pensions, IRAs (including IRA-based retirement plans), and state-facilitated retirement savings programs. Pension plans vary along a number of dimensions, such as whether the employer that sponsors the plan is in the public or private sector and whether the benefit is paid according to a specified formula or is based on

---

[1] Social Security also provides benefits for the eligible family members of insured deceased workers. More informationabout Social Security is available in CRS In Focus IF10426, *Social Security Overview*.

[2] Annuities are insurance products that provide regular—typically monthly—payments for a specified number of yearsor for an individual's and spouse's life, if married. Annuities can be purchased either as a lump sum or as an ongoing purchase and either as a standalone product, in a retirement plan, or in an IRA. For example, individuals can convert part or all of their retirement savings for monthly payments for life or use part or all of their regular retirement contributions to purchase annuities that will provide monthly payments in retirements. For more information, see Investor.gov, "Annuities," https://www.investor.gov/introduction-investing/investing-basics/glossary/annuities.

funds that accumulate in a worker's individual account. In 2021, nearly three-quarters (71%) of U.S. workers had access to, and more than half (56%) participated in, pension plans at theirworkplaces. Pensions and retirement policy is an area of ongoing congressional interest as lawmakers seek ways to improve the retirement system for both employers and employees.

History of Pensions

The earliest pensions in what later became the United States were provided by several of the colonies and then by the Continental Congress for disabled members of the military. The U.S. Army pension plan was funded out of general revenue (current benefits were paid from current government revenue) while the U.S. Navy pension plan was funded by prizes from captured ships. The prizes that funded the U.S. Navy pension plan were invested in an effort to provide aconsistent source of revenue for the plan.[3]

The first private-sector pension plan appears to have been created by the American Express Company in 1875. By 1925, about 400 pension plans covering about 4 million employees hadbeen established, mostly by large companies in the railroad and utility industries.[4] During the Second World War, wage and price controls prevented employers from using higher wages toattract scarce labor. Instead, an increasing number of employers offered other forms of compensation, such as pensions, to recruit and retain employees.[5]

The bankruptcy of the Studebaker automobile company in 1963 resulted in a number of pensionplan participants receiving either a fraction of their promised benefits or losing their benefits entirely. The incident became the catalyst for pension reform, eventually leading to the passage ofthe Employee Retirement Income Security Act of 1974 (ERISA, P.L. 93-406).[6] When ERISA

---

[3] As a result of poor investment returns, in 1841, Congress passed legislation that began paying Navy pensions from thegeneral fund of the U.S. Treasury again. See *Public Statutes at Large*, ed. Richard Peters, vol. 5 (Boston: Charles C. Little and James Brown, 1848), p. 440. See Robert L. Clark, Lee A. Craig, and Jack W. Wilson, *A History of Public Sector Pensions in the United States* (Pension Research Council, 2003).

[4] See Raymond Schmitt, *The Historical Development of the Private Pension System*, Congressional Research Service,72-77 ED, March 24, 1972, pp. 6-7.

[5] See Patrick W. Seaburn, "Evolution of Employer Provided Defined Benefit Pensions," Bureau of Labor Statistics,December 1991, https://www.bls.gov/mlr/1991/12/art3full.pdf.

[6] See James Wooten, "'The Most Glorious Story of Failure in the Business': The Studebaker-Packard Corporation andthe Origins of ERISA," in *The Employee Retirement Income Security Act of 1974: A Political History* (Berkley: University of California Press, 2005).

wasenacted, defined benefit (DB) pension plans had more participants than defined contribution (DC)pension plans did, though by 1984, the number of active participants in DC plans surpassed the number of active participants in DB plans and was six times as large in 2019.[7]

In the public sector, the earliest pensions were provided by some cities for disabled police and firefighters. The first pension plan to cover general state employees was in Massachusetts in 1911.[8] Because government workers were generally excluded from Social Security when it was created in 1935 due to concerns about the constitutionality of the federal government taxing state governments, and because some states already provided pensions for their employees, an increasing number of states created pension plans to cover their employees. By 1950, nearly halfof the largest state pension plans had been established.[9] State and local government employees continue to be covered mostly by DB pension plans.[10] Since the late 1990s, an increasing number of states and localities have modified their pension plans, with many offering hybrid *cash balance* plans or DC plans as alternatives or enhancements to traditional DB benefits.[11]

Congress passed the Civil Service Retirement Act of 1920 (P.L. 66-215) to provide pension benefits for federal employees. Federal employees were not covered by Social Security when itwas created in 1935 and remained outside of it until Congress passed the Social Security Amendments of 1983 (P.L. 98-21), which required all civilian federal employees hired after 1983 to

---

[7] Active participants are individuals who are earning credit under DB plans or are making, or are eligible to make, contributions to DC plans. See CRS In Focus IF12007, *A Visual Depiction of the Shift from Defined Benefit (DB) toDefined Contribution (DC) Pension Plans in the Private Sector*.

[8] See Clark, Craig, and Wilson, A History of Public Sector Pensions in the United States.

[9] Clark, Craig, and Wilson, A History of Public Sector Pensions in the United States.

[10] See, for example, Urban Institute, *State and Local Finance Initiative: State and Local Government Pensions*, https://www.urban.org/policy-centers/cross-center-initiatives/state-and-local-finance-initiative/projects/state-and-local-backgrounders/state-and-local-government-pensions.

[11] A cash balance plan is a type of DB plan in which participants' benefits are calculated using a formula, but the benefit is expressed as an account balance that is paid as an annuity (or lump sum, if offered by the plan). See Alicia H.Munnell, Jean-Pierre Aubry, and Mark Cafarelli, *Defined Contribution Plans in the Public Sector: An Update*, Center for Retirement Research at Boston College, April 2014, https://crr.bc.edu/wp-content/uploads/2014/04/SLP_37-1.pdf; Jean-Pierre Aubry and Kevin Wandrei, *Have Localities Shifted Away from Traditional Defined Benefit Plans?*, Center for State and Local Government Excellence, April 2020, https://slge.org/wp-content/uploads/2020/04/local-dc-brief- april-2020.pdf.

participate in Social Security.[12] As a result, the Federal Employees' Retirement System (FERS)Act of 1986 (P.L. 99-335) created a new retirement plan that is fully integrated with Social Security. The FERS benefit package has three elements: Social Security benefits; the FERS DB pension (which provides smaller benefits than the CSRS standalone DB pension does); and the Thrift Savings Plan (TSP), a DC pension.[13]

Types of Retirement Plans

Pension plans can be classified along several dimensions, such as whether the employee receives a monthly payment in retirement (*DB pensions*) or accrues funds in an individual account (*DC pensions*), whether the plan sponsor is a *private-sector* or *public-sector* employer, and whether the plan is *sponsored by one employer* or *more than one employer.*

Pension discussions also frequently include *IRAs*, which are tax-advantaged accounts for individuals to save for retirement outside of employer-sponsored plans. Often individuals with savings in DC plans, or with lump sum payments from DB plans, roll over their savings to IRAs at job change or retirement. In addition, Congress has authorized several types of IRA-based retirement plans that employers can offer, such as SIMPLE IRAs and SEP-IRAs (described below). In IRA-based plans, employers establish IRAs for employees at financial institutions.

Employers may also offer payroll deduction IRAs, which are available to employers who want toprovide their employees a retirement savings option while limiting employer involvement. In addition, some states have established state-facilitated retirement savings programs, often IRA-based, for private-sector employees.

---

[12] The Servicemen's and Veterans' Survivor Benefits Act of 1956 (P.L. 84-881) granted Social Security wage credits for all military service performed before 1957 and brought military service performed after 1956 fully under the Social Security Act. Since 1957, military service has been subject to Social Security payroll taxes and has been counted as covered employment for all Social Security benefits. See CRS Report 98-810, *Federal Employees' Retirement System:Benefits and Financing.*

[13] See CRS Report 98-810, Federal Employees' Retirement System: Benefits and Financing.

Defined Benefit and Defined Contribution Pension Plans

The two types of pension plans based on benefit structure are (1) plans in which participants typically receive their benefits as monthly payments in retirement (DB plans) and (2) plans in which participants' benefits accrue in individual savings accounts (DC plans).

Defined Benefit (DB) Plans

In DB plans (sometimes referred to as *traditional* pension plans), participants typically receive monthly payments in retirement based on a formula that uses either (1) a combination of length ofservice, accrual rate, and average of final years' salary; or (2) a flat dollar amount times the number of months or years in the plan.[14] Some plans offer participants the option to receive their benefits as a lump-sum amount.

Generally, DB plans are meant to be fully funded, meaning that sufficient funds are set aside in order to pay for promised future benefits. Employer contributions to a DB plan consist of benefits earned by participants during the year (called *normal cost*) and a portion of plan underfunding (for example, due to investment losses, called *amortization cost*).

Some DB plans require employee contributions. In 2011 (the most recent data available), 4% of private-sector workers with DB plans were in plans that required employee contributions.[15] In contrast, in 2021, 91% of state and local government workers in DB plans were in plans that required employee contributions.[16] This percentage has steadily increased since 2011, when 79% of state and local employees were in plans requiring employee contributions.[17]

---

[14] For example, a plan might specify that retirees receive an annual amount equal to (1) 1.5% of their pay for each yearof service, where the pay is the average of a worker's salary during a specified number of years (for example, a participant who worked for 30 years, with an average salary of $100,000 during his or her highest-paid five years, would receive $45,000 per year in retirement), or (2) $40 multiplied by the number of months worked in the plan (for example, a worker who worked for 30 years [i.e., 360 months] would receive $14,400 per year in retirement).

[15] See U.S. Department of Labor (DOL), Bureau of Labor Statistics (BLS), "National Compensation Survey: EmployeeBenefits in the United States, March 2011," Table 3, https://www.bls.gov/ncs/ebs/benefits/2011/ebbl0048.pdf.

[16] See BLS, " National Compensation Survey: Employee Benefits in the United States, March 2021," Table 4, https://www.bls.gov/ncs/ebs/benefits/2021/employee-benefits-in-the-united-states-march-2021.pdf.

[17] See BLS, "National Compensation Survey: Employee Benefits in the United States, March 2011," Table 3.

The DB plans that cover nearly all federal employees require employee contributions.

Cash Balance Plans

Instead of a traditional DB plan, some companies have established "hybrid" cash balance plans. Cash balance plans combine features of DB and DC plans: Participants' benefits are calculated using a formula, but the benefit is expressed as an account balance that is paid as an annuity (or lump sum, if offered by the plan). About 46% of DB plans in the private sector were cash balanceplans in 2019, and 30.6% of DB plan participants in 2019 were in cash balance plans.[18]

Defined Contribution (DC) Plans

In DC plans, workers are provided individual accounts funded by their own contributions, contributions from their employers, or both. The funds in the account may accrue investmentearnings, which can then be used as a source of income in retirement.

The type of DC plan that an employer may offer depends on the type of employer (for example, the types of plans offered by public-sector employers are different from those offered by private-sector employers), as well as the employer's choices regarding plan features (for example, private-sector employers have a number of types of DC plans they can offer). The plan sponsor has to make various decisions about plan features. These include, for example, whether to fund the accounts solely with employee contributions, solely with employer contributions, or with both; whether and how much to match employee contributions; and whether to allow distributions before retirement such as through hardship withdrawals or loans.

Employers may have several types of DC plans from which to choose, as outlined below:

- *401(k) plan.* A 401(k) plan allows employees to contribute a portion of their wages to their individual accounts. Employers can also contribute to the accounts as a match of the employee's contributions or as a profit-sharing contribution.

---

[18] The remainder were in traditional DB pension plans in which the benefit is expressed as a monthly payment in retirement. See DOL, *Private Pension Plan Bulletin*, Table A1, https://www.dol.gov/sites/dolgov/files/EBSA/researchers/statistics/retirement-bulletins/private-pension-plan-bulletins-abstract-2019.pdf.

- Employers must demonstrate that their 401(k) plans benefit a wide variety ofemployees (and not just well-paid employees) through a process called *nondiscrimination testing.*[19]
- Additionally, there are several types of 401(k) plans available to certainemployers:
  - *Safe Harbor 401(k)* plans are available to employers of any size. These plansare exempt from nondiscrimination testing, provided they follow certain contribution rules.
  - *SIMPLE 401(k)* plans are available to employers with 100 or fewer employees and are exempt from nondiscrimination requirements. Employers are required to make either (1) matching contributions up to 3% of each employee's pay or (2) nonelective contributions of 2% of each employee's pay.
  - *Solo 401(k)* plans cover a business owner with no employees (or the owner and spouse, if applicable).
- *Profit-sharing plans and stock bonus plans.* In a profit-sharing plan, an employer makes a contribution to each eligible participant's account based on a formula established by the employer.[20] Employee contributions are not permitted. Profit-sharing plans provide flexibility to employers because they can choose whether to contribute to employees' accounts each year. Profit-sharing contributions do not need to be tied to a company's profits, if any. A stock bonusplan is a type of profit-sharing plan in which employer contributions are paid in employer stock rather than cash. Profit-sharing plans and stock bonus plans mayhave a 401(k) component, in which case employee contributions are allowed.
- *Money purchase plan.* In a money purchase plan, the employer contributes an amount to each eligible employee's account as a percentage of compensation. Employees are not permitted to contribute to the plan.
- *Employee stock ownership plan (ESOP).* An ESOP is a type of DC plan inwhich the investments are primarily in employer stock.

---

[19] Nondiscrimination tests are used to demonstrate that the plans are being used by both highly compensated employeesand rank-and-file employees.

[20] For more information, see Internal Revenue Service (IRS), "Choosing a Retirement Plan: Profit-Sharing Plan," https://www.irs.gov/retirement-plans/choosing-a-retirement-plan-profit-sharing-plan.

- *403(b) plan.* A 403(b) plan (or tax-sheltered annuity plan) is a pension plan offered by public schools, 501(c)(3) tax-exempt organizations, and churches. Investment options for 403(b) plans were originally restricted to annuity contracts until 1974, after which investments in mutual funds were also permitted.
- *457(b) plan.* State and local governments and tax-exempt 501(c)(3) employers can establish 457(b) plans. While they share many features with 401(k) plans, they differ in some respects—for example, investments in 457(b) plans are limited to purchases of annuity contracts and mutual funds, and some withdrawalrules differ.

Public-Sector Pension Plans

Both private- and public-sector employers offer pension plans to their employees.[21] Some provisions of the Internal Revenue Code (IRC, Title 26 of the *U.S. Code*) apply to both private- and public-sector plans, while some apply to one. For example, taxes on most distributions are deferred until the funds are received—this provision applies to both private- and public-sector plans. Public-sector employers are more likely to offer DB plans, while private-sector employers are more likely to offer DC plans.

To try to protect the interests of pension plan participants and beneficiaries, Congress enacted ERISA (P.L. 93-406). ERISA covers most private-sector pension plans and is included in both theIRC and in the Labor Code (Title 29 of the *U.S. Code*). State and local pension plans are exempt from ERISA, and thus, ERISA provisions in the IRC (such as funding requirements for DB plans)and in the Labor Code (such as standards of conduct for individuals who make decisions within a plan) do not apply. However, state and local plans are subject to certain pre-ERISA IRC provisions, such as vesting requirements (how long a person must work for an employer to be covered) in place as of September 1, 1974.

State and Local Government Pension Plans

Most public-sector employees are covered by pension plans. Those covered are more likely to becovered by DB plans than by DC plans. In March 2021, 92% of all state and local government workers had *access* to a pension plan,

[21] Plans sponsored by nonprofit companies are included in the discussion of private-sector pensions.

with 86% having access to DB plans and 38% having access to DC plans.[22] In the same month, 82% of state and local government workers *participated* in a pension plan.[23]

State and Local DB Plans

In FY2020, state and local government entities—including municipalities, townships, counties, school districts, and special districts—administered 5,340 DB plans with 33.2 million participantscovering workers such as police officers, firefighters, teachers, and city and state government employees.[24] Most participants are in the largest DB plans: 95% of state and local plan participants are in the 210 largest state and local DB plans (119 state, 91 local).[25]

While nearly all private-sector workers are covered by Social Security, 28.4% of state and localDB plan participants were *not* covered by Social Security in 2018.[26] The states with the largest *number* of state and local government employees not covered by Social Security in 2018 were California, Texas, Ohio, Illinois, and Massachusetts.[27] The states with the highest *percentage* of state and local government employees not covered by Social Security in 2018 were Ohio, Massachusetts, Nevada, Louisiana, and Colorado.[28] Most noncovered local government employees are police officers, firefighters, and teachers.[29]

State and local plans are governed by state laws, contract law, and/or state constitutions, whichprovide protections for accrued and prospective benefits. Accrued benefits in many states are protected from the beginning of

---

[22] Total does not sum to 100% because some workers have access to both types of plans.

[23] Among state and local government workers, 75% participated in DB plans and 18% participated in DC plans in March 2021. See BLS, *National Compensation Survey: Employee Benefits in the United States, March 2021*, September 2021, state and local government tables, Table 2, https://www.bls.gov/ncs/ebs/benefits/2021/home.htm.

[24] The fiscal year for most states begins on July 1. See U.S. Census Bureau, *2020 Annual Survey of Public Pensions: State and Local Tables*, https://www.census.gov/data/tables/2020/econ/aspp/aspp-historical-tables.html.

[25] Center for Retirement Research at Boston College, "Public Plans Data," https://publicplansdata.org/public-plans- database.

[26] See CRS Report R46961, Social Security Coverage of State and Local Government Employees.

[27] Ibid.

[28] Ibid.

[29] IRS Publication 963, *Federal-State Reference Guide*, Rev. 7-2020, p. 1, https://www.irs.gov/pub/irs-pdf/p963.pdf.

employment or once plan vesting requirements have been met.Future benefit accruals for current participants are typically protected in many states as well.

Cost-of-living adjustments (COLAs) are generally less protected than benefit accruals.[30] Between 2009 and 2018, DB pension systems in most states implemented reforms to improve plan funding, including increased employee contribution rates, reduced benefit levels, and reduced COLAs. Given the pension protections mentioned above, many of these reforms primarily affect new hires.[31]

State and Local DC Plans

In March 2021, 38% of all state and local government workers had access to DC plans and 18%participated in DC plans.[32] State and local DC plans had about $500 billion in assets in 2020.[33] Since the financial crisis and recession of 2007-2009, states and localities have modified their pension plans, with many offering hybrid cash balance plans or DC plans as alternatives or enhancements to traditional DB plans.[34] In 2019, 18 states offered retirement benefits other thansole DB plans. Between 2001 and 2018, the proportion of local governments offering retirementbenefits outside traditional DB plans increased from 11% to 19%.[35]

Depending on the employer, state and local DC plan types include 401(a), 401(k), 403(b), and 457(b) plans. Employee participation and contributions may be mandatory or optional, dependingon the structure of the plan as determined by the employer.[36] A *401(a) plan* may be available to state and local government workers as part of a DB-DC combination plan or a hybrid cash balance plan.[37] A *403(b) plan* may be offered to employees of public

---

[30] American Academy of Actuaries Pension Webinar Series, Retirement Plan Coverage in America Part Two: Focuson Public Pension Plans, April 23, 2020.

[31] Keith Brainard and Alex Brown, *Spotlight on Significant Reforms to State Retirement Systems*, National Association of State Retirement Administrators, December 2018, https://www.nasra.org/files/Spotlight/Significant%20Reforms.pdf.

[32] BLS, *National Compensation Survey: Employee Benefits in the United States, March 2021*, state and localgovernment tables, Table 2.

[33] See CRS Insight IN11659, *U.S. Retirement Assets in 2020.*

[34] Munnell, Aubry, and Cafarelli, *Defined Contribution Plans in the Public Sector.*

[35] Aubry and Wandrei, *Have Localities Shifted Away from Traditional Defined Benefit Plans?*

[36] State and local government 401(k) plans are legacy plans that were implemented before the Tax Reform Act of 1986,after which the implementation of such plans was prohibited. National Association of State Retirement Administrators, *Defined Contribution Plans Administered by State Retirement Systems or Available to State Employees*, April 2019, https://www.nasra.org/files/Topical%20Reports/DC%20plans/statewidedcplans.pdf.

[37] MissionSquare Retirement, "401(a) Money Purchase Plan," https://www.icmarc.org/products-and-services/ 401%28a%29-defined-contribution-plans.html. PRRL, "The State of Public

schools, churches, and certain charitable tax-exempt entities.[38] A *457(b) plan* is a voluntary, supplementary DC savingsvehicle, often offered to state and local government employees in conjunction with a traditional DB pension.[39]

Federal Pension Plans[40]

In its role as an employer, the federal government sponsors a number of DB and DC pension plans for civilian federal employees. The vast majority of these federal employees are covered bytwo DB plans funded through the Civil Service Retirement and Disability Fund: the older, now- closed Civil Service Retirement System (CSRS) and FERS. In addition, most employees are eligible to participate in a DC plan for federal employees, the TSP.

A number of smaller DB and DC plans have been established for certain employees within various agencies. There are a few additional plans that provide federal pensions to a non-trivialnumber of civilian federal employees. The Foreign Service Retirement and Disability System (FSRDS) and the Foreign Service Pension System (FSPS) are DB plans that cover Foreign Service Officers (FSOs) based on their date of hire in a similar way to CSRS and FERS. The Federal Reserve also operates its own DB and DC plans on behalf of its bank and board employees and certain other employees.[41]

Sector DC Plans: A First Look at the PRRL Database," February 25, 2021, https://www.nagdca.org/wp-content/uploads/2021/02/PRRL-Study_The-State-of-DC-Plans_A-First-Look_FINAL.pdf.

[38] IRS, *IRC 403(b) Tax-Sheltered Annuity Plans*, https://www.irs.gov/retirement-plans/irc-403b-tax-sheltered-annuity-plans.

[39] IRS, *457(b) Plans for State or Local Governments: Key Characteristics*, https://www.irs.gov/retirement-plans/457b-plans-for-state-or-local-governments-key-characteristics. IRS, *Comparison of Governmental 457(b) Plans and 401(k) Plans: Features and Corrections*, https://www.irs.gov/retirement-plans/comparison-of-governmental-457b-plans-and- 401k-plans-features-and-corrections.

[40] For additional information on pension plans for civilian federal employees, see CRS Report R47084, *Federal Retirement Plans: Frequently Asked Questions*. Military servicemembers are covered by a separate retirement system,which is not discussed in this report. For details on retirement benefits for military servicemembers, see CRS Report RL34751, *Military Retirement: Background and Recent Developments*.

[41] The Central Intelligence Agency Retirement and Disability System (CIARDS), which covered certain special category employees, has been closed to new entrants since 1984. Special category CIA employees first hired in 1984 orlater are covered by FERS (like other CIA employees). The last time that an audit of all "federal pension plans" (using a definition of *pension plan* subject to reporting requirements under P.L. 95-595) was in 1996 by the Government Accountability Office (GAO). This GAO investigation identified 34 federal DB plans and 17 federal DC plans. Some of these identified plans provide retirement coverage for federal entities that do not employ federal employees (e.g., employees of the Tennessee Valley Authority [Tennessee Valley Authority Retirement System]) or for individual employees (e.g., the former heads of the GAO [Comptrollers' General

Defined Benefit Plans for Civilian Federal Employees

Most civilian federal employees who were first hired before 1984 are covered by CSRS. CSRS was created by the Civil Service Retirement Act of 1920 (P.L. 66-215). Under CSRS, employeesdo not pay Social Security taxes or earn Social Security benefits but may be eligible for a standalone DB annuity if they make required contributions and meet age and years of service conditions.[42] Monthly CSRS retirement benefits are calculated based on a formula that multiplies years of service, the average of the highest three consecutive years of basic pay, and an accrual rate set out under statute.[43] Most civilian federal employees first hired in 1984 or later are coveredby FERS, which was created under the Federal Employees' Retirement System Act of 1986 (P.L. 99-335). All federal employees who are enrolled in FERS pay Social Security taxes and earn Social Security benefits along with a monthly DB annuity under FERS that is calculated using a formula similar to CSRS but replaces a lower amount of earnings than does the CSRS benefit dueto smaller benefit accrual rate.[44] The Office of Personnel Management administers CSRS and FERS, although employing agencies handle pre-retirement paperwork and provide retirement counseling to employees. According to the FY2020 Actuarial Report of the Civil Service Retirement and Disability Fund, at the beginning of FY2020, there were 70,000 active CSRS employees, 2,474,000 active FERS employees, 1,717,000 CSRS annuitants, and 966,000 FERSannuitants.[45]

Two additional federal pension plans run by the State Department provide retirement benefits to FSOs.[46] These plans are authorized under current law: FSRDS was created by Section 18 of the Foreign Service Act of 1924 (P.L. 68-135); FSPS was created by the Foreign Service Act of 1980(P.L. 96-465). Similar to the distinction between CSRS and FERS, FSRDS is the older

Retirement Plan]). See GAO, *Public Pensions: Summary of Federal Pension Plan Data*, AIMD-96-6, February 16, 1996, https://www.gao.gov/assets/aimd-96-6.pdf.

[42] For details on CSRS eligibility requirements, see CRS Report R47084, *Federal Retirement Plans: Frequently AskedQuestions*.

[43] For details on the calculation of CSRS benefits, see CRS Report R47084, *Federal Retirement Plans: FrequentlyAsked Questions*.

[44] For details on FERS eligibility requirements and benefit calculations, see CRS Report R47084, *Federal RetirementPlans: Frequently Asked Questions*.

[45] Office of Personnel Management, *Annual Report of the Board of Actuaries, Civil Service Retirement and DisabilityFund, Fiscal Year Ended September 30, 2020*, February 2021, p. 16, https://www.opm.gov/about-us/budget- performance/other-reports/fy-2020-csrdf-annual-report.pdf. Counts of annuitants include both retirees and survivors. FY2020 data are the most recently available program data from the Office of Personnel Management.

[46] Other employees of the State Department (i.e., civil service employees) are covered by CSRS or FERS, depending ontheir date of hire.

retirementsystem that is not integrated with Social Security and provides a standalone DB pension for FSOsfirst hired before 1984. FSPS, which is integrated with Social Security, provides a retirement benefit package to FSOs hired in 1984 or later. FSRDS and FSPS also have eligibility requirements and benefit calculations set out under current law.[47] According to the FY2020 Actuarial Report of the Foreign Service Retirement and Disability Fund, as of June 2020, there were 33 active FSRDS employees, 15,208 active FSPS employees, 9,209 FSRDS annuitants, and7,220 FSPS annuitants.[48]

Under general authority provided by Title 10 of the Federal Reserve Act of 1913 (P.L. 63-43), theFederal Reserve operates its own pension plan—the Federal Reserve System (FRS)—for employees of Federal Reserve Banks, the Office of Employee Benefits, the Federal Reserve Board of Governors, and the Consumer Financial Protection Bureau. The FRS provides a DB benefit, and covered employees also participate in Social Security. Unlike CSRS, FERS, FRDS, and FSPS, the FRB DB plan does not require any contributions from covered employees. As ofJanuary 1, 2020, there were 23,675 active FRB employees and 21,085 FRB annuitants.[49]

Defined Contribution Plans for Civilian Federal Employees

Federal employees enrolled in either CSRS or FERS may also contribute to the TSP, a DC pension plan similar to the 401(k) plans provided by many private-sector employers. However, only employees enrolled in FERS are eligible for employer matching contributions under TSP. Newly hired FERS employees are automatically enrolled in TSP and contribute 5% of their pay, though they have the option to decline participation or change the amount of their contributions. TSP participants may contribute up to the lesser of (1) their salary or (2) the DC contribution limit.[50] Employees covered by FERS receive an automatic 1% contribution and a match equal to 100% of the worker's first 3% of basic pay and 50% of the next 2% of basic pay.[51]

---

[47] For FRSDS, see 22 U.S.C. Chapter 52, Subchapter 8, Part I (i.e., 22 U.S.C. §§4041-4069); for FSPS, see 22 U.S.C.Chapter 52, Subchapter 8, Part II (i.e., 22 U.S.C. §§4071 et seq.).

[48] U.S. Department of State, Foreign Service Retirement and Disability Fund, Actuarial Report for the September 30,2020 Valuation Fiscal Year Ended September 30, 2020, December 8, 2020, Table 1.1, p. 4. Counts of annuitants include both retirees and survivors. FY2020 data are the most recently available program data from the State Department.

[49] CRS email communication with FRB, April 28, 2021.

[50] Contribution limits are available at IRS, "Retirement Topics—Contributions," https://www.irs.gov/retirement-plans/plan-participant-employee/retirement-topics-contributions.

[51] Participants are fully vested in the 1% agency automatic contributions to the TSP after three years (two years for congressional employees and executive-branch political appointees).

Also similar to CSRS and FERS, FSDRS employees may contribute to TSP, but only FSPS employees are eligible for TSP employer matching contributions. The Federal Reserve also operates its own DC plan: the Thrift Plan, which is distinct from TSP. Employees covered by FRS are eligible for employer matching under the Thrift Plan.

Private-Sector Pension Plans

Private-sector pension plans, which include those sponsored by nonprofit companies, are subject to ERISA and the tax code. ERISA sets standards that private-sector pension plans must follow with regard to (1) plan participation (who must be covered); (2) minimum vesting requirements (how long a person must work for an employer to be covered); (3) fiduciary duties (how individuals who oversee the plan must behave, such as operating the plan in the sole interest of plan participants); and (4) DB plan funding (how much employers must set aside to pay for future benefits).

Most pension-related legislation is targeted to private-sector plans, which are governed by ERISA, unlike public-sector plans.

Private-sector pension plans are classified by whether they are sponsored by one or more than one employer:

- A *single-employer plan* is sponsored by one employer.
- A *multiple-employer plan* has more than one participating employer but is *not* maintained as part of a collective bargaining agreement. These plans are generally treated as single-employer plans for the purposes of pension funding rules and federal disclosure requirements.
- A *multiemployer plan* is sponsored by more than one employer and maintainedas part of a collective bargaining agreement.

Single-employer plans, multiple-employer plans, and multiemployer plans can be either DB plans or DC plans. Private-sector DB plans are subject to funding rules found in ERISA, which outline requirements for how much an employer must contribute to the plan each year.[52] Typically, an employer's

---

See CRS Report RL30387, Federal Employees'Retirement System: The Role of the Thrift Savings Plan.

[52] DC plans do not have funding rules.

required contribution consists of the present value of benefits earned by participants in the year and a share, as determined by the law, of past amounts of underfunding (such as from a plan's investment losses).

Private-Sector DB Pension Plans

ERISA provisions in the IRC outline funding requirements for private-sector DB plans to ensurethat plans generally have sufficient funds from which to pay participants' earned benefits.

Separate funding rules apply to (1) single- and multiple-employer plans and (2) multiemployer plans. The Pension Benefit Guaranty Corporation (PBGC) insures private-sector DB plans.

PBGC is a government corporation that pays participants' benefits in the case of (1) employerbankruptcy in the case of single-employer plans or (2) plan insolvency in the case of multiemployer plans.

Single-Employer DB Plans

Most private-sector DB plans are single-employer plans.

Generally, plans must be fully funded. If a plan is underfunded, it must become fully funded overtime. This can be done through various methods, including increases in employer contributions orchanges to funding rules, such as increases in the discount rate that plans use to calculate benefitsor increases in the time period over which plans can amortize their losses.

A plan sponsor that has a fully funded DB plan can terminate the plan by purchasing annuities from an insurance company for all participants. Employers can also purchase annuities for a portion of the plan participants without terminating the plan (known as *de-risking*). This is designed to accomplish two goals: (1) relieve the employer of having to make up for potential investment losses in the future, and (2) reduce their per-participant premiums owed to the PBGC(described later in this report).[53]

Community Newspaper Plans. Community newspaper plans are those maintained by certain private community newspaper organizations that are family-controlled and have been in existencefor 30 or more years. Section 115 of the Setting Every Community up for Retirement Enhancement Act of 2019 (SECURE Act, enacted as Division O of the Further Consolidated Appropriations Act of 2020; P.L. 116-94) provided special funding rules for

---

[53] As described later in this report, when an underfunded DB plan terminates due to, for example, employer bankruptcy,PBGC becomes the trustee of the plan and pays the participants' benefits up to a statutory maximum.

pension plans operated by certain community newspapers that had no benefit increases for participants afterDecember 31, 2017.[54]

Multiple-Employer DB Plans

Private-sector multiple-employer DB plans are fairly uncommon. In 2019, Department of Labor(DOL) data indicated that there were 202 such plans (representing 0.4% of private-sector DB plans) covering 1.8 million participants.[55] The most widely known type of multiple-employer DB plan is the Cooperative and Small Employer Charity plan. These plans covered 539,000participants in 2017.[56]

Cooperative and Small Employer Charity (CSEC) Pension Plans. CSEC pension plans aregenerally multiple-employer pension plans established by certain cooperative and charitable organizations. Plans that meet the criteria to be CSEC plans follow special funding rules.

The Cooperative and Small Employer Charity Pension Flexibility Act of 2013 (P.L. 113-97) established funding rules for and provided a definition of CSEC pension plans.[57] Among other provisions, this act permanently exempted these plans from the Pension Protection Act's (P.L. 109-280) funding rules and outlined minimum funding standards for CSEC plans.[58] Plans mustindicate if they use the CSEC-specific funding rules in their required annual reporting to DOL.

Multiemployer DB Plans

While most private-sector DB plans are single-employer plans, about 3% are multiemployer plans(as of 2019).[59] Multiemployer DB plans covered 11.2 million union participants in 2019. They are commonly sponsored by employers in unionized industries such as construction, manufacturing, and transportation.

Workers in multiemployer plans might work for a number of employers over a career and wouldcontinue to earn pension benefits—provided those

---

[54] For these plans, the SECURE Act increased the interest rate to 8% and extended the amortization period from sevento 30 years.

[55] See DOL, *Private Pension Plan Bulletin*, Table B1.

[56] See the Appendix of CRS Report R46366, Single-Employer Defined Benefit Pension Plans: Funding Relief andModifications to Funding Rules.

[57] The sponsors of two single-employer DB plans are included as CSEC plans.

[58] The Pension Protection Act outlined new funding standards for pension plans. See CRS Report R46366, *Single- Employer Defined Benefit Pension Plans: Funding Relief and Modifications to Funding Rules.*

[59] See DOL, *Private Pension Plan Bulletin*, Table B1.

employers were signatories to the collective bargaining agreement. Multiemployer pension plans pool risk so that the withdrawal of a few employers from the plan typically does not place the plan in financial jeopardy.

Since 2001, the financial position of multiemployer plans has generally worsened, becoming, onaverage, 42% funded in 2019.[60] In 2018, about 10%-15% of participants were in plans that werelikely to become insolvent within 19 years.

Most recently, the American Rescue Plan Act of 2021 (P.L. 117-2) contained a provision authorizing federal financial assistance to qualifying financially troubled multiemployer plans.

For more information about multiemployer plans, see CRS Report R43305, *MultiemployerDefined Benefit (DB) Pension Plans: A Primer.*

Pension Benefit Guaranty Corporation (PBGC)

PBGC is a government corporation established by ERISA (P.L. 93-406). It was created to protect the pensions of participants and beneficiaries in private-sector pension plans by paying participants' benefits up to a statutory maximum if the pension plan is unable to do so. PBGC insures only private-sector DB plans and is chaired by the Secretary of Labor, with the Secretaries of the Treasury and Commerce serving as board members.

PBGC is required by ERISA to be self-supporting and receives no appropriations from federalgeneral revenue. ERISA Section 4002(g)(2) states that the "United States is not liable for any obligation or liability incurred by the corporation," and some Members of Congress have expressed reluctance about providing financial assistance to PBGC. The most reliable source of PBGC revenue is the premiums set by Congress and paid by the private-sector employers that sponsor DB pension plans. Other sources of income are (1) assets from terminated single-employer plans taken over by PBGC, (2) investment income, and (3) recoveries collected fromcompanies when they end underfunded pension plans.

PBGC operates two distinct insurance programs: one for single-employer DB plans and a secondfor multiemployer DB plans. PBGC maintains separate reserve funds for each program. In the case of a single-employer DB plan in financial distress, PBGC becomes the trustee of the plan and continues to pay participants' benefits up to a statutory maximum. PBGC does not become

[50] In the 1990s, multiemployer DB plans were generally well-funded: Except for 1996, these plans were funded at 90% or better. See PBGC, *PBGC 2019 Data Tables*, Table M-9, https://www.pbgc.gov/sites/default/files/2019-pension-data-tables.pdf.

trustee of multiemployer plans. An insolvent multiemployer plan does not have sufficient resources from which to pay promised benefits. PBGC provides financial assistance to insolvent multiemployer plans in the form of loans, although PBGC does not expect the loans to be repaid.As in the case of single-employer plans, participants in insolvent multiemployer DB plan receivetheir benefits up to a statutory maximum. The statutory maximums differ between single and multiemployer plans. For more information on PBGC, see CRS Report 95-118, *Pension Benefit Guaranty Corporation (PBGC): A Primer.*

PBGC also operates the Special Financial Assistance (SFA) program for multiemployer DB plans. Section 9704 in Title IX, Subtitle H, of the American Rescue Plan Act of 2021 (P.L. 117-2) provides financial assistance to qualifying financially troubled multiemployer DB plans. Eligibleplans may apply for SFA through December 31, 2025. If approved, the amount of SFA that an eligible plan receives is the amount needed to pay participants' full plan benefits through the 2051 plan year. For more information about SFA, see CRS In Focus IF11765, *Special FinancialAssistance to Multiemployer Plans*.

Private-Sector DC Plans

Over the past five decades, private-sector employees have become less likely to be covered by DB pensions and more likely to be covered by DC pensions.[61] This general shift occurred for a number of possible reasons. First, employer costs are generally higher for DB plans than for DCplans, because the benefit in a DB plan is typically funded entirely by the employer, while a smaller portion of the typical DC plan benefit is from employer contributions. Second, from an employer's perspective, contributions to DC plans tend to be a more predictable cost than contributions to DB plans are. This is because employer contributions to DB plans may includeadditional contributions to make up for investment losses, whereas in DC plans employer contributions are typically based on a set formula that uses employee compensation.

Third, DC plans may be easier to administer than DB plans are. DB plan actuaries determine thevalue of benefits earned by participants in a year and how much the plan must set aside to fund those benefits, incorporating factors

[61] For an illustration of this shift, see CRS In Focus IF12007, A Visual Depiction of the Shift from Defined Benefit (DB)to Defined Contribution (DC) Pension Plans in the Private Sector.

such as likely retirement ages and mortality rates. DC plansdo not use any of these actuarial projections.

For some employees, DC plans may be preferable to DB plans because DC plan account balancesare portable. When individuals change jobs, they can transfer (i.e., roll over) their account balances to IRAs or, often, to their new employers' plans. In contrast, DB plan benefits are not portable, and the benefit formula typically takes into account the number of years a worker has worked for an employer. Employees who change jobs and might earn benefits in several plans do not accumulate the same benefits as employees who stay with one employer and remain in a single plan. On the other hand, workers have more decisions to make in DC plans, such as the amount to contribute, investments to choose, and how much and how often to withdraw funds in retirement. In addition, retirees with DC plans face the risk of outliving their assets. Retirees receiving DB plan benefits do not face this risk; DB plan payments continue for the life of theparticipant and, if applicable, the spouse.

As a result of the shift, some have noted that the growth of DC plans since 1974 may have resulted in a greater share of private-sector workers receiving income from retirement plans.[62] The reasons may include (1) lengthy vesting provisions that may have prevented some individuals in DB plans from qualifying for benefits and (2) the overall lower costs of DC plans,which may have resulted in more employers offering these plans.

Private-Sector Single-Employer and Multiemployer DC Plans

Single-employer DC plans are the most common type of pension plan.[63] The types of plans thatemployers offer include profit-sharing and stock bonus plans—typically with a 401(k) component—ESOPs, and, for nonprofit employers, 403(b) plans. Plans may include a Roth component, which allows employees to make contributions with after-tax income and tax-free withdrawals in retirement.

In DC plans, workers traditionally needed to actively choose to participate, though many DC plans have adopted *automatic enrollment*

---

62 See Investment Company Institute (ICI), "A Look at Private-Sector Retirement Plan Income After ERISA, 2015," December 2016, https://www.ici.org/doc-server/pdf%3Aper22-08.pdf.

63 In many respects, single-employer and multiemployer DC plans are similar, so this report does not focus on themseparately.

provisions in which new employees are enrolled in theplan but have the option to decline participation (also referred to as *opting out*).[64]

Multiple-Employer DC Plans

Multiple-employer plans (often called MEPs) can be attractive to employers because administrative expenses can be shared, potentially leading to lower costs. In addition, certainfiduciary duties can be handled by the sponsor rather than the employers. Prior to 2019, employers in a multiple-employer plan had to have a common business interest (such as an organizational relationship), referred to as a *common nexus*. These plans are referred to as *closedMEPs*. In addition, the entire plan could be disqualified if one participating employer violated a qualification requirement, called the *unified plan rule* (informally referred to as the "one-bad-apple" rule).

In an effort to increase the number of employers offering pension plans, in July 2019, DOL published a rule that, while leaving in place the common nexus requirement, expanded the definition of *associations* so that more associations could sponsor multiple-employer DC plans (referred to as *Association Retirement Plans*, or ARPs). The rule also clarified the definition of *employer* so that certain employer groups and professional employer organizations (PEOs) areemployers within the meaning of ERISA and could sponsor multiple-employer DC plans.[65]

The SECURE Act (P.L. 116-94; December 20, 2019) eliminated the requirement that employersthat participate in a multiple-employer plan must have a business connection. As a result, unrelated employers are now able to join multiple-employer 401(k) plans.[66] The SECURE Act authorized a new type of open MEP called a Pooled Employer Plan (PEP) organized by a Pooled

---

[64] Prior to the widespread adoption of automatic enrollment, about 30% of employees eligible for a DC plan opted out. See, for example, these reports with data prior to the widespread adoption of automatic enrollment in DC plans: Patrick Purcell, *Retirement Plan Participation and Contributions: Trends from 1998 to 2006*, Congressional Research Service, January 2009, https://ecommons.cornell.edu/bitstream/handle/1813/78093/RL33116_20090130.pdf; and Vanguard, *How America Saves 2009: A Report on Vanguard 2008 Defined Contribution Plan Data*, August 2009, p. 20, https://www.pionline.com/assets/docs/CO68397126.PDF.

[65] See Employee Benefits Security Administration, "Definition of 'Employer' Under Section 3(5) of ERISA- Association Retirement Plans and Other Multiple-Employer Plans," 84 *Federal Register* 37508-37544, July 31, 2019.The rule left the commonality requirement in place, as that could not be changed by regulation.

[66] Currently, 403(b) plans may not form multiple-employer plans. Several bills in the 117th Congress include aprovision that would permit them to do so.

Plan Provider (PPP).[67] Additionally, the SECURE Act eliminated the one-bad-apple rule.

The SECURE Act also permitted individual DC plans that share similar features (such as trustees,administrators, and investment options), referred to as a *Group of Plans*, to file a single, consolidated return.[68]

Church Plans

Pension plans established and maintained primarily for the benefit of employees of (1) churches or (2) conventions or associations of churches are referred to as *church plans*.[69] Church plans canbe either DB or DC plans and are exempt from ERISA coverage, which means they are not subject to funding rules, nondiscrimination tests, fiduciary obligations, and PBGC insurance. Onerationale for this exemption stemmed from a constitutional concern: A 1973 Senate report notes concern that "the examination of books and records that may be required in any particular case aspart of the care and responsible administration of the [PBGC's] insurance system might be regarded as an unjustified invasion of the confidential relationship that is believed to be appropriate with regard to churches and their religious activities."[70] While church plans can choose to be covered by ERISA (thus becoming *electing* church plans), those that do not (called *non-electing* church plans) must follow certain pre-ERISA requirements in the IRC.[71]

The definition of what constitutes a church or association or convention of churches for the purpose of ERISA coverage has been the subject of litigation. For example, the Supreme Courtruled in 2017 that the pension plans

---

67 One advantage of a PEP is that it can file a single Form 5500 instead of one for each participating employer.

68 One issue with the Group of Plans is whether they would be able to have a single audit or if each plan would be required to have separate audits. See Austin R. Ramsey, "Audits Are Cause for Pause in DOL Group Retirement PlanProposal," *Bloomberg Law*, September 17, 2021, https://www.bloomberglaw.com/bloomberglawnews/daily-labor- report/X4BB75B K000000.

69 See 29 U.S.C. §1002(33).

70 U.S. Congress, Senate Committee on Finance, *Private Pension Plan Reform*, 93rd Cong., 1st sess., August 21, 1973,S. Rpt. 93-383, p. 81.

71 See IRS, "Issue Snapshot—Qualification Requirements for Non-Electing Church Plans Under IRC Section 401(a)," https://www.irs.gov/retirement-plans/issue-snapshot-qualification-requirements-for-non-electing-church-plans-under- irc-section-401a. In addition, non-electing church plans may be subject to state law in the states in which they operate.See Groom Law Group, "View from Groom: After Advocate—Practical Considerations for Church Plan Sponsors," June 13, 2017, https://www.groom.com/ resources/view-from-groom-after-advocate-practical-considerations-for-church-plan-sponsors/.

of certain religiously affiliated nonprofits that operate hospitals and other health care facilities qualified as church plans.[72]

Because the plans are not subject to ERISA funding rules, there have been instances where participants in church plans have lost part or all of their DB pension benefits promised. Becausethese plans are not covered by PBGC, participants may be unable to recover their benefits.[73]

Individual Retirement Accounts (IRAs)

IRAs are tax-advantaged savings accounts that, in most cases, are unconnected to individuals' workplaces. IRAs were first authorized by ERISA (P.L. 93-406) for two reasons: (1) to encourageworkers without access to employer-sponsored plans to save for retirement and (2) to allow workers with employer plans to roll over their savings and retain tax advantages.[74] Though eligibility was originally limited to workers without pension coverage, subsequent legislationexpanded eligibility to nearly all workers.

Congress has authorized two types of IRAs: traditional and Roth. Contributions to traditional IRAs may be deductible from taxable income (depending on household adjusted gross income and workplace pension coverage), and withdrawals are included in taxable income. Contributionsto Roth IRAs are not tax-deductible, but qualified distributions (those made after age 59½, death,or disability from an account that is at least five years old) are tax free. An individual can move traditional IRA savings to a Roth IRA in what is referred to as a *conversion*.[75]

Most inflows to traditional IRAs are from rollovers of pension plan savings from employer- sponsored plans rather than from contributions. Rollovers preserve the tax benefits of retirement savings. In 2018 (the latest year for which data are available), about 97% of inflows to traditionalIRAs

---

[72] See CRS Legal Sidebar WSLG1837, *Supreme Court Delves into What Constitutes a "Church Plan" under ERISA*.

[73] See, for example, Groom Law Group, "Church Plan Litigation—Out of the ERISA Woods into the State Law Forest," December 28, 2021, https://www.groom.com/resources/church-plan-litigation-out-of-the-erisa-woods-into-the-state-law-forest/.

[74] Congressional discussions cited increasing mobility of the workforce as reason for this provision. Prior to rolloversinto IRAs, employees who changed jobs may have been able to transfer assets from one employer plan to another, provided both employers agreed to the transfer. See *Congressional Record*, vol. 120, part 4 (February 26, 1974), p. 4300.

[75] At the time of conversion, the individuals must include the amount of the conversion in his or her taxable income.

were from rollovers, while about 52% of Roth IRA inflows came from rollovers and conversions.[76] For more information on IRAs, see CRS Report RL34397, *Traditional and Roth Individual Retirement Accounts (IRAs): A Primer* and CRS Report R46635, *Individual Retirement Account (IRA) Ownership: Data and Policy Issues*.

IRA-Based Retirement Plans

Most individuals with IRAs independently established and contributed directly to them throughfinancial institutions or because they rolled over savings from employer-sponsored plans.

However, some individuals have IRAs because their employers established IRA-based retirement plans. IRA-based plans include payroll deduction IRAs, Salary Reduction Simplified Employee Pension Plans (SARSEPs), Simplified Employee Pensions (SEPs), and Savings Incentive Match Plan for Employees (SIMPLE) IRAs. Among other factors, these plans vary in the degree of employer involvement.

Data from year-end 2020 indicated that assets in SARSEPs, SEPs, and SIMPLE IRAs totaled anestimated $710 billion, or 5.8% of total IRA assets.[77]

Payroll Deduction IRA

In a payroll deduction IRA, an employer establishes a program through a financial institution. Employees open either traditional or Roth IRAs and authorize the employer to deduct pay from their paychecks to fund the IRAs. Contributions may not exceed the IRA contribution limit ($6,000 in 2022; $7,000 for individuals aged 50 and over). Employer involvement is minimal and is limited to transmitting employees' authorized contributions to the financial institution that holds the employees' IRAs. Employers do not make any contributions to employees' IRAs.[78]

Salary Reduction Simplified Employee Pension Plan (SARSEP)

Under a SARSEP, employees elect to enter into a salary reduction agreement, in which part of their compensation is contributed to their SEP-IRAs. Starting in 1997, employers were no longerpermitted to establish SARSEPs. SARSEPs

---

[76] CRS analysis of data in ICI, "The US Retirement Market," Third Quarter 2021, Table 11.

[77] CRS analysis of data in ICI, "The US Retirement Market," Third Quarter 2021, Table 10.

[78] For more information about payroll deduction IRAs, see IRS, "Payroll Deduction IRA," https://www.irs.gov/retirement-plans/plan-sponsor/payroll-deduction-ira.

could be established only by employers with 25 or fewer eligible participants.[79]

Some SARSEPs established before 1997 are still in existence and must continue to follow SARSEP requirements.[80] In addition, an employee hired in 1997 or later by an employer thatoperates a SARSEP may participate in the SARSEP.

Employee contributions may not exceed the lesser of (1) $20,500 in 2022 or (2) 25% of the employee's compensation. Employees aged 50 and older may make catch-up contributions up to an additional $6,500. Employers may make non-elective contributions to their employees' SEP- IRAs.[81] Employer and employee contributions (excluding catch-up contributions) may not exceedthe lesser of (1) 25% of the employee's compensation or (2) $61,000 in 2022.[82]

Simplified Employee Pension (SEP)

Under a SEP, employers set up and contribute to employees' traditional IRAs (referred to as SEP-IRAs).[83] Employers of any size, including self-employed individuals, may establish SEPs.

Employer contributions to an employee's SEP-IRA are excluded from the employee's gross income and may not exceed the lesser of (1) 25% of the employee's compensation or (2) $61,000in 2022. Employers may decide whether and how much to contribute each year by the tax filing deadline. If an employer decides to contribute, it must do so proportionally for all employees whoworked for the business during the year for which contributions are made.

---

[79] In addition, state or local governments or any of their political subdivisions, agencies, or instrumentalities, or tax-exempt organizations could not establish SARSEPs.

[80] For example, if an employee's elective deferrals equal 25% of compensation, then the employee would not receive an employer contribution. For more information about SARSEP requirements, see IRS, "Salary Reduction SimplifiedEmployee Pension Plan (SARSEP)," https://www.irs.gov/retirement-plans/plan-sponsor/salary-reduction-simplified-employee-pension-plan-sarsep, and IRS, "Retirement Plan FAQs Regarding SARSEPs," https://www.irs.gov/retirement-plans/retirement-plans-faqs-regarding-sarseps.

[81] Non-elective contributions are those made to an employee's account regardless of whether the employee contributesto his or her own account.

[82] See IRS, "SEP Contribution Limits (Including Grandfathered SARSEPs)," https://www.irs.gov/retirement-plans/plan-participant-employee/sep-contribution-limits-including-grandfathered-sarseps.

[83] For more information on SEPs, see IRS, "Simplified Employee Pension Plan (SEP)," https://www.irs.gov/retirement-plans/plan-sponsor/simplified-employee-pension-plan-sep.

Employee contributions (and, thus, catch-up contributions) are not permitted in SEP-IRAs.

Savings Incentive Match Plan for Employees (SIMPLE) IRA

Small employers (i.e., those with 100 or fewer employees who received at least $5,000 in compensation from the employers for the preceding year) may establish SIMPLE IRA plans.

Employees may contribute up to $14,000 in 2022. (Employees aged 50 and older may make additional catch-up contributions up to $3,000.) Each year, employers are required to contribute (1) *matching contributions* up to 3% of an employee's compensation or (2) *nonelective contributions* of 2% of compensation for each eligible employee.[84] Employers that establish SIMPLE IRA plans may not operate any other retirement plans for their employees.[85]

State-Facilitated Retirement Savings Programs for Private-Sector Workers

While Congress addresses retirement security at the national level and establishes federal pensionlaw and savings incentives, several states have enacted or implemented state-administered retirement savings programs to increase retirement plan access and savings among private-sectorworkers. Additional states are considering similar programs.[86] States have taken a variety of approaches to these programs, such as payroll deduction IRAs, retirement marketplaces, andmultiple-employer plans.[87]

In some state programs, employer participation (with some exceptions) is mandatory. In other state programs, employer participation is voluntary. Typically, eligible employees of participatingemployers are automatically enrolled in state programs but can opt out at any time.

---

[84] For purposes of the 2% nonelective contribution, the compensation taken into account must be limited to $290,000for 2021 ($285,000 for 2020), subject to COLAs.

[85] For more information on SIMPLE IRAs, see IRS, "SIMPLE IRA Plan," https://www.irs.gov/retirement-plans/plan-sponsor/simple-ira-plan.

[86] See, for example, John Scott, "Pennsylvania and Hawaii Consider Auto-IRA Savings Opportunities for PrivateSector Workers," Pew Charitable Trusts, January 18, 2022, https://www.pewtrusts.org/en/research-and-analysis/ articles/2022/01/18/pennsylvania-and-hawaii-consider-auto-ira-saving-opportunities-for-private-sector-workers.

[87] For more information on state retirement initiatives, see Georgetown University's Center for Retirement Initiatives,at https://cri.georgetown.edu/states/.

- *Payroll deduction IRAs.* Payroll deduction IRA programs are the most common state-facilitated program. The four state-administered payroll deduction IRA programs in place as of the date of this report (California, Connecticut, Illinois, Oregon) automatically enroll employees. Because of the automatic enrollmentfeature, these plans are sometimes referred to as *automatic, or auto, IRAs*. For more information, see CRS In Focus IF11611, *State-Administered IRA Programs: Overview and Considerations for Congress.*
- Retirement marketplaces. In a retirement marketplace, employers and individuals (including, for example, sole proprietors and "gig" workers) can purchase savings plans through different state-approved providers. For example,the State of Washington operates a retirement marketplace.[88]
- *Multiple-employer plans.* In a multiple-employer plan, unrelated businesses may jointly sponsor a 401(k) plan. For example, Massachusetts's state-administered multiple-employer plan permits eligible small nonprofit organizations to join the plan.[89] The Office of the State Treasurer and ReceiverGeneral acts as sponsor of the plan and performs most administrative and investment responsibilities.

Tax Treatment of Retirement Plans

To encourage preparation for retirement, Congress makes certain tax advantages available to employers and individuals. Contributions to retirement plans may be excluded from or deductedfrom an individual's or an employer's taxable income, investment earnings in the plan may accrue on a tax-deferred or tax-free basis, and distributions from the plan may or may not beincluded in taxable income.

Pension plans are generally *tax qualified*, which means that the plan receives certain tax advantages provided it meets IRC requirements.[90] Depending on the plan, these requirements include determining when

[88] See Retirement Marketplace, https://retirement-marketplace.com/.

[89] See Commonwealth of Massachusetts, "CORE Plan for Nonprofits," https://www.mass.gov/core-plan-for-nonprofits.

[90] Nonqualified plans (also referred to as nonqualified deferred compensation plans) are typically for corporate executives to enable them to save above the tax-qualified plan contribution limits. Nonqualified plans often have sometax advantages, such as the deferral of income taxes until the funds are received by the individual.

participants have a legal right to their benefits (vesting schedules) and determining the amounts employers must contribute to the plans they sponsor (funding requirements).

IRAs and IRA-based plans also receive certain tax advantages but are not considered tax- qualified plans. IRAs must follow requirements outlined in Title 26, Sections 408 and 408A, ofthe *U.S. Code*.

DB Pension Plan Tax Treatment

Employer contributions to DB plans are tax-deductible expenses in the year they are made.

Employee contributions to DB plans are not excluded from taxable income (i.e., they are madewith after-tax income).[91] Relatively few private-sector DB pensions require employee contributions. In 2011 (the most recent data available), 4% of private-sector workers with DB plans were in plans that required employee contributions.[92] In contrast, in 2021, 91% of state and local government workers in DB plans were in plans that required employee contributions.[93] BothCSRS and FERS for federal employees require employee contributions.

DB plan payments to participants in retirement are included in their taxable income except forany portions that are attributable to employee contributions.

DC Pension Plan Tax Treatment

Employer contributions to tax-qualified DC plans are tax-deductible.

Employee contributions can be made on a pre-tax or an after-tax basis. Most contributions aremade on a pre-tax basis, and taxes are *deferred*, which means that taxes are not paid until distributions are made from the account.

---

[91] State and local plans with employee contributions often *pick up* employee contributions, effectively making them employer contributions and therefore excluded from the employees' taxable income.

[92] See BLS, "National Compensation Survey: Employee Benefits in the United States, March 2011," Table 3.

[93] See BLS, "National Compensation Survey: Employee Benefits in the United States, March 2021," Table 4.

Upon withdrawal, pre-tax contributions and any investment earnings are included in taxable income.

Contributions to DC plans that are made on an after-tax basis—such as *designated Roth contributions* or *after-tax, non-Roth contributions*—are not excluded from taxable income.[94]Distributions from designated Roth accounts and those attributable to after-tax, non-Roth contributions are made on a *pro-rata* (or proportional) basis combination of contributions and earnings.

Qualified distributions (those made after age 59½, death, or disability, from accounts that are at least five years old) from designated Roth accounts, which include contributions and any investment earnings, are tax free in retirement. Withdrawals attributable to after-tax, non-Rothcontributions are not included in taxable income, but investment earnings attributable to those contributions are included in taxable income.

IRA Tax Treatment

IRA tax treatment is similar to DC plan tax treatment. Traditional IRAs are funded by workers'contributions, which may be tax deductible (depending on the IRA owner's household income and workplace pension coverage). Taxes are paid on both contributions and any interest earnings when funds are distributed. Contributions to Roth IRAs are made with after-tax funds, and qualified distributions are not included in taxable income. Investment earnings accrue free of taxes.

Effect on U.S. Treasury

Provisions in the tax code that create revenue losses for the U.S. Treasury (e.g., through exclusions and deductions from income) are referred to as tax expenditures. Examples include excluding employer contributions for employee health care, the tax deduction for mortgage interest on an individual's residence, and the variety of tax deductions and exclusions related toretirement plans and savings. Unlike, for example, the mortgage interest

---

[94] Employer matching contributions for an individual who makes designated Roth contributions are always made on apre-tax basis.

deduction, which represents a permanent loss to the Treasury,[95] retirement-related tax expenditures, in most cases,represent a *deferral* of taxes.

- Income taxes are deferred on contributions to traditional DC plans and traditional IRAs. Investment earnings also accrue on a tax-deferred basis. Distributions from these accounts are included in taxable income.
- Benefits earned in DB plans are also not taxed until received in retirement.
- While contributions to designated Roth accounts within DC plans and Roth IRAs are *not* excluded from taxable income, investment earnings accrue on a tax-free basis.[96]

The tax preferences for retirement savings are one of the largest federal tax expenditures. The Treasury Department estimated the following tax expenditures in FY2022:

- $73.4 billion for DB plans,
- $102.9 billion for DC plans, and
- $19.9 billion for IRAs.[97]

The Joint Committee on Taxation (JCT) estimated the following tax expenditures in FY2022:

- $131 billion for DB plans,
- $199.5 billion for DC plans, and
- $27.2 billion for IRAs.[98]

---

[95] See CRS In Focus IF11540, The Mortgage Interest Deduction.

[96] See Peter Brady, "The Tax Benefits and Revenue Costs of Tax Deferral," ICI, 2012, pp. 29-34, https://www.ici.org/pdf/ppr_12_tax_benefits.pdf.

[97] See U.S. Department of the Treasury, "Tax Expenditures," Table 1, https://home.treasury.gov/system/files/131/Tax- Expenditures-FY2023.pdf. Treasury also estimated a tax expenditure of $33.2 billion for self-employer plans, which refer to Keogh plans (IRA-based plans for self-employed individuals).

[98] See JCT, "Estimates of Federal Tax Expenditures for Fiscal Years 2020-2024," https://www.jct.gov/publications/2020/jcx-23-20/. JCT also estimated a tax expenditure of $15.1 billion for Keogh plans.

The difference in the estimates may be due to differences in assumptions and methodologies.Unlike, for example, the student loan interest deduction, which is a one-time deduction and relatively easy to calculate, taxation on retirement plan contributions is deferred until a futuredate, and the actual tax expenditure depends on many factors, such as the rate of return on investments and the difference in marginal income tax rates at the time of contribution and withdrawal for any given individual. Some researchers have identified issues with the calculationmethods used by Treasury and JCT and have proposed alternative methods.[99]

Appendix. Selected CRS Resources on Pension Plans and Individual Retirement Accounts

The following CRS resources provide additional background on the different types of pensions discussed in this report.

- *CRS In Focus IF12008, Private-Sector Pensions in 2019: Number of Plans,Participants, and Amount of Assets*
- *CRS Insight IN11659, U.S. Retirement Assets in 2020*

Private-Sector Defined Benefit Plans

- *CRS Report R46366, Single-Employer Defined Benefit Pension Plans: FundingRelief and Modifications to Funding Rules*
- *CRS Report R43305, Multiemployer Defined Benefit (DB) Pension Plans: APrimer*
- *CRS Report R45187, Data on Multiemployer Defined Benefit (DB) PensionPlans*

---

[99] For example, see Judy Xanthopoulos and Mary Schmitt, "Retirement Savings and Tax Expenditure Estimates,"Retirement Saving Association, September 2016, https://www.asppa.org/sites/asppa.org/files/Comm_2016/16.09%20ARA%20Report%20-%20Retirement%20Savings%20and%20Tax%20Expenditure%20Estimates%20FINAL.pdf. The authors state that current tax expenditure measures overstate costs for provisions that defer taxes compared to provisions that permanently reduce taxes (e.g., a tax credit). The authors suggest that estimates should be made for groups based oncontribution level, age, and income to measure the effects of tax deferral (i.e., the benefit that results from taxpayers facing a different tax rate in retirement compared to when the contributions are made) and the benefits of future earnings (assuming a 4% rate of return).

- *CRS Report R45311, Policy Options for Multiemployer Defined Benefit PensionPlans*
- *CRS In Focus IF11765, Special Financial Assistance to Multiemployer Plans*

Private-Sector Defined Contribution Plans

- *CRS In Focus IF12007, A Visual Depiction of the Shift from Defined Benefit (DB) to Defined Contribution (DC) Pension Plans in the Private Sector*
- *CRS Insight IN11721, Data on Retirement Contributions to Defined Contribution(DC) Plans*

Federal, State, and Local Government Pension Plans

- *CRS In Focus IF10243, Civilian Federal Retirement: Current Law, RecentChanges, and Reform Proposals*
- *CRS Report 98-810, Federal Employees' Retirement System: Benefits andFinancing*
- *CRS Report RL30387, Federal Employees' Retirement System: The Role of theThrift Savings Plan*
- *CRS Report R47084, Federal Retirement Plans: Frequently Asked Questions*

Individual Retirement Accounts

- *CRS Report RL34397, Traditional and Roth Individual Retirement Accounts(IRAs): A Primer*
- *CRS Report R41476, Ownership of Individual Retirement Accounts (IRAs) andPolicy Options for Congress*
- *CRS Insight IN11722, Data on Contributions to Individual Retirement Accounts(IRAs)*
- *CRS In Focus IF11611, State-Administered IRA Programs: Overview andConsiderations for Congress*

Chapter 2

Pensions and Individual Retirement Accounts (IRAs): Investment Issues*

Katelin P. Isaacs
Elizabeth A. Myers
and John J. Topoleski

Summary

Employer-sponsored pensions and individual retirement accounts (IRAs) are important sources of income security in retirement for American households. Recent congressional interest in retirement policy has focused on several aspects of pension investments. Some of this interest involves pension investment policy spanning the state and local, federal, and private sectors. For example, several hearings in the 118th Congress have examined the role of environmental, social, and governance (ESG) investing in pension plans with regard to investment managers and retirement policy generally. Some other recent developments in pension investment policy have focused on a particular sector. For instance, recent regulatory and congressional responses to private sector pension issues have addressed investment advice and investment fees. Similarly, the investment practices of the Thrift Savings Plan (TSP), a retirement plan covering the civilian federal workforce and the uniformed services, have been legislatively active over recent Congresses, including the 118th Congress.

This report provides an overview of pension investment issues across state and local pensions, federal pensions (with a focus on TSP), private

* This is an edited, reformatted and augmented version of Congressional Research Service Publication No. R47996, dated April 3, 2024.

In: Retirement Strategies: Analysis of Policies, Investments, and Security
Editor: Ryan M. Powell
ISBN: 979-8-89530-366-5

sector pension plans, and IRAs. For each of these types of pensions or retirement accounts, this report explains relevant federal authorities (if any), relevant federal oversight (if any), and administrative issues. For example, while current TSP investment options are set out specifically under federal law (5 U.S.C. §8438), state and local pension plans are generally governed by state laws, contract law, and/or state constitutions. Moreover, state and local pension plans are exempt from many, but not all, requirements under the Employee Retirement Income Security Act of 1974 (ERISA; P.L. 93-406), the federal law that covers most private sector pension plans.

Understanding the relevant authorities and administration of different types of pension plans and retirement accounts is crucial to untangling policy proposals to address pension investment issues.

This report also identifies and synthesizes key pension investment issues for Congress, many of which have received regulatory and congressional responses or have involved legislative activity in the 118th Congress. Specifically, lawmakers have expressed interest in the following policy issues related to pension investments, by sector:

- State and local pensions: ESG investing, alternative investments, geopolitical considerations, and diverse asset managers;
- Federal pensions, specifically with regard to TSP: the International "I" Fund benchmark and investments in Chinese companies, ESG investment issues, the mutual fund window, diverse asset managers, and the exercise of shareholder rights;
- Private sector pensions: investments based on non-pecuniary factors, exercise of shareholder rights, alternative investments, collective investment trusts in 403(b) plans, investment advice, investment fees, and qualified professional asset managers; and
- IRAs: investment restrictions and prohibited transactions.

For background on other aspects of these pension plans and retirement accounts, see CRS Report R47119, *Pensions and Individual Retirement Accounts (IRAs): An Overview*.

Introduction

A pension is a benefit offered by employers to assist employees in providing for their financial security in retirement.[1] Pensions are a type of deferred

[1] For a discussion of retirement income security more generally, see CRS In Focus IF12330, *Retirement Income Security: Issues and Policies*.

compensation intended to replace income when individuals separate from the paid labor force at older ages. Employers in the public sector—state and local governments as well as the federal government—and in the private sector may provide pensions to their employees.[2]

Pension plans can be classified along several dimensions. In defined benefit (DB) plans (sometimes referred to as traditional pension plans), participants typically receive monthly payments in retirement based on a formula that uses either (1) a combination of length of service, accrual rate, and average of final years' salary or (2) a flat dollar amount times the number of months or years in the plan. Some plans offer participants the option to receive their benefits as a lump-sum amount.

In defined contribution (DC) plans, workers are provided individual accounts funded by their own contributions, contributions from their employers, or both. The funds in the account may accrue investment earnings, which can then be used as a source of income in retirement. The type of DC plan that an employer may offer depends on the type of employer (for example, the types of plans offered by public sector employers are typically different from those offered by private sector employers), as well as the employer's choices regarding plan features (for example, private sector employers have a number of types of DC plans they can offer). Examples of DC plans include profit-sharing plans, money purchase plans, 401(k) plans, 403(b) plans, and employee stock ownership plans (ESOPs).

Individual retirement accounts (IRAs) are tax-advantaged accounts that allow individuals to save for retirement outside of employer-sponsored plans or to roll over savings from employer- sponsored plans.[3] Traditional and Roth IRAs differ based on their tax treatment. Contributions to traditional IRAs may be deductible from taxable income, while withdrawals are included in taxable income. Contributions to Roth IRAs are not deductible and are limited by income, but qualified withdrawals are not included in taxable income; investment earnings grow tax free.

Most inflows to IRAs come from rollovers of savings in workplace pension plans (such as 401(k) plans) at job change or retirement.[4]

---

[2] For background on the various types of pension plans, see CRS Report R47119, *Pensions and Individual Retirement Accounts (IRAs): An Overview*.

[3] For background on IRAs, see CRS Report R46635, *Individual Retirement Account (IRA) Ownership: Data and Policy Issues*, and CRS Report RL34397, *Traditional and Roth Individual Retirement Accounts (IRAs): A Primer*.

[4] For example, in 2020 (the latest year for which data is available), over 96% of the inflows to traditional IRAs came from rollovers. More inflows to Roth IRAs came from contributions rather than rollovers, but Roth IRA inflows ($85.0 billion) were much smaller than

In March 2023, nearly three-quarters (72%) of U.S. civilian workers had access to, and more than half (56%) participated in, DB or DC pension plans at their workplaces.[5] Additionally, in 2019, about 25% of U.S. households owned IRAs.[6] Pensions and retirement policy is an area of ongoing congressional interest as lawmakers seek ways to improve the retirement system for both employers and employees. Congress may be interested in a number of issues related to pensions, such as proposals to expand pension coverage or the tax treatment of retirement plans. One pension policy issue that has received considerable attention recently is the investment practices of different types of retirement plans. For example, in May and June of 2023, the House Committee on Oversight and Accountability held two joint subcommittee hearings to examine the role of environmental, social, and governance (ESG) investing,[7] including with regard to investment managers and retirement policy.[8] On November 7, 2023, the House Committee on Ways and Means held a hearing on "Ensuring That 'Woke' Doesn't Leave Americans Broke: Protecting Seniors and Savers from ESG Activism,"[9] which also focused on the role of ESG investments in retirement policy. Additionally, legislation to make changes to the investment practices of the Thrift Savings Plan (TSP), a defined contribution retirement plan for the civilian federal workforce and the uniformed services, has been introduced in recent Congresses.[10]

This report synthesizes information on selected pension investment issues so Congress can understand existing legislative proposals as well as develop

---

traditional IRA inflows ($616.9 billion) in 2020. See Investment Company Institute, "The U.S. Retirement Market, Third Quarter 2023," https://www.ici.org/research/stats/retirement.

[5] See Bureau of Labor Statistics, National Compensation Survey, March 2023, https://www.bls.gov/ebs/publications/employee-benefits-in-the-united-states-march-2023.htm.

[6] See CRS Report R47213, *Ownership of Retirement Assets: Data in Brief.*

[7] For background on ESG investing, see CRS In Focus IF11716, Introduction to Financial Services: Environmental, Social, and Governance (ESG) Issues.

[8] See U.S. Congress, House Committee on Oversight and Accountability, ESG Part I: An Examination of Environmental, Social, and Governance Practices with Attorneys General, May 10, 2023, https://oversight.house.gov/ hearing/esg-part-i-an-examination-of-environmental-social-and-governance-practices-with-attorneys-general/; and ESG Part II: The Cascading Impacts of ESG Compliance, June 6, 2023, https://oversight.house.gov/hearing/esg-part-ii-the- cascading-impacts-of-esg-compliance/.

[9] See U.S. Congress, House Committee on Ways and Means, *Hearing on Ensuring That "Woke" Doesn't Leave Americans Broke: Protecting Seniors and Savers from ESG Activism*, November 7, 2023, https://waysandmeans.house.gov/event/hearing-on-ensuring-that-woke-doesnt-leave-americans-broke-protecting- seniors-and-savers-from-esg-activism/.

[10] For examples of legislation that would have made changes to TSP investments in the 117th Congress, see CRS In Focus IF12110, *Thrift Savings Plan: Investment Issues*.

new legislative proposals. This report provides background information on pension investment issues generally, including differences across sectors and types of pension plans.

Overview of Pension Plans

Pensions vary across a number of dimensions that are relevant for the purposes of investment policy considerations. First, and most significantly, the sector of the employer that sponsors the pensions matters for the purposes of pension investments. Therefore, this report considers public sector pension plans sponsored by governments at the (1) state and local level and (2) federal level and discusses (3) private sector pensions, all on their own terms. Pensions sponsored by employers across these three sectors differ meaningfully for the purposes of investment policy, including the role of federal laws (if any), the role of federal oversight (if any), and plan administration. Similarly, IRAs are subject to their own federal authorities, federal oversight, and account administration.

Second, as previously mentioned, there are two types of pension plans based on benefit structure: (1) DB plans, in which participants typically receive their benefits as monthly payments in retirement, and (2) DC plans, in which participants' benefits accrue in individual savings accounts. The different features of these two types of pension plans lend themselves to different policy issues with regard to investment practices. In addition, DB plan investment decisions may be influenced by plans' funded statuses, which differ by sector.[11] For example, both private sector and state and local DB plans have historically been underfunded, although in recent years, private sector plans' funding status has improved, in part due to changes in law that affect the discount rate used by plans.[12] State and local DB plans continue to

---

[11] Plans' funded statuses, which differ by sector, may be a result of different funding rules between private and public sector plans. Private sector DB plans are subject to funding rules in federal law—ERISA sets out requirements for the minimum required contribution, which is the amount of money that must be contributed each year to a DB pension plan (see CRS Report R46366, *Single-Employer Defined Benefit Pension Plans: Funding Relief and Modifications to Funding Rules*). State and local pension plans are not subject to federal pension funding requirements and generally follow pension accounting standards set by the Governmental Accounting Standards Board. In some cases, state and local plans may not make their full required contributions to the pension plans each year, which contributes to plan underfunding.

[12] See CRS Report R46366, Single-Employer Defined Benefit Pension Plans: Funding Relief and Modifications to Funding Rules.

be underfunded.[13] Federal DB pensions are not underfunded because they are generally invested in risk-free Treasury securities.[14]

Pension plans hold a variety of investments.[15] The Federal Reserve publishes quarterly data on the holdings of pension plans in the Financial Accounts of the United States.[16] These holdings include short-term securities (such as checking and savings deposits), corporate equities (such as company stock), debt (such as mortgages and bonds issued by governments and companies), mutual funds (such as investment companies that pool money from investors in securities such as stocks and bonds), and, for DB plans, the claims of the pension funds on plan sponsors (plans' unfunded benefits).[17] Not every pension plan holds every type of asset.[18] For example, the DB pension plans for nearly all federal employees hold only U.S. Treasury securities.

Total assets held in DB retirement plans, DC accounts, and IRAs totaled $40.0 trillion as of June 30, 2023.[19] Because assets in pension plans and IRAs comprise a significant portion of U.S. households' wealth, changes to pension investment policies could affect both the amount and the distribution of household wealth.[20] Figure 1 shows (1) the amount of financial assets (in trillions of dollars) in pension plans sponsored by private sector employers, state and local governments, and the federal government; (2) the amount of assets in IRAs; and (3) the components of these assets.

---

[13] See Public Plans Data, "Actuarial Funded Ratio for State and Local Pensions, 2001-," https://publicplansdata.org/ quick-facts/national/#.

[14] See "Federal Pension Plans" later in this report.

[15] For additional information, see CRS Report R47699, U.S. Retirement Assets: Data in Brief.

[16] The Financial Accounts of the United States are available at https://www.federalreserve.gov/releases/z1/.

[17] DB plan underfunding is in plan assets because the plans expect to receive the funds that are owed by plan sponsors.

[18] The financial accounts data does not have a separate category for international holdings. International holdings are included in their respective categories. (For example, the sovereign debt of a foreign nation would be under "debt.")

[19] See CRS Report R47699, U.S. Retirement Assets: Data in Brief.

[20] In Q3 2023, household net worth totaled $142.4 trillion. See Board of Governors of the Federal Reserve System (US), "Households; Net Worth, Level [BOGZ1FL192090005Q]," retrieved from Federal Reserve Bank of St. Louis, https://fred.stlouisfed.org/series/BOGZ1FL192090005Q, January 7, 2024.

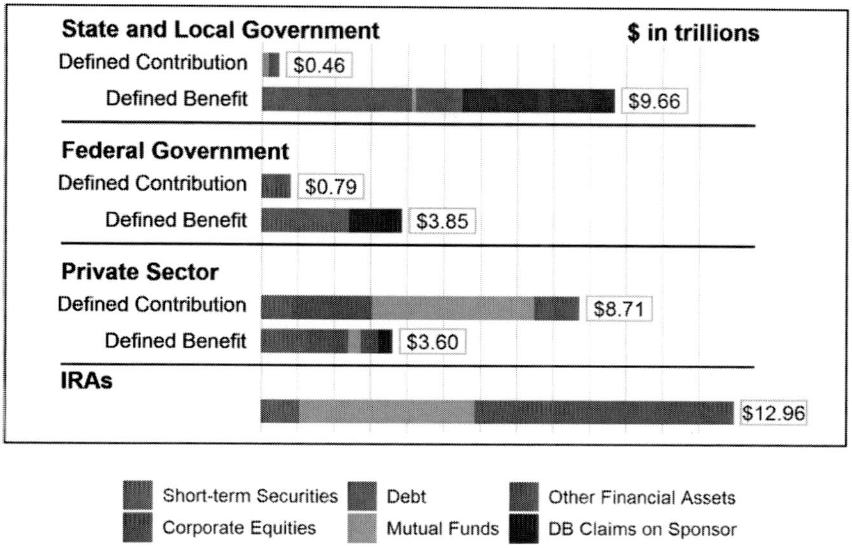

Source: Figure constructed by CRS from Board of Governors of the Federal Reserve System, Financial Accounts of the United States, https://www.federalreserve.gov/apps/fof/FOFTables.aspx. See tables L.118.b, L.118.c, L.119.b, L.119.c, L.120.b, L.120.c, and L.229.

Notes: IRAs include employer-sponsored IRAs and state-administered IRA programs. Mutual funds invest in a variety of assets, including corporate equities and debt. As a result, the total amount of corporate equities and debt held by pension plans likely exceeds the values presented in the Corporate Equities and Debt categories in the figure. DB claims on sponsors are funds owed but unpaid by plan sponsors to the plans. Unpaid funds are treated as financial assets. Short-term securities include checkable deposits, savings deposits, money market funds, and security repurchase agreements. Debt is composed of securities such as commercial paper, U.S. Treasury securities, U.S. government agency and government-sponsored-enterprise-backed securities, foreign bonds, and corporate bonds. Corporate equities include publicly traded shares and private equity. Mutual funds pool money from investors and invest the money in securities such as stocks, bonds, and debt. DB claims on sponsors are funds owed but unpaid by plan sponsors to the plan. Unpaid funds are treated as financial assets. Other financial assets include, but are not exclusively composed of, insurance contracts and contributions receivable.

Figure 1. Total Holdings and Components of Financial Assets in U.S. Pension Plans and Individual Retirement Accounts (IRAs). (In Trillions of Dollars, as of June 30, 2023)

State and Local Government Pension Plans

Most state and local employees (such as police officers, firefighters, teachers, and other state and local government employees) are covered by pension plans and, among those with plans, they are more likely to be covered by DB plans than by DC plans. In March 2023, 91% of all state and local government workers had access to pension plans, with 86% having access to DB plans and 39% having access to DC plans. In the same month, 81% of state and local government workers participated in pension plans (75% DB, 18% DC; some workers participated in both types of plans).[21]

Authority and Administration

State and local pension plans are not covered by the Employee Retirement Income Security Act of 1974 (ERISA; P.L. 93-406), which covers most private sector pension plans and is included in the U.S. Code in both Title 26 (the Internal Revenue Code, or IRC) and in Title 29 (often called the Labor Code). Relatedly, state and local pension plans are not covered by the Pension Benefit Guaranty Corporation (PBGC), which is a government corporation established by ERISA that insures private sector DB plans.[22] Finally, state and local pension plans are exempt from many, but not all, IRC requirements (such as minimum funding requirements). Instead, these plans are governed by state laws, contract law, and/or state constitutions.

Many (if not nearly all) state and local government plans follow the accounting and financial standards set by the Governmental Accounting Standards Board (GASB).[23] GASB publishes accounting and financial reporting standards for state and local governmental pension plans using U.S. Generally Accepted Accounting Principles. These standards govern how public pensions calculate and report their assets and liabilities and are intended to promote transparency, consistency, and comparability across state and local pension plans.

---

[21] Bureau of Labor Statistics, "National Compensation Survey: Employee Benefits in the United States," March 2023, September 2023, https://www.bls.gov/ebs/publications/employee-benefits-in-the-united-states-march-2023.htm.

[22] For background on the PBGC, see CRS Report 95-118, *Pension Benefit Guaranty Corporation (PBGC): A Primer.*

[23] See Governmental Accounting Standards Board, "About the GASB," https://gasb.org/about-us/about-the-gasb.

In FY2020, 14.7 million active (working) members and 11.5 million total beneficiaries were covered by 5,340 DB plans administered by state and local government entities, including municipalities, townships, counties, school districts, and special districts.[24] The Center for Retirement Research indicated that the 219 largest state and local DB plans (121 state, 108 local) in its Public Plans Data accounted for 95% of state and local DB pension assets and members in the United States.[25]

Most public sector employees are covered by DB plans, but DC plans are becoming more common.[26] Some states have shifted to a hybrid system that combines DB and DC plans. Others, such as Alaska, have closed their DB plans and instead offer a DC plan to new hires.[27] Depending on the employer, state and local DC plan types include 401(a), 401(k), 403(b), and 457(b) plans. Employee participation and contributions may be mandatory or optional, depending on the structure of the plan as determined by the employer. A 401(a) plan may be available to state and local government workers as part of a DB-DC combination plan or a hybrid cash balance plan. A 403(b) plan may be offered to employees of public schools, churches, and certain charitable tax- exempt entities. A 457(b) plan is a voluntary, supplementary DC savings vehicle, often offered to state and local government employees in conjunction with a traditional DB pension.

State and Local Pension Plan Investment Issues

Investment issues for state and local pensions include those related to

- ESG investing,

---

[24] U.S. Census Bureau, *2020 Annual Survey of Public Pensions: State and Local Tables*, https://www.census.gov/data/ tables/2020/econ/aspp/aspp-historical-tables.html. Fiscal year dates vary by state. Between 25% and 30% of state and local DB plan members and beneficiaries are not covered by Social Security. See National Conference on Public Employee Retirement Systems and Cobalt Community Research, *2019 NCPERS Public Retirement Systems Study*, January 21, 2020, https://www.ncpers.org/files/ 2019%20 NCPERS%20Public%20Retirement%20Systems%20Study%20Report%20Final.pdf.

[25] Center for Retirement Research at Boston College, "Public Plans Data," https://public plansdata.org/public-plans-database. Data retrieved from website on February 16, 2024.

[26] See CRS Report R43439, *Worker Participation in Employer-Sponsored Pensions: Data in Brief.*

[27] See American Society of Pension Professionals and Actuaries, "Snapshot: The Effect of the DB to DC Shift in Alaska," June 5, 2023, https://www.asppa-net.org/news/snapshot-effect-db-dc-shift-alaska.

- geopolitical concerns,
- alternative investments, and
- diverse asset managers.

Most state and local pension investment issues have been focused on DB plans.[28] In comparison with private sector pensions, which use company resources to make up for DB plan underfunding, state and local pension plans could have different investment risk tolerances because plan underfunding is generally made up through increased taxation or reductions in other public spending.[29]

Congress has expressed interest in issues affecting state and local pension plan investments— particularly those related to ESG investing. However, because state and local plans are not subject to the part of federal pensions law governing plan investments, Congress may have fewer options to influence state and local pension plan investments.[30]

ESG Investment Issues

There is no universally agreed-upon definition of what constitutes ESG.[31] In addition, inconsistent disclosure standards make it harder for investors to measure a firm's performance on ESG issues. In general, the *E* means that investors and stakeholders may examine a firm's impact on the environment, the *S* refers to the consideration of a firm's effects on its various stakeholders, such as consumers, employees, suppliers, contractors, and the local and broader communities; and *G* refers to the consideration of policies, processes, and controls implemented by a firm.[32]

---

[28] This might be because DC plan assets comprise a small portion of state and local pension assets (less than $500 billion compared to $9.5 trillion for DB).

[29] For a discussion of the different incentives of participants and stakeholders in the public pension plan system, see American Academy of Actuaries, ***Risk Management and Public*** *Plan Retirement Systems*, https://www.actuary.org/sites/default/files/files/PPPTF_Final_Report_c_0.pdf.

[30] One example of federal legislation that would have affected public sector pensions is the Public Employee Pension Transparency Act, first introduced by Representative Devin Nunes in the 111th Congress (see H.R. 6484) and later introduced in subsequent Congresses. This bill would have required state and local pension plans to file annual reports with the Department of the Treasury disclosing pension liabilities based on a specified (typically lower) interest rate. State and local governments not in compliance with the reporting requirements would lose their ability to issue tax- exempt bonds.

[31] For information about ESG, see CRS In Focus IF11716, Introduction to Financial Services: Environmental, Social, and Governance (ESG) Issues.

[32] For more details on what ESG investment factors might include, see Securities and Exchange Commission, "Environmental, Social, and Governance (ESG) Funds—Investor Bulletin,"

State and local pension plans are taking different approaches to ESG issues. Some plans specifically incorporate ESG factors into their investment choices; others limit the consideration of ESG factors in the investment process, such as by requiring plan fiduciaries to choose investments solely based on factors that balance risk and return or to divest from companies or asset managers as state law might dictate. Some examples include New York, which integrates ESG considerations in its investment decisions;[33] Texas, which barred state governmental entities (which include public pension funds) from contracting with companies that boycott fossil fuel companies;[34] and Kansas, which passed a law that prevents the use of ESG considerations in state contracts and investments.[35]

Pensions and Investments 1000 Summary Report includes data on DB plans among the top 200 funds that use ESG factors. Public sector plans included in this list include those based in Alabama, California, Illinois, Iowa, Maryland, New Jersey, New York, Ohio, Washington, and Wisconsin.[36]

Advocates of ESG investing note that portfolios that consider ESG factors may lead to greater portfolio diversification and improved corporate performance and can align with investors' goals.[37] Opponents of ESG

February 26, 2021, https://www.sec.gov/ oiea/investor-alerts-and-bulletins/environmental-social-and-governance-esg-funds-investor-bulletin.

[33] See New York Common Retirement Fund, *Environmental, Social and Governance (ESG) Strategy*, https://www.osc.ny.gov/files/common-retirement-fund/2020/pdf/ESG-strategy-report-2020.pdf. In addition, California's CalPERS plan, which has nearly 2.2 million participants, operates a Sustainable Investments Program, which assists the investment office by integrating ESG risks and opportunity consideration into investment decisionmaking and engages with companies and managers to manage ESG risks. See CalPERS, *2021-22 Annual Comprehensive Financial Report*, https://www.calpers.ca.gov/docs/forms-publications/acfr-2022.pdf, and CalPERS, "Sustainable Investments Program," https://www.calpers.ca.gov/page/investments/sustainable-investments-program.

[34] See Texas Comptroller of Public Accounts, "Texas Comptroller Glenn Hegar Announces List of Financial Companies That Boycott Energy Companies," August 24, 2022, https://comptroller.texas.gov/about/media-center/ news/20220824-texas-comptroller-glenn-hegar-announces-list-of-financial-companies-that-boycott-energy-companies-166126 7815099; and Oklahoma State Treasurer, "Financial Institutions Remain on Oklahoma Treasurer's List of Restricted Companies," August 15, 2023, https://oklahoma.gov/treasurer/news-releases/financial-institutions-remain-on-oklahoma-treasurers-list-of-restricted-companies.html.

[35] See Kansas legislature, HB 2100, https://www.kslegislature.org/li/b2023_24/measu res/hb2100/.

[36] See Pensions and Investments, *The P&I 1000 Summary Report*, https://www.pionline.com/pi1000.

[37] See, for example, Tensie Whelan et al., "ESG and Financial Performance: Uncovering the Relationship by Aggregating Evidence from 1,000 Plus Studies Published Between 2015-2020," New York University Stern Center for Sustainable Business, August 2021,

investment point out the higher costs associated with ESG investing, lower returns, and misalignment with the goal of maximizing investment returns instead of pursuing social policy.[38]

Geopolitical Considerations

Related to ESG issues are geopolitical issues, on which some plans base investment decisions.[39] In recent years, two general trends in state and local pension investment policies have been to (1) divest from certain countries (e.g., Russia, Belarus, China) and entities based in those countries and (2) bar investments in companies that support the Boycott, Divestment and Sanctions (BDS) movement.[40] In the past, there have been efforts to divest from Sudan, Northern Ireland, and Iran.[41]

For example, Indiana, New Jersey, and New York have introduced legislation and/or undertaken executive actions to divest from Russia.[42] In 2023, Indiana's public pension system divested from investments controlled by the People's Republic of China or the Chinese Community Party.[43] In 2015, Illinois was the first state to divest its public pensions from companies that participate in the BDS movement.[44] In some cases, the pension plans are making divestment decisions. In other cases, sanctions in state laws require all public funds, including pension funds, to divest from certain countries or entities in specified countries.

---

https://www.stern.nyu.edu/sites/default/files/assets/documents/ESG%20Paper%20Aug%202021.pdf.

[38] See, for example, testimony of the Hon. Jason Isaac, in *Ensuring That "Woke" Doesn't Leave Americans Broke*, https://gop-waysandmeans.house.gov/wp-content/uploads/2023/11/Isaac-Testimony.pdf, and testimony of the Hon. Marlo M. Oaks, , in *Ensuring That "Woke" Doesn't Leave Americans Broke*, https://gop-waysandmeans.house.gov/wp-content/uploads/2023/11/Oaks-Testimony.pdf.

[39] There is no universally agreed-upon definition of what constitutes ESG. Investors and other stakeholders consider a wide-ranging array of topics as part of ESG. Some might categorize geopolitical concerns as an ESG issue; this report discusses them separately.

[40] The BDS movement, according to its website, is a global movement made up of unions, academic associations, churches, and grassroots movements that seeks to employ boycotts, divestment, and sanctions against Israel. See BDS, https://bdsmovement.net/.

[41] See National Association of State Retirement Administrators, "Divestment," https://www.nasra.org/files/Topical%20Reports/Governance%20and%20Legislation/Pension%20Reform/divestment.pdf.

[42] In general, news reports suggest that state plan holdings in Russia account for approximately 1% or less of total pension assets.

[43] See Indiana Senate Bill 268, https://iga.in.gov/legislative/2023/bills/senate/268/details.

[44] See Illinois.gov, "Governor Signs Historic Anti-BDS Law in Illinois," press release, July 23, 2015, https://www.illinois.gov/news/press-release.13202.html.

Alternative Investments

In the past 30 years, many state and local DB pension plans have increased the allocation of alternative investments (i.e., financial assets that are not stocks, bonds, or cash, including assets such as private equity, hedge funds, real estate, and commodities) in their investment portfolios. Alternative investments might be perceived as being less regulated and transparent or having higher fees compared to traditional investments. On the other hand, advocates note that alternative investments' low correlation with traditional investments could strengthen diversification of investment portfolios.[45] The CRR indicated that the plans in the Public Plans database had about 9% of their assets invested in alternatives in 2001 and that the percentage increased to 34% in 2022.[46] State and local pension plans typically have a greater percentage of their investments allocated to private equity than do private sector plans.[47] It is unclear why state and local and private sector DB plans differ in the percentages of plan assets allocated to alternatives, but it might be related to plan sponsors' different risk tolerances due to a variety of factors.[48]

Diverse Asset Managers

Some policymakers have expressed interest in growing the diversity of professional asset managers in the public pension investment space, including minority- and women-owned business enterprises. Several states have enacted laws, implemented programs, or established goals to encourage the utilization of diverse asset managers under the notion that diversity among asset managers can enhance financial outcomes and lead to better risk-adjusted returns on plan assets. For example, Maryland's State Retirement and Pension System

---

[45] See CFA Institute, "Introduction to Alternative Investments," https://www. cfainstitute.org/en/membership/professional-development/refresher-readings/introduction-alternative-investments.

[46] See Jean-Pierre Aubry, "Public Pension Investment Update: Have Alternatives Helped or Hurt?," Center for Retirement Research at Boston College, November 22, 2022, https://crr.bc.edu/public-pension-investment-update- have-alternatives-helped-or-hurt/.

[47] For example, WTW indicated that at the end of 2021, the 100 largest private sector DB plans that are sponsored by publicly traded corporations had about 9.5% of their investments allocated to alternative investments. See Brendan McFarland, "WTW Pension 100: Year-End 2021 Disclosures of Funding, Discount Rates, Asset Allocations and Contributions," WTW, May 4, 2022, https://www.wtwco.com/en-us/insights/2022/05/wtw-pension-100-year-end- 2021-disclosures-of-funding-discount-rates-asset-allocations.

[48] Some note that one reason may be that public pension plans "have become optimistic about the so-called alpha of alternatives relative to public equities." See Juliane Begenau, Pauline Liang, and Emil Siriwardane, "The Rise of Alternatives," January 18, 2024, Stanford University Graduate School of Business Research Paper, https://papers.ssrn.com/sol3/papers.cfm?abstract_id=4105813.

operates a program that "seeks to identify promising smaller or developing managers."[49] At the local level, the Chicago Teachers' Pension Fund's annual financial report noted that, during the year ending June 30, 2019, "approximately 44% ($4.8 billion) of the Fund's investment portfolio was managed by qualified minority, women, and disabled-person owned investment managers."[50]

These actions at the state and local level have also been a model for interest in diverse asset managers at the federal pension level, especially as a consideration for TSP (see the discussion in the federal pension section below on "Diverse Asset Managers").[51]

Federal Pension Plans

Most of the civilian federal workforce is covered by one of two DB retirement plans: the Civil Service Retirement System (CSRS) for employees first hired prior to 1984, or the Federal Employees' Retirement System (FERS) for employees first hired in 1984 or later.[52] Both CSRS and FERS are financed through the Civil Service Retirement and Disability Fund (CSRDF). The CSRDF is similar to the Social Security trust funds in that, by law, 100% of its assets are invested in special-issue U.S. Treasury bonds or other bonds backed

---

[49] See Maryland State Retirement and Pension System, *Terra Maria: Developing Manager Program in Public Markets and Private Equity*, updated February 2011, https://sra.maryland.gov/sites/main/files/file-attachments/terramariadevelopingmanagerprogram-description.pdf.

[50] See Chicago Teachers' Pension Fund, *124th Comprehensive Annual Financial Report, 2019*, p. 12, https://www.ctpf.org/sites/files/2020-10/2019_ctpf_cafr_final_post.pdf.

[51] At the federal level, the House Financial Services Committee held a hearing in 2019 about challenges, solutions, and opportunities for inclusion of diverse asset managers. See U.S. Congress, House Committee on Financial Services, *Diverse Asset Managers: Challenges, Solutions and Opportunities for Inclusion*, 117th Cong., 1st Sess., June 25, 2019, https://financialservices.house.gov/calendar/eventsingle.aspx?EventID=407321.

[52] Military servicemembers are covered by a separate retirement system, which is not discussed in this report. For details on retirement benefits for military servicemembers, see CRS Report RL34751, *Military Retirement: Background and Recent Developments*. A number of smaller DB and DC plans have been established for certain civilian federal employees within various agencies. There are a few additional plans that provide federal pensions to a non-trivial number of civilian federal employees. For example, the Foreign Service Retirement and Disability System (FSRDS) and the Foreign Service Pension System (FSPS) are DB plans that cover Foreign Service Officers (FSOs) based on their dates of hire in a similar way to CSRS and FERS. The Federal Reserve also operates its own DB and DC plans on behalf of its bank and board employees and certain other employees. For more information all of these federal pension plans, including CSRS and FERS, see CRS Report R47084, *Federal Retirement Plans: Frequently Asked Questions*.

by the full faith and credit of the U.S. government.[53] When the trust fund needs cash to pay retirement benefits, it redeems the bonds and the Treasury disburses an equivalent dollar value of payments to CSRS and FERS beneficiaries.[54]

Federal employees enrolled in either CSRS or FERS may also contribute to the TSP, a DC pension plan similar to the 401(k) plans provided by many private sector employers.[55] However, only employees enrolled in FERS are eligible for employer matching contributions under TSP. Newly hired FERS employees are automatically enrolled in TSP and contribute 5% of their pay, though they have the option to decline participation or change the amount of their contributions. TSP participants may contribute from their salaries up to the current contribution limits.[56] An employee covered by FERS receives an automatic 1% agency contribution and an agency match equal to 100% of the worker's first 3% of basic pay and 50% of the next 2% of basic pay.[57]

Because the CSRDF investments are restricted to Treasury securities, the remaining discussion about federal pension plans focuses on TSP investment issues. Below is an explanation of the authority for and administration of TSP investments as well as an explanation of current TSP investment options.

TSP Investments: Authority and Administration

The Thrift Savings Plan (TSP) was created under the Federal Employees' Retirement System Act (FERSA; P.L. 99-335; June 6, 1986). The Federal Retirement Thrift Investment Board (FRTIB) administers TSP.[58] FRTIB is an independent agency that receives no appropriations from Congress. Instead, administrative expenses for FRTIB are paid through TSP loan fees, 1% agency automatic contributions forfeited by certain employees who leave federal

---

[53] See 5 U.S.C. §8348(c). For information on the investment practices of the Social Security trust funds, see CRS In Focus IF10564, *Social Security Trust Fund Investment Practices*.

[54] For more information on the CSRDF, see CRS Report RL30023, *Federal Employees' Retirement System: Budget and Trust Fund Issues*.

[55] Military servicemembers and FSOs may also contribute to the TSP.

[56] Contribution limits are available at TSP.gov, "Contribution Limits," https://www.tsp.gov/making-contributions/ contribution-limits/.

[57] Participants are fully vested in the 1% agency automatic contributions to the TSP after three years (two years for congressional employees and certain senior political appointees). There is no vesting requirement for other contributions (i.e., employee or agency matching contributions). See 5 U.S.C. §8432(g). (*Vesting* refers to ownership, or amounts not being subject to forfeiture.)

[58] For more information on FRTIB, see https://www.frtib.gov/.

service before they have vested, and administrative charges against participant accounts.[59]

FRTIB is composed of five board members chosen by the President and confirmed by the Senate. The Board also selects an Executive Director who manages daily operations.[60] Under current law, members of the FRTIB and the Executive Director serve as fiduciaries, legally obligated to act "solely in the interest of the [TSP] participants and beneficiaries … and for the exclusive purpose of providing benefits to participants and their beneficiaries."[61]

All TSP investment options are set out under current law.[62] In order to offer these investment options to participants, FRTIB develops specific investment policies—for example, selecting benchmarks for the index fund investment options—that provide for "prudent investments suitable for accumulating funds for payment of retirement income; and low administrative costs."[63] Thus, in addition to its fiduciary responsibilities, FRTIB must adhere to its statutory mandates to keep administrative costs low and prudently manage returns for TSP account holders.

At its creation in 1986, the TSP was designed to be passively managed in order to avoid political manipulation—in particular, using the large pool of assets managed by FRTIB for political purposes.[64] Thus, TSP index funds are all passively managed by professional fund managers, each with an investment objective of matching the performance of a specific, benchmark index fund.

TSP fund managers do not actively select a fund's portfolio assets. Currently, BlackRock and State Street Global Advisors both hold fund manager contracts for all TSP index funds.[65]

Three investment options—the "C" Fund (a common stock index fund), the "F" Fund (a fixed income index fund), and the "G" Fund (a government

---

[59] For more information on TSP administrative expenses, see TSP.gov, "Expenses and Fees," https://www.tsp.gov/tsp- basics/expenses-and-fees/.

[60] For information on current FRTIB board members as well as the Executive Director, see https://www.frtib.gov/ board-members/. The FRTIB currently has one vacancy.

[61] 5 U.S.C. §8477(b)(1)).

[62] 5 U.S.C. §8438.

[63] 5 U.S.C. §8475.

[64] House Conference Report 99-906 (May 16, 1986).

[65] For the announcement of the most recent BlackRock fund manager contract, see FRTIB, "Federal Retirement Thrift Investment Board Awards the First of Two Fund Manager Contracts," press release, February 24, 2020, https://www.frtib.gov/pdf/reading-room/PressRel/PR_2020-02-26_Fund_Manager_Contract.pdf. For the announcement of the State Street Global Advisors fund manager contract, see FRTIB, "Federal Retirement Thrift Investment Board Awards the Second of Two Fund Manager Contracts," press release, October 22, 2020, https://www.frtib.gov/pdf/reading-room/PressRel/PR_2020-10-27_Multi_Manager_Selection.pdf.

security fund)—were authorized at TSP's creation under FERSA. Two additional index funds, the "S" Fund (a small cap stock index fund) and the "I" Fund (an international stock index fund), were added in 2001 in accordance with the Thrift Savings Plan Act of 1996 (P.L. 104-208; September 30, 1996).

In 2005, FRTIB introduced "Lifecycle Funds" (L Funds), which are invested in various combinations of the five core TSP funds with allocations based on the year that the participant expects to begin withdrawing money from the TSP. The Smart Savings Act (P.L. 113-255; December 18, 2014) changed the default investment option to the age-appropriate Lifecycle Fund for automatic contributions to TSP. Prior to P.L. 113-255, TSP default contributions were automatically invested in the "G" Fund of the TSP. (The default contribution rate for most employees is 5% if enrolled in TSP after October 1, 2020, or 3% if enrolled between August 1, 2010, and September 30, 2020.)

Title I of Division B of P.L. 111-31, the Thrift Savings Plan Enhancement Act (June 22, 2009), provided FRTIB with the authority to set up a mutual fund window (MFW) "if the Board determines that such addition would be in the best interests of participants."[66] The TSP mutual fund window opened to eligible participants in June 2022.[67] (Additional details on this TSP investment option are provided below in the "Current TSP Investment Options" and "Mutual Fund Window" sections.)

Current TSP Investment Options

Participants in the TSP may currently choose among five core funds in which they can invest their TSP contributions:

- The "C" Fund replicates the Standard and Poor's 500 Index of 500 large to medium-sized U.S. companies.[68]
- The "F" Fund invests in bonds in the same proportion as they are represented by the Barclays Capital U.S. Aggregate Bond Index.[69]

---

[66] 5 U.S.C. §8438(b)(5)(A)).
[67] See TSP.gov, "Mutual Fund Window," at https://www.tsp.gov/mutual-fund-window/.
[68] For additional details, see TSP.gov, "C Fund," https://www.tsp.gov/funds-individual/c-fund/.
[69] For additional details, see TSP.gov, "F Fund," https://www.tsp.gov/funds-individual/f-fund/.

- The "G" Fund invests in U.S. government securities and pays interest equal to the average rate of return on government securities with maturities of four years or more.[70]
- The "S" Fund tracks the Dow Jones U.S. Completion Total Stock Market Index of small to medium-sized U.S. companies not included in the "C" Fund.[71]
- The "I" Fund currently replicates the Morgan Stanley Capital International (MSCI) EAFE (Europe, Australasia, Far East) Index.[72]
- On November 14, 2023, FRTIB announced that it had voted to change the I Fund benchmark to replicate the MSCI All Country World ex USA ex China ex Hong Kong Investable Market Index.[73] (Implementation of this change is scheduled for 2024 but has not occurred as of the date of this report.[74])

Additionally, the L Funds are composed of the five core TSP funds and consist of L2025 through L2065 in five-year increments and the L Income Fund, which is a low-risk option designed to achieve asset preservation for participants making withdrawals or nearing retirement.[75] As the participant approaches retirement, the proportion of contributions invested in the C, I, and S funds—which invest in stocks—is reduced. The proportion invested in the G and F funds—which invest in bonds—is increased. This helps to protect participants who are nearing retirement from investment losses that would occur from a sharp decline in stock prices.

Finally, eligible TSP participants may invest in the mutual fund window (MFW). According to the final rule implementing the TSP MFW

> A mutual fund window is a type of brokerage window. A brokerage window is a retirement plan feature that allows participants to open a

---

[70] For additional details, see TSP.gov, "G Fund," https://www.tsp.gov/funds-individual/g-fund/.

[71] For additional details, see TSP.gov, "S Fund," https://www.tsp.gov/funds-individual/s-fund/.

[72] For additional details, see TSP.gov, "I Fund," https://www.tsp.gov/funds-individual/i-fund/.

[73] FRTIB, "Federal Retirement Thrift Investment Board Approves a New Benchmark Index for the I Fund," press release, November 14, 2023, https://www.frtib.gov/pdf/reading-room/PressRel/PR_2023-11-14_I-Fund-Benchmark- Change.pdf. *Ex* means "excluding."

[74] FRTIB has stated that it plans to announce when the I Fund benchmark transition is complete no later than December 31, 2024. See FRTIB, "I Fund Benchmark Change in 2024," February 5, 2024, https://www.tsp.gov/plan-news/2024- 02-05-I-Fund-benchmark-index-change-in-2024/.

[75] For additional details, see TSP.gov, "Lifecyle Funds," https://www.tsp.gov/funds-lifecycle/.

brokerage account to put some of their retirement savings in investments that are not curated by their retirement plan's fiduciaries.[76]

FRTIB set out the following terms and conditions for MFW participation:[77] (1) a minimum initial transfer of $10,000 into the MFW; (2) a limit of no more than 25% of a TSP account holder's balance into the MFW (thus, a minimum balance of $40,000 is required); and (3) inclusion of transfers to and from the MFW in the overall limit on interfund transfers (two per month). FRTIB also specified fees for TSP participants who choose to invest in the MFW: an annual $55 administrative fee, an annual $95 maintenance fee, a per-trade fee of $28.75, and any fees and expenses imposed by the specific mutual fund(s). According to the FRTIB, "The MFW offers roughly 5,000 mutual funds in roughly 300 mutual fund families, including those offered by Fidelity, T. Rowe Price, and Vanguard. For funds with multiple classes, the lowest expense ratio class is offered."[78]

TSP Investment Issues

Several TSP investment-related policy issues have been legislatively active in recent Congresses. Below is a discussion of key TSP investment issues, including

- the TSP "I" Fund benchmark and investments in Chinese companies,
- ESG investment issues,
- the TSP mutual fund window (MFW),
- diverse asset managers, and
- the exercise of shareholder rights and proxy voting on behalf of TSP assets. Examples of relevant legislation from the 118th Congress are also provided.

---

76 FRTIB, "Mutual Fund Window," 87 *Federal Register* 27917, May 10, 2022, https://www.govinfo.gov/content/pkg/ FR-2022-05-10/pdf/2022-09972.pdf.

77 FRTIB, "Mutual Fund Window," 87 *Federal Register* 27917-27923, May 10, 2022, https://www.govinfo.gov/ content/pkg/FR-2022-05-10/pdf/2022-09972.pdf.

78 FRTIB, "Facts About the TSP's Mutual Fund Window," press release, June 2022, https://www.frtib.gov/pdf/reading-room/FactSheets/FS_2022-06-01_MFW_Fact_Sheet_ June_2022.pdf.

"I" (International) Fund Benchmark and Investments in Chinese Companies

TSP I Fund investment practices have drawn attention from policymakers over recent years. Specifically, there has been FRTIB deliberation surrounding changes to the I Fund benchmark, including concerns from policymakers about potential investments in Chinese companies. In November 2017, after consulting with experts,[79] FRTIB made the decision to move from the current I Fund benchmark—the Morgan Stanley Capital International (MSCI) EAFE (Europe, Australasia, Far East) Index—to a new benchmark: the MSCI ACWI ex U.S. IMI (All Country World ex USA Investable Market Index).[80] FRTIB justified this decision using the following arguments: (1) the MSCI ACWI ex. U.S. IMI represents 99% of the international equity market (vs. the MSCI EAFE Index, which represents only 58%) and, thus, is a more representative benchmark that better fulfills the statutory requirement of a complete representation of the international equity markets; and (2) the MSCI ACWI ex. U.S. IMI would be more in line with the investment policies of other large retirement plans in the private and public sectors, which offer the ability to invest in Canada and emerging markets.

Before the change to the I Fund benchmark could be implemented, however, this FRTIB decision received attention from policymakers. This interest focused on issues raised by investments in certain Chinese companies. For example, in August 2019, Senators Rubio and Shaheen sent a letter to FRTIB outlining concerns with the proposed I Fund benchmark change as

> a decision to invest in China-based companies, including many firms that are involved in the Chinese government's military, espionage, human rights abuses and 'Made in China 2025' industrial policy, and therefore poses fundamental questions about the board's statutory and fiduciary responsibilities to American public servants who invest in federal retirement plans.[81]

---

[79] See Aon Hewitt, "Benchmark Study: Federal Retirement Thrift Investment Board, Thrift Savings Plan," November 2017, https://www.frtib.gov/pdf/reading-room/InvBMarks/2017Oct_Benchmark-Evaluation-Report.pdf.

[80] See TSP.gov, "Investment Benchmark Update," November 13, 2019, https:// www.tsp.gov/plan-news/2024-02-05-I- Fund-benchmark-index-change-in-2024/.

[81] Office of Sen. Rubio, "Rubio, Shaheen Urge TSP Board to Reverse Decision to Steer Federal Retirement Savings to China," press release, August 26, 2019, https://www.rubio.senate.gov/rubio-shaheen-urge-tsp-board-to-reverse-decision-to-steer-federal-retirement-savings-to-china/.

In November 2019, FRTIB reviewed its decision and announced that it was moving ahead to finalize the I Fund benchmark change.[82] In May 2020, however, FRTIB announced that it was deferring any action on the I Fund benchmark due to (1) the "meaningfully different economic environment related in large part to the impact of the global COVID-19 pandemic" and (2) the nominations of new FRTIB members.[83] The current I Fund benchmark, the MSCI EAFE Index, does include investments in Hong Kong, which FRTIB claims has been less than 4% of the I Fund since its creation in 2001.[84] But the current I Fund benchmark (the MSCI EAFE Index) does not, nor has it ever, included investments in mainland China.[85] Among the dynamic offering of more than 5,000 mutual funds available through the TSP MFW, however, there is likely exposure to investments in Chinese companies (for additional details on this issue, see "Mutual Fund Window," below).

Most recently, in November 2023, FRTIB announced that it had voted to change the I Fund benchmark to replicate the MSCI All Country World ex USA ex China ex Hong Kong Investable Market Index (MSCI ACWI IMI ex USA ex China ex Hong Kong Index).[86] According to FRTIB, this new index represents 90% of non-U.S. market capitalization and is expected to outperform the current I Fund benchmark on a "risk-adjusted basis over the

---

[82] See TSP.gov, "Investment Benchmark Update."

[83] FRTIB, "Federal Retirement Thrift Investment Board Defers Action on I Fund Transition," press release, May 13, 2020, https://www.frtib.gov/pdf/reading-room/PressRel/PR_2020-05-13_Defer_I_Fund_Implementation.pdf.
On June 9, 2022, the Senate confirmed four nominees to the FRTIB, including three new Board Members (Leona Bridges, Michael Gerber, and Stacie Olivares) and one Board Member who received another term (Dana Bilyeu). See FRTIB, "Federal Retirement Thrift Investment Board Announces the Confirmation of Dana Bilyeu, Leona Bridges, Michael Gerber and Stacie Olivares as New Members of the Board," press release, June 28, 2022, https://www.frtib.gov/pdf/reading-room/PressRel/PR_2022-06-28_Board_Members_Bilyeu _Bridges_Gerber_Olivares.pdf.
On September 1, 2022, David Jones announced his resignation from the FRTIB, effective September 15, 2023. See FRTIB, "Federal Retirement Thrift Investment Board Announces Resignation of Board Member David A. Jones," press release, September 1, 2022, https://www.frtib.gov/pdf/reading-room/PressRel/PR_2022-08- 01_DAJ_Resignation.pdf. For more information on current Board Members, see https://www.frtib.gov/board-members/.

[84] FRTIB, "TSP Fact Sheet—Investment in China," press release, August 2023, https://www.frtib.gov/pdf/reading-room/FactSheets/FS_2023-08-04_TSP_Investment_in_ China.pdf.

[85] FRTIB, "TSP Fact Sheet—Investment in China."

[86] FRTIB, "Federal Retirement Thrift Investment Board Approves a New Benchmark Index for the I Fund," press release, November 14, 2023, https://www.frtib.gov/pdf/reading-room/PressRel/PR_2023-11-14_I-Fund-Benchmark- Change.pdf.

long term."[87] Thus, the MSCI ACWI IMI ex USA ex China ex Hong Kong Index will provide a more representative benchmark that better fulfills the statutory requirement for the I Fund of a complete representation of the international equity markets. At the same time, this new benchmark will exclude China and Hong Kong, thus addressing concerns related to Chinese investments. Implementation for the new I Fund benchmark is scheduled for 2024. (As of the publication of this report, it has not yet occurred.[88])

Examples of Legislation in the 118th Congress[89]

Several pieces of legislation have been introduced in the 118th Congress that would have the effect of prohibiting any TSP investment in Chinese firms. For example, S. 1650, the TSP Act of 2023 (introduced by Senator Rubio), and H.R. 3455, the TSP Act (introduced by Representative Waltz), would both amend TSP law to prohibit any investments in "countries of concern," defined as a country identified as a threat to the national security of the United States in the most recent Annual Threat Assessment report submitted to Congress by the Director of National Intelligence.[90] In addition, S. 149, the TSP Fiduciary Security Act of 2023 (introduced by Senator Rubio), would amend FRTIB fiduciary duties under current law to include national security concerns and would prohibit TSP investments in entities on certain lists maintained by the Department of Defense and the Department of Commerce (e.g., Chinese military companies).

This type of legislation would have prevented the I Fund benchmark change to the MSCI ACWI ex USA (i.e., due to its exposure to Chinese investments). However, it is not clear that it would prevent the proposed I Fund benchmark change to the MSCI ACWI IMI ex USA ex China ex Hong Kong, as it does not have exposure to Chinese companies. These bills would, however, likely require FRTIB to make changes to the TSP mutual fund window, which does currently have exposure to Chinese companies. (For additional discussion on this issue, see the section on "Mutual Fund Window.")

---

[87] FRTIB, "Federal Retirement Thrift Investment Board Approves a New Benchmark Index for the I Fund," p. 1.

[88] For more information, see FRTIB, "I Fund Benchmark Change in 2024."

[89] Examples of TSP-related legislation here and below are provided for illustrative purposes and should not be considered exhaustive.

[90] The legislative text in these bills was also offered as S. Amdt. 523 to S. 2226, the National Defense Authorization Act for Fiscal Year 2024, but this amendment was not agreed to in the Senate.

ESG Investment Issues

Policymakers have also been interested in ESG issues with regard to TSP investments.[91] For example, in a May 2021 report, the Government Accountability Office (GAO) recommended that FRTIB evaluate TSP investment risks with regard to climate change:

> Investment risks associated with climate change are expected to impact the global economy and cause unprecedented disruption to the financial markets, and investors, including retirement plans, are considering how their portfolios may be exposed to these risks. Passive investment strategies, like those used by TSP, are generally seen as providing the important benefits of broad diversification and low costs, leading to greater risk-adjusted returns when compared to active investment strategies. However, even passive investment strategies are exposed to financial risks from climate change as the impacts are expected to be widespread across all economic sectors. Climate and financial experts urge passive investors and others to consider the unique and systemic risks posed by climate change.[92]

In its comments responding to this GAO report, FRTIB did not agree or disagree with GAO's recommendation—although it did provide a response that challenged some of GAO's conclusions and asserted that its current investment strategy already prices in risk:

> The draft report states that the FRTIB "does not currently have any knowledge" of the risks of climate change. We disagree with that characterization. As we discussed several times with the GAO representatives and as is mentioned in the report, the FRTIB subscribes to a strict indexing discipline using the broadest possible market opportunity set. As such, individual companies are held in the TSP index funds at their market weights, in line with the theory that markets are generally efficient and that the market portfolio is the most efficient from a risk and return perspective. The theory has proven to hold true over decades of empirical studies. Indeed, we build our 10 Lifecycle Funds using that analysis. The efficient market theory concludes that the market is pricing all risks into its valuation in an

---

[91] For background on ESG, see CRS In Focus IF11716, Introduction to Financial Services: Environmental, Social, and Governance (ESG) Issues.

[92] GAO, Retirement Savings: Federal Workers' Portfolios Should Be Evaluated for Possible Financial Risks Related to Climate Change, GAO-21-327, May 25, 2021, p. 39, https://www.gao.gov/assets/gao-21-327.pdf.

on-going basis. It also posits that a broad index fund with all assets held at market weight provides the highest return to risk ratio.[93]

Prior to the opening of the TSP MFW in June 2022, there were no ESG investment options available to TSP participants, as the core funds are all passively managed with the investment objective of matching the performance of a specific, benchmark index fund selected by the FRTIB. In authorizing the MFW in 2009, Congress acknowledged that some TSP participants may wish to access "socially responsible funds" as part of their investment options.[94] In TSP annual reports from 2020 and 2021, FRTIB acknowledged that offering ESG investment would be part of the MFW: "Of the more than 5,000 mutual funds available through the MFW, there will be funds that are designed for ESG investment (however a participant may define that), as well as commodity specific funds, actively managed funds, and emerging manager funds."[95] Thus, with the current availability of the MFW, eligible TSP participants have access to ESG investment options (for additional information on the TSP MFW, see "Mutual Fund Window," below).

Examples of Legislation in the 118th Congress

There has been legislation introduced in the 118th Congress that would both expand and prohibit ESG investing through TSP. For example, Representative Schiff introduced H.R. 1261, the Federal Employees Sustainable Investment Act, which would create a new TSP index fund, the Corporate Responsibility Stock Index Fund. This new index fund would be invested in a stock portfolio designed to replicate the performance of a commonly recognized, passively managed index comprised of stocks that meet certain minimum criteria related to corporate responsibility. In terms of anti-ESG legislation, Representative Roy introduced H.R. 3612, the No ESG in TSP Act, which would prohibit any ESG mutual funds from being offered as part of the TSP MFW. Senator Lee introduced S. 2147, the Senate companion bill. Additionally, a policy rider (Section 754) in H.R. 4664, the Financial Services and General Government Appropriations Act, 2024, would prevent any funding to be used "to make investments under the Thrift Savings Plan in certain mutual funds that make

---

93 GAO, Retirement Savings, p. 50.

94 See H.Rept. 111-58 Part 2, P.L. 111-31, Division B, Thrift Savings Plan Enhancement Act of 2009, p. 5.

95 FRTIB, "TSP Annual Report 2020," p. 2, https://www.frtib.gov/pdf/reading-room/congress/annual/TSP-Annual- Report_2020.pdf; and FRTIB, "TSP Annual Report 2021, p. 2, https://www.frtib.gov/pdf/reading-room/congress/annual/TSP-Annual-Report_2021.pdf.

investment decisions based primarily on environmental, social, or governance criteria."

Mutual Fund Window

In a 2008 TSP participant survey, 39% of participants—and 46% of TSP participants who were military servicemembers—reported that the addition of a self-directed mutual fund window would improve TSP.[96] In 2009, P.L. 111-31 provided the FRTIB with an authority to set up an MFW "if the Board determines that such addition would be in the best interests of participants."[97]

In providing this authority, the House Committee on Oversight and Government Reform noted that

> The Committee recognizes some investors today have sophisticated or specialized investment needs. Participants may want added diversity by investing in funds comprised of real estate investment trusts, emerging markets, or inflation-protected bonds. Other participants may want to align their portfolio with their personal convictions by investing in socially responsible funds. The self-directed investment options are intended to provide a vehicle for meeting these needs of plan participants without complicating the basic structure of the Thrift Savings Plan.[98]

From 2009 until its decision to offer an MFW in April 2015, FRTIB deliberation about this issue included consultations with relevant subject matter experts and the Employee Thrift Advisory Council (ETAC).[99] In November 2020, FRTIB announced that the recordkeeping contract to implement the MFW, along with other TSP service delivery features, was

---

[96] FRTIB, "2008 TSP Participant Survey Results," pp. 57-58, https://www.frtib.gov/pdf/reading-room/SurveysPart/satisfaction/TSP-Survey-Results-2008.pdf.

[97] 5 U.S.C. §8438(b)(5)(A)).

[98] H.Rept. 111-58 Part 2, P.L. 111-31, Division B, Thrift Savings Plan Enhancement Act of 2009, p. 5.

[99] For a legislative and program history of the TSP MFW, see FRTIB, "Mutual Fund Window," 87 *Federal Register* 3940-3943, January 26, 2022, https:// www.govinfo.gov/content/pkg/FR-2022-01-26/pdf/2022-01312.pdf.
As explained at https://www.frtib.gov/board-members/: "The Employee Thrift Advisory Council (ETAC) is comprised of representatives from Federal and Postal unions and management associations, as well as a representative from the Department of Defense on behalf of uniformed service members. ETAC provides advice on matters relating to TSP investment policies and plan administration. The Board and the Executive Director meet with ETAC at least annually."

awarded to Accenture Federal Services.[100] FRTIB published the final regulations for the MFW on May 10, 2022.[101] The TSP MFW opened to eligible participants in June 2022.[102]

With regard to the mutuals funds offered through the TSP MFW, FRTIB has explained that

> All the mutual funds on the platform comply with all applicable U.S. laws and regulations, including those promulgated by the Securities and Exchange Commission (SEC) and the Office of Foreign Assets Control (OFAC). The mutual funds on the TSP MFW platform will follow the same rules applicable to any other mutual fund offered in any other public or private retirement plan in the United States.[103]

Additionally, FRTIB is not providing fiduciary oversight over the MFW, which it noted mirrors the practice of private sector retirement plans[104] and could "place unreasonable cost and resource burdens on the FRTIB."[105] Instead, eligible TSP participants may create MFW accounts to view the

---

[100] FRTIB, "Federal Retirement Thrift Investment Boards Awards Recordkeeping Contract," press release, November 16, 2020, https://www.frtib.gov/pdf/reading-room/PressRel/PR_2020-11-17_RKSA_Award_Announcement_FINAL.pdf.

[101] FRTIB, "Mutual Fund Window," 87 *Federal Register* 27917-27923, May 10, 2022, https://www.govinfo.gov/content/pkg/FR-2022-05-10/pdf/2022-09972.pdf.

[102] See TSP.gov, "Mutual Fund Window," https://www.tsp.gov/mutual-fund-window/. As of December 2023, out of a total of 6,997,017 TSP accounts, FRTIB reports that there were slightly over 4,000 MFW accounts with funds in them (i.e., approximately 0.06% of all TSP accounts). See FRTIB, "Thrift Fund Statistics: December 2023," https://www.frtib.gov/pdf/minutes/2024/Jan/Att1-Participant-Activity-Report-December-2023.pdf. More generally, FRTIB estimates that 2%-3% of TSP account holders will be using the MFW two to three years after implementation (see FEDweek Staff, "TSP Projects Just 2-3% of Investors Will Use Mutual Fund Window," *FEDweek*, March 22, 2024, https://www.fedweek.com/fedweek/tsp-projects-just-2-3-of-investors-will-use-mutual-fund-window/).

[103] FRTIB, "Facts about the TSP's Mutual Fund Window," p. 1.

[104] See, for example, Department of Labor, *Understanding Brokerage Windows in Self- Directed Retirement Plans*, report to Honorable Martin Walsh, Secretary of the Department of Labor, Advisory Council on Employee Welfare and Pension Benefit Plans (2021), p. 47, https://www.dol.gov/sites/dolgov/files/EBSA/about-ebsa/about-us/erisa-advisory-council/2021-understanding-brokerage-windows-in-self-directed-retirement-plans.pdf ("Investments accessible through a brokerage window are not routinely monitored by plan fiduciaries, and most experts conclude that, except perhaps in extraordinary circumstances, plan fiduciaries are not obligated to monitor brokerage window investments nor do their fiduciary duties apply with respect to those investments.").

[105] FRTIB, "Mutual Fund Window," 87 *Federal Register* 27920, May 10, 2022, https://www.govinfo.gov/content/pkg/ FR-2022-05-10/pdf/2022-09972.pdf.

complete list of available mutual funds and use a Morningstar tool to sort and review funds.[106] According to the FRTIB, the TSP MFW

> provides TSP participants with access to roughly 4,700 commercially available mutual funds, including funds from Berkshire, BNY Mellon, Calvert, Cohen & Steers, Fidelity, Franklin Templeton, Goldman Sachs, John Hancock, JPMorgan, Morgan Stanley, Schwab, T Rowe Price, TIAA, Vanguard, and Voya, among many others.[107]

Examples of Relevant Legislation in the 118th Congress

In general, any legislation that would require major investment changes, including divestment for any reason (e.g., from Chinese companies [S. 149, S. 1650, and H.R. 3455]), would affect the TSP mutual fund window. Additionally, as described above, there are three bills that would prohibit ESG investments specifically in the mutual fund window: H.R. 3612 and S. 2147, the No ESG in TSP Act, as well as Section 754 in H.R. 4664, the Financial Services and General Government Appropriations Act, 2024.

Diverse Asset Managers

Some policymakers have also expressed interest in expanding professional services contracts to minority- and women-owned business enterprises in the arena of public pension investment, including TSP investment. At a July 2008 hearing held by the House Oversight and Government Reform Committee's Subcommittee on the Federal Workforce, Postal Service, and the District of Columbia on "Investing in the Future: Minority Opportunities and the Thrift Savings Plan," Representative Danny Davis stated

> The debate over minorities participating in the TSP funds has been a concern for quite some time; yet, the issue came to the forefront during last year's Congressional Black Caucus legislative conference. The executive director of the Federal Retirement Thrift Investment Board revealed that there are minority firms with talent in long-term financial management. However, most of these firms gravitate toward the active fund management business, which is not an investment strategy of the

---

106 FRTIB, "Facts About the TSP's Mutual Fund Window," p. 1.

107 FRTIB, "TSP Fact Sheet—Investment in China," p. 2.

TSP. Research by the TSP indicates that there may be only one minority-owned firm that deals with passive-management of index funds.[108]

After this hearing, Section 105 of the Thrift Savings Plan Enhancement Act of 2009 (enacted as part of P.L. 111-31) created annual reporting requirements for FRTIB, which included reporting on "the diversity demographics of any company, investment adviser, or other entity retained to invest and manage the assets of the Thrift Savings Fund."[109]

A September 2017 GAO report, *Investment Management: Key Practices Could Provide More Options for Federal Entities and Opportunities for Minority- and Women-Owned Asset Managers*, examined how federal entities, including TSP, were using minority- and women- owned asset managers and identified key practices to increase opportunities for these asset managers: (1) "top leadership commitment," (2) "remove potential barriers," (3) "outreach," and (4) "communicate priorities and expectations."[110] This report concluded that FRTIB did not intend to use any of these best practices in setting up the TSP MFW.[111]

In October 2021, Senators Menendez, Padilla, Luján, Brown, Merkley, Kaine, and Booker sent a letter urging the FRTIB "to create opportunities for federal workers to invest in funds run by racially, ethnically, and gender diverse asset managers. When it comes to their retirement investments, federal workers deserve the chance to make the strategic and values-driven choice to prioritize diversity."[112] The signatories of this letter highlighted the opportunity for diverse asset managers in the MFW.[113]

---

108 U.S. Congress, House Committee on Oversight and Government Reform, Subcommittee on the Federal Workforce, Postal Service, and the District of Columbia, *Investing in the Future: Minority Opportunities and the Thrift Savings Plan*, 110th Cong., 2nd sess., July 10, 2008, Serial No. 110-133, p. 2.

109 See, for example, Appendix A (BlackRock) and Appendix B (State Street) in FRTIB, *TSP Annual Report 2022*, https://www.frtib.gov/pdf/reading-room/congress/annual/TSP-Annual-Report_2022.pdf.

110 GAO, Investment Management: Key Practices Could Provide More Options for Federal Entities and Opportunities for Minority- and Women-Owned Asset Managers, GAO-17-726, September 13, 2017, https://www.gao.gov/products/ gao-17-726.

111 See also Appendix V in GAO-17-726 for FRTIB's response to GAO.

112 See Office of Sen. Menendez, "Menendez, Booker, Colleagues Urge for Diversity Among Federal Retirement Asset Managers," press release, October 21, 2021, https://www.menendez.senate.gov/newsroom/press/menendez-booker-colleagues-urge-for-diversity-among-federal-retirement-asset-managers.

113 In terms of the contracting rules, including for professional services such as asset managers, FRTIB states:

There has been legislation introduced in prior Congresses related to the use of diverse asset managers by federal institutional investors, including FRTIB (e.g., S. 4097 and H.R. 7594 in the 117th Congress). At this time, no such legislation has been introduced in the 118th Congress.

Exercise of Shareholder Rights

Under current law, FRTIB, the Executive Director, and TSP participants are all prohibited from exercising shareholder voting rights associated with TSP assets.[114] Therefore, TSP fund managers (i.e., BlackRock and State Street Global Advisors) are the only parties currently exercising voting rights, with oversight provided by the FRTIB. According to the FRTIB:

> [T]he FRTIB does not set proxy voting policy for its Fund managers. The FRTIB does, however, require that the Fund managers conform to their stated proxy voting policy. The FRTIB receives quarterly reports from an independent organization hired by the money manager to audit that their proxy voting complies with their policy. Those reports are sent to the FRTIB by the money manager. Our Chief Investment Officer reports on this issue quarterly to the Board in our monthly, public Board meetings.[115]

FRTIB is a self-funded federal agency with independent budgetary authority that receives no annual appropriations from Congress. Due to our unique status, FRTIB is not strictly bound to adhere to the Federal Acquisition Regulation (FAR). While subject to many of the same procurement laws as other government agencies, FRTIB also works under the mandate of its enabling statute, the Federal Employees' Retirement System Act (FERSA), which requires that FRTIB fiduciaries manage Thrift Savings Fund (TSF) assets in the sole interest of the TSF participants and beneficiaries, and expend funds for the exclusive purpose of providing benefits to participants and beneficiaries and defraying reasonable expenses of administering the TSP. To that end, FRTIB procurements will largely adhere to the FAR, unless doing so might infringe upon the Agency's fiduciary obligations under FERSA. FRTIB has adopted the FAR as its primary contracting policy and procedures for procuring its goods and services.

FRTIB designed the Thrift Federal Acquisition Supplement (T-FAS) as a supplement to the FAR, which specifies when the Agency's policies and practices deviate from the FAR. See link to T-FAS below. The T-FAS provides an efficient blend of the FAR and federal procurement law while allowing the Agency to be more flexible to accomplish its mission under FERSA (FRTIB, "Doing Business with FRTIB," https://www.frtib.gov/procurement/).

[114] See 5 U.S.C. §8438(f): "The Board, other Government agencies, the Executive Director, an employee, a Member, a former employee and a former Member may not exercise voting rights associated with the ownership of securities by the Thrift Savings Fund."

[115] Email communication with FRTIB, January 14, 2021.For FRTIB's quarterly reporting on the proxy voting by asset managers, see "Meeting Minutes," available at http://www.frtib.gov for the month after each quarter (i.e., January, April, July, and October). See, for example,

It should be noted that there is additional federal oversight over TSP fiduciary duties. The U.S. Department of Labor's (DOL's) Employee Benefits Security Administration (EBSA) is responsible for establishing a program to carry out audits to determine the level of compliance with the requirements related to TSP fiduciary responsibilities and prohibited activities of TSP fiduciaries.[116] EBSA provides regular fiduciary audits of TSP.[117]

Some policymakers have expressed concerns about proxy voting by TSP asset managers— particularly with regard to ESG issues. For example, in July 2021, Senators Toomey and Johnson wrote a letter to FRTIB expressing their concerns:

> Specifically, recent statements by the CEOs of BlackRock and State Street Global Advisors (SSGA) indicate they are using their control of proxy votes for federal employees' Thrift Savings Plan ("the Plan") investments to pressure other companies to adhere to their own environmental and social policy views. We are concerned that BlackRock and SSGA may be prioritizing their CEOs' personal policy views over retirees' financial security. Federal law explicitly requires all fiduciaries of the [TSP], including BlackRock and SSGA, to discharge their responsibilities "*solely* in the interest of the participants and beneficiaries and for the *exclusive* purpose of providing benefits to participants and their beneficiaries."[118]

Examples of Relevant Legislation in the 118th Congress

In the 118th Congress, for example, Representative Buck introduced H.R. 3406, the Stop TSP ESG Act, which would add "a qualified professional asset manager" to the entities and individuals prohibited from exercising shareholder voting rights associated with securities held by TSP. Senator Rubio introduced the Senate companion bill as S. 1891. This proposal would effectively prevent any TSP proxy voting.

FRTIB, "Monthly Meeting," October 2020, Attachment 4, pp. 10-13, https://minutes.frtib.gov/.

[116] This authority is provided by the statutory reference to the Secretary of Labor; see 5 U.S.C. §8477(g).

[117] See, for example, EBSA, "FY2022 Thrift Savings Plan Fiduciary Oversight Program," April 26, 2022, https://www.frtib.gov/pdf/minutes/2022/Apr/MM-2022Apr-Att7.pdf.

[118] Sens. Pat Toomey and Ron Johnson, letter to David A. Jones, Acting Chairman, Federal Retirement Thrift Investment Board, June 30, 2021, https://www.banking.senate.gov/imo/media/doc/toomey_johnson_letter_to_frtib.pdf.

Private Sector Pension Plans

Pension plans can be classified along several dimensions, such as whether the employee receives a monthly payment in retirement (DB pensions) or accrues funds in an individual account (DC pensions), and whether the plan sponsor is a private-sector or public-sector employer. To protect the interests of pension plan participants and beneficiaries, ERISA was enacted (P.L. 93-406).

ERISA covers most private-sector pension plans and is included in the *U.S. Code* in both Title 26 (the Internal Revenue Code, or IRC) and in Title 29 (often called the Labor Code).[119]

Nearly all private sector pension plans are required to file Form 5500 with the Internal Revenue Service (IRS), DOL, and the PBGC. The Form 5500 includes breakdowns on the number of plan participants, financial information about the plan, and details of companies providing services to the plan. Though information on plan investments is included in the Form 5500, this information is not aggregated into downloadable Form 5500 datasets nor presented in a standardized manner. To see information on an individual plan's investments, individuals must download the plan's Form 5500 and examine the corresponding schedule.[120]

Duties of Plan Sponsors Regarding Plan Investments Under ERISA

ERISA contains provisions governing many aspects of pension plans (e.g., reporting and disclosure requirements, participation standards, funding requirements). ERISA also contains fiduciary standards, which require that individuals who make decisions in and for private sector pension plans and their participants (referred to as fiduciaries) adhere to specified standards of conduct, including

- The duty of loyalty, which requires fiduciaries to discharge their duties "solely in the interest of the participants and beneficiaries" and for the "exclusive purpose" of providing benefits to participants and

[119] For an overview of ERISA, see CRS Report RL34443, Summary of the Employee Retirement Income Security Act (ERISA).

[120] Schedule H of the Form 5500 provides financial information for the plan. A plan must provide details on plan investments as an attachment to Schedule H.

beneficiaries and defraying reasonable expenses of administering the plan;

- The duty of prudence, which requires fiduciaries to also act "with the care, skill, prudence, and diligence under the circumstances then prevailing that a prudent man would use in the conduct of an enterprise of a like character with like aims;"
- The duty to diversify investments, which requires fiduciaries to diversify the investments of plans "so as to minimize the risk of large losses, unless under the circumstances it is clearly prudent not to do so;" and
- The duty to act in accordance with plan documents, which requires fiduciaries to discharge their duties "in accordance with the documents and instruments governing the plan insofar as such documents and instruments are consistent with" ERISA.[121]

ERISA also prohibits fiduciaries from engaging in transactions deemed likely to injure pension plans, referred to as prohibited transactions. ERISA bars certain transactions between a plan and a party in interest with respect to a plan, and between a plan and a plan fiduciary.[122] In order to facilitate transactions between pension plans and service providers that would otherwise be prohibited by ERISA, a number of prohibited transaction exemptions (PTEs) exist, either in statute or as issued by DOL.[123]

[121] See ERISA §404 and 29 C.F.R. §2550.404a-1.

[122] These transactions include sale, exchange, or leasing of any property; lending of money or other extension of credit; furnishing of goods, services, or facilities; transfer or use of any plan assets; and acquisition, on behalf of the plan, of any employer security or employer real property in violation of ERISA Section 407, which limits the amount of employer securities and property that may be held by a plan. A fiduciary may not deal with the assets of the plan in his own interest or for his own account; act in any transaction involving the plan on behalf of a party (or represent a party) whose interests are adverse to the interests of the plan or the interests of its participants or beneficiaries, or receive any consideration for his own personal account from any party dealing with such plan in connection with a transaction involving the assets of the plan. See 29 U.S.C. §1106.

[123] A list of class exemptions is available at https://www.dol.gov/agencies/ebsa/laws-and-regulations/rules-and- regulations/exemptions/class.

Private Sector Pension Plan Investment Considerations

Few explicit restrictions on private sector pension plan investments exist.[124] Because the fiduciary duty is such a high standard (and fiduciaries can be held personally liable for violating their duties), plan sponsors tend to be cautious about which types of investments are included in their plans. Among those who are fiduciaries are individuals who choose plan investments. The roles of fiduciaries in DB plans and DC plans are described in more detail below.

Defined Benefit Plans

Private sector DB plan sponsors are responsible for choosing how plans' assets are invested. While DB plan participants can file claims for breach of fiduciary duty, because participants have a claim on their monthly benefits they receive and not on the assets on the plans, they generally cannot take action for fiduciaries' investment choices unless they experience loss of benefits.

Defined Contribution Plans

Most private sector DC plans are those in which participants have individual accounts and choose their investments from among the options provided by the plan sponsors, referred to as 404(c) plans.[125]

DC plan sponsors make various decisions about plan features, including which investment options to include in the plans (referred to *designated investment alternatives*).[126] The investment options usually include mutual funds with varying characteristics such as index funds (which mirror the performance of a stock market index such as the S&P 500), small and large cap funds (which invest in small or large firms as measured by market capitalization), bond funds (which invest in debt obligations), real estate funds (which invest in real estate), and target date funds (which change the

---

[124] One investment restriction that exists for DC plans and IRAs is collectibles, such as artwork, rugs and antiques, metals, gems, stamps, alcoholic beverages, and most coins. Amounts invested in collectibles are treated as distributions and may be subject to income tax and a 10% penalty (26 U.S.C. §408(m)). Gold, silver, and platinum coins issued by the U.S. Treasury and gold, silver, palladium, and platinum bullion are permissible. Nonfungible tokens, or NFTs, are digital certificates of ownership that represent digital or physical assets. In March 2023, Treasury and the IRS announced that they were soliciting feedback for upcoming guidance regarding the tax treatment of an NFT as a collectible. Certain plans, such as DC plans in which participants direct the investments of their accounts, may be subject to other restrictions, such as limitations on the amount of employer stock held in a plan.

[125] See ERISA 404(c).

[126] See 29 C.F.R. §2550.404a-5.

investment mix between bonds and stocks as an individual gets closer to retirement). DC plans may also offer participants collective investment trusts (CITs), which are pooled investment vehicles managed by bank and trust companies, and annuities, which provide a monthly payment in retirement that lasts until the death of the participant or, if married, the surviving spouse.

In addition to mutual fund investments, less than one-third of private sector DC plans allow participants to invest via *brokerage windows.*[127] A brokerage window allows plan participants to invest in options beyond those provided by the plan, such as individual stocks and a wide variety of mutual funds. Some plans place restrictions on participants' investments within brokerage windows, such as limiting the percentage of an individual's account balance that can be invested in the brokerage window or prohibiting investments in the stock of the employee's company.[128]

At job change or retirement, many individuals with DC plans roll over their savings into IRAs. IRA investment restrictions and policy issues are described later in this report.

---

[127] Although one-quarter to one-third of DC plans offer brokerage windows, a small fraction of participants use them. Plan Sponsor Council of America found that 31.2% of plans in its survey offered brokerage windows. See Plan Sponsor Council of America, "65th Annual Survey of Profit Sharing and 401(k) Plans," https://www.psca.org/research/401k/ 65thAR. An ERISA advisory report on brokerage windows cited data from various financial services firms. In that report, brokerage window offer rates varied by firm: Fidelity (17.4% in 2016), Vanguard (20% of all plans; 38% of plans with 5,000 or more participants), and Alight Solutions (46%). Vanguard's data stated that while 33% of all participants had access to brokerage windows, less than 0.5% of all participants used them. Alight's data stated that 2.4% of participants used brokerage windows. See Advisory Council on Employee Welfare and Pension Benefit Plans, *Understanding Brokerage Windows in Self-Directed Retirement Plans*, December 2021, https://www.dol.gov/sites/ dolgov/files/EBSA/about-ebsa/about-us/erisa-advisory-council/2021-understanding-brokerage-windows-in-self-directed-retirement-plans.pdf.

[128] DOL regulations state that a brokerage window is *not* a designated investment alternative. See 29 C.F.R.§2550.404a-5(h)(4). In "Field Assistance Bulletin (FAB) 2012-02," DOL clarified that investments in a brokerage window could be considered a designated investment alternative if chosen by a significant number of participants (see Q30 at https://www.dol.gov/agencies/ebsa/employers-and-advisers/guidance/field-assistance-bulletins/2012-02). However, DOL subsequently removed that in an update to the FAB (see Q39 at https://www.dol.gov/agencies/ebsa/employers-and-advisers/guidance/field-assistance-bulletins/2012-02r).

Private Sector Pension Plan Investment Issues

This section describes several issues related to private sector pension plan investments that have been topics of discussion in recent Congresses. Each issue is comprised of two parts: an overview and a discussion of relevant regulatory or congressional responses, if any. The following issues are discussed:

- Investments based on non-pecuniary factors,
- Exercise of shareholder rights,
- Investment advice,
- Alternative investments in retirement plans,
- Collective investment trusts in 403(b) plans,
- Investment fees, and
- Qualified professional asset managers (QPAMs).

ESG Investment Issues

Over the years, investors—including pension plan sponsors and participants—have taken an interest in investment features beyond the standard risk and return relationship. Examples of such investments include those that consider the effects of climate change (e.g., preferring renewable energy companies to fossil fuel companies), a firm's supply chain practices (e.g., ensuring that seafood is not caught with forced labor), faith-based approaches (e.g., investing based on the Bible or Sharia law), corporate governance structures (e.g., considering the diversity of a corporation's board of directors), or geopolitical circumstances (e.g., avoiding countries that are perceived to be hostile to U.S. interests). These investments have been referred to with various names, such as economically targeted investments, socially responsible investments, and ESG investing. Policymakers' opinions vary as to the appropriateness of these types of investments within pension plans. Some Members of Congress are interested in facilitating these investments; others are interested in limiting them.

In 1994, 2008, and 2015, DOL issued guidance in the form of Interpretive Bulletins and, in 2018, a Field Assistance Bulletin on the extent to which pension plan fiduciaries can consider factors beyond an investment's risk and return relationship.[129] The guidance generally emphasized that investment

---

[129] See Pension and Welfare Benefits Administration, "Interpretive Bulletin Relating to the Employee Retirement Income Security Act of 1974," https://www.govinfo.gov/content/

decisions must be made with the objective to provide economic benefits to plan participants. The guidance also described scenarios in which consideration of investments that have goals beyond providing income to participants could be consistent with a fiduciary's duties. For example, if a plan found that two investments were equal on an economic basis, then the plan could—but would not be required to—choose based on noneconomic factors. DOL, in Interpretive Bulletin (IB) 2015-01, construed that ERISA prohibits "a fiduciary from subordinating the interests of participants and beneficiaries in their retirement income to unrelated objectives."[130]

Regulatory and Congressional Responses

On November 13, 2020, under the Trump Administration, DOL issued a final rule relating to the selection of investments by a pension plan fiduciary.[131] The DOL rule said that the evaluation of an investment by a pension plan fiduciary must be based on economic factors only—what the regulation called pecuniary factors—and that a pension plan could not subordinate the interests of participants and their retirement income to non-pecuniary objectives.

On December 1, 2022, under the Biden Administration, DOL issued a final rule that it said would clarify the application of fiduciary duty when selecting plan investments.[132] DOL said that the November 2020 regulation had a "chilling effect and other potential negative consequences" on the appropriate use of ESG factors in investment decisions in pension plans. While the regulation removed some of the barriers from the 2020 regulation to make it easier to consider factors beyond the risk-return relationship, the 2022 regulation retains what it calls "the core principle" that the duties of prudence and loyalty require ERISA plan fiduciaries to focus on relevant risk- return

pkg/FR-1994-06-23/html/94-15162.htm; EBSA, "Interpretive Bulletin Relating to Economically Targeted Investments," 73 *Federal Register* 61734-61736, October 17, 2008, https://www.govinfo.gov/content/pkg/FR-2008-10-17/pdf/E8-24551.pdf; EBSA, "Interpretive Bulletin Relating to the Fiduciary Standard Under ERISA in Considering Economically Targeted Investments," 80 *Federal Register* 65135-61736, October 26, 2015, https://www.govinfo.gov/content/pkg/FR-2015-10-26/pdf/2015-27146.pdf; and EBSA, "Interpretive Bulletins 2016-01 and 2015-01," https://www.dol.gov/sites/dolgov/files/ebsa/employers-and- advisers/guidance/field-assistance-bulletins/2018-01.pdf.

[130] EBSA, "Interpretive Bulletin Relating to the Fiduciary Standard Under ERISA in Considering Economically Targeted Investments," 80 *Federal Register* 65135-61736, October 26, 2015, https://www.govinfo.gov/content/pkg/ FR-2015-10-26/pdf/2015-27146.pdf.

[131] See EBSA, "Financial Factors in Selecting Plan Investments," 85 *Federal Register* 72846-72885, November 13, 2020, https://www.federalregister.gov/documents/2020/11/13/2020-24515/financial-factors-in-selecting-plan- investments.

[132] See EBSA, "Prudence and Loyalty in Selecting Plan Investments and Exercising Shareholder Rights," 87 *Federal Register* 73882-73886, December 1, 2022.

factors. It stated that ERISA fiduciaries cannot subordinate the interests of participants and beneficiaries (such as by sacrificing investment returns or taking on additional investment risk) to objectives unrelated to the provision of benefits under the plan.

In the 118th Congress, H.J.Res. 30, which would use the Congressional Review Act (CRA; enacted in P.L. 104-121) to nullify the 2022 regulation, was passed by the House and Senate and vetoed by President Biden on March 20, 2023.[133]

H.R. 4008, the Protecting Americans' Retirement Savings Act, introduced by Representative Jim Banks on June 12, 2023, would prohibit private sector pension plans from making newinvestments in specified countries (China, Russia, North Korea, and Iran) or in entities operated by individuals or organizations in these specified countries.[134]

Exercise of Shareholder Rights

Among other responsibilities, pension plan fiduciaries must manage plan assets that involve shares of corporate stock and, thus, may be required to make and monitor decisions about voting proxies and exercising shareholder rights. DOL has published guidance over the past few decades outlining these responsibilities.

Pension plans typically hold stocks as part of their investment portfolios. Ownership of a company's stock confers partial ownership and grants the investor certain rights. One of these rights may include the right to vote on matters such as electing the board of directors and the approval of mergers and acquisitions. Shareholders can exercise their votes in person. However, most shareholders do not attend corporate annual meetings. Typically, shareholders have the right to appoint proxies. A proxy is a written authorization that delegates the shareholder's voting power to another person or, more typically, an institution.

DOL's long-standing position is that plan fiduciaries should engage in proxy voting activities in discharging their fiduciary obligation to prudently manage plan investments. A pension plan fiduciary is subject to fiduciary responsibility when deciding whether to vote or not to vote (via proxy or in person) and when deciding how to vote. The details of how fiduciaries

---

133 The House failed to override the veto. For more information, see CRS In Focus IF12328, Department of Labor Guidance and Regulations on Selecting Private-Sector Pension Plan Investments.

134 Pension plans would not be required to divest current investments in these specified countries or entities but would be subject to disclosure requirements.

determine whether and how to vote have been the subject of various regulations.

Due to the large number and diverse array of issues that shareholders may vote on, institutional investors, such as mutual funds and pension plans, frequently use proxy advisory firms for proposal voting recommendations. Proxy advisory firms provide institutional investors with research and recommendations on management and shareholder proposals that are voted on at annual corporate meetings. Two firms—Institutional Shareholder Services (ISS) and Glass Lewis—control much of the proxy advisory business. Pension plan fiduciaries are subject to fiduciary responsibility in the selection and monitoring of proxy advisory firms and ensuring that any proxy advisory firm votes in the best interest of plan participants.

Regulatory and Congressional Responses

In the 118th Congress, H.J.Res. 30, which would use the CRA (enacted in P.L. 104-121) to nullify the 2022 regulation, was passed by the House and Senate and vetoed by President Biden on March 20, 2023.[135]

Investment Advice

Retirement plans are complex, and individuals often rely on financial services professionals to assist them with their decisionmaking. For example, an employer might seek assistance in determining what investments to offer in a 401(k) plan it has established, participants in a 401(k) plan might seek assistance in choosing their investments from among the options offered by the plan, or a worker who participates in an employer-sponsored 401(k) plan might seek assistance on whether to leave his or her 401(k) account balance in the plan or roll it over into an IRA or into another employer's DC plan either upon job change or at retirement.

The compensation structure of some financial services professionals may give rise to conflicts of interest, particularly if these professionals' recommendations result in larger commissions or otherwise benefit them. These potential conflicts could lead to recommendations that are not in the interests of their clients. By contrast, some financial services professionals have compensation structures that do not vary based on which products clients

---

[135] The House failed to override the veto. For more information, see CRS In Focus IF12362, Department of Labor Guidance and Regulations on the Exercise of Shareholder Rights by Private-Sector Pension Plans.

choose. This type of compensation structure could mitigate any conflicts of interest.

Individuals who transact with a pension plan may be required to meet certain standards. The standard that applies depends on the individuals' roles and the actions they are taking. For example, an individual providing investment advice is subject to the high fiduciary standard, whereas an individual who is acting on the direction of the plan participant to buy or sell a particular security or mutual fund may have a lower standard of duty.

Following the passage of ERISA, DOL issued regulations in 1975 that created a five-part test to determine whether an individual provided investment advice and thus was subject to the fiduciary standard.[136] In addition, DOL issued a PTE to ensure that fiduciaries can continue to engage in practices that would otherwise be prohibited (such as brokers receiving commissions).

To be held to the 1975 fiduciary standard with respect to his or her advice, an individual must (1) make recommendations on investing in, purchasing, or selling securities or other property or give advice as to the value (2) on a regular basis, (3) pursuant to a mutual understanding that the advice (4) serves as a primary basis for investment decisions and (5) is individualized to the particular needs of the plan regarding such matters as, among other things, investment policies or strategy, overall portfolio composition, or diversification of plan investments. An investment adviser is not treated as a fiduciary unless each of the five elements of the test is satisfied for each instance of advice.

In October 2010, DOL proposed, and subsequently withdrew in September 2011, an expansion of the definition of *fiduciary advice* that would have made more individuals and their actions subject to the fiduciary advice regulation. In April 2015, DOL issued a revised proposal to broaden the definition of *investment advice* and in April 2016 issued a final rule and PTE. In March 2017, DOL issued a Temporary Enforcement Policy that indicated it would not initiate enforcement actions against financial advisers or financial institutions that failed to satisfy the conditions of the regulation or PTE.[137]

In March 2018, a U.S. district court ruled that the 2016 rule was improperly promulgated, and in March 2018, the U.S. Court of Appeals for

---

[136] See 29 C.F.R. §2510.3-21.

[137] See DOL, "Temporary Enforcement Policy on Fiduciary Duty," March 10, 2017, https://www.dol.gov/sites/dolgov/files/ebsa/employers-and-advisers/guidance/field-assistance-bulletins/2017-01.pdf.

the Fifth Circuit vacated the 2016 rule. This meant that the five-part test was reinstated.[138]

In October 2020, DOL issued PTE 2020-02 which, as with previous PTEs, allows fiduciaries to conduct transactions that are otherwise prohibited.[139] Investment advice fiduciaries who rely on PTE 2020-02 must comply with Impartial Conduct Standards, which require them to provide advice that is in the best interest of the retirement investor, charge no more than reasonable compensation, and make no misleading statements about investment transactions. In addition, PTE 2020-02 noted that rollover recommendations from an employer plan to an IRA could be considered investment advice if specified conditions are met—for example, if the investment recommendation is expected to be part of an ongoing relationship.[140] On February 13, 2023, a federal district court struck down the portion of PTE 2020-02 related to the rollover recommendations, and on June 30, 2023, in a different federal district court, a magistrate judge recommended that the guidance related to rollover advice be vacated.[141]

Regulatory and Congressional Responses

In November 2023, DOL issued a proposed rule that would change the definition of an investment advice fiduciary under ERISA.[142] The rule was accompanied by several other amendments to existing PTEs, including PTE 2020-02.[143] A public hearing on the rule and associated PTE amendments was

---

[138] See EBSA, "Conflict of Interest Rule—Retirement Investment Advice: Notice of Court Vacatur," 85 *Federal Register* 40589-40594, July 20, 2020.

[139] EBSA, "Prohibited Transaction Exemption 2020–02, Improving Investment Advice for Workers and Retirees," 85 *Federal Register* 82798-82866, December 18, 2020, https://www.govinfo.gov/content/pkg/FR-2020-12-18/pdf/2020- 27825.pdf.

[140] See EBSA, *New Fiduciary Advice Exemption: PTE 2020-02 Improving Investment Advice for Workers and Retirees Frequently Asked Questions*, April 2021, https://www.dol.gov/sites/dolgov/files/ebsa/about-ebsa/our-activities/resource-center/faqs/new-fiduciary-advice-exemption.pdf.

[141] See https://www.bloomberglaw.com/product/blaw/document/X1VIAADDLGV944QLQJHAF66N3JO/download.

[142] See EBSA, "Retirement Security Rule: Definition of an Investment Advice Fiduciary," 88 *Federal Register* 75890-75979, November 3, 2023, https://www.federalregister.gov/documents/2023/11/03/2023-23779/retirement-security-rule-definition-of-an-investment-advice-fiduciary.

[143] See EBSA, "Proposed Amendment to Prohibited Transaction Exemption 84-24," 88 *Federal Register* 76004-76032, November 3, 2023, https://www.federalregister.gov/ documents/2023/11/03/2023-23781/proposed-amendment-to-prohibited-transaction-exemption-84-24; EBSA, "Proposed Amendment to Prohibited Transaction Exemptions 75-1, 77-4, 80-83, 83-1, and 86-128," 88 *Federal Register* 76032-76045, November 3, 2023, https://www.federalregister.gov/documents/2023/11/03/2023-23782/proposed-amend ment-

held in December 2023.[144] Comments on the proposed rule and amendments were due January 2, 2024.

As of the date of this report, congressional responses include

- separate letters opposing the proposed regulation from Dr. Virginia Foxx, the chairwoman, and 10 members of the majority on the House Education and Workforce Committee;[145] a bipartisan group of 50 members of the House of Representatives; Representative Roger Williams, Chairman, and three members of the House Committee on Small Business Committee;[146] and Senator Roger Marshall and 10 other Senators;[147]
- a letter supporting the proposed regulation from Senator Bernie Sanders, chair of the Senate Committee on Health, Education, Labor, and Pensions; and Representative Bobby Scott, ranking member of the House Education and Workforce Committee;[148]
- press releases opposing the proposed regulation from Representative Ann Wagner, chair of the House Financial Services Subcommittee on Capital Markets, and supporting the proposed regulation from Representative Scott, ranking member of the House Committee on

to-prohibited-transaction-exemptions-75-1-77-4-80-83-83-1-and-86-128; and EBSA, "Proposed Amendment to Prohibited Transaction Exemption 2020-02," 88 *Federal Register* 75979-76003, November 3, 2023, https://www.federalregister.gov/documents/2023/11/03/2023-23780/proposed-amendment-to-prohibited-transaction-exemption-2020-02.

144 For unofficial transcripts of the hearing, see DOL, "US Department of Labor Publishes Transcripts of Online Hearing on Proposed Retirement Security Rule, Related Proposed Exemption Amendments," press release, December 22, 2023, https://www.dol.gov/newsroom/releases/ebsa/ebsa20231222.

145 See letter to Acting Secretary Su from Reps. Foxx, Good, Walberg, Grothman, Stefanik, Allen, Banks, Smucker, McClain, Bean, and Houchin, December 21, 2023, at https://edworkforce.house.gov/uploadedfiles/12.21.23_final_comment_ltr_house_committee_on_education_and_the_workforce.pdf.

146 See letter to Acting Secretary Su from Senators Marshall, Barrasso, Braun, Collins, Cornyn, Ernst, Grassley, Hagerty, Hyde-Smith, Rounds, and Thune, December 18, 2023, at https://www.marshall.senate.gov/wp-content/uploads/Letter-to-DOL-Fiduciary-Rule-12.18.23.pdf.

147 See letter to Acting Secretary Su and Assistant Secretary Gomez from multiple Members of Congress, January 8, 2024, at https://si-interactive.s3.amazonaws.com/prod/planadviser-com/wp-content/uploads/2024/01/08165414/2024.1.8_Bipartisan_Hill_DScott_DOL_Retirement_Security_Proposed_Rule_Comment_Letter-FINAL-SIGNED.pdf.

148 See Sen. Sanders and Rep. Scott, letter to Acting Secretary Su, January 2, 2024, https://democrats-edworkforce.house.gov/imo/media/doc/scott_sanders_comment_letter_to_dol_re_retirement_security_rule.pdf.

Education and the Workforce, and Representative Maxine Waters, ranking member of the House Financial Services Committee;[149]

- a hearing from the House Financial Services committee on January 10, 2024, entitled *Examining the DOL Fiduciary Rule: Implications for Retirement Savings and Access*;[150] and
- a hearing from the Subcommittee on Health, Employment, Labor, and Pensions of the House Education and Workforce committee on February 15, 2024, entitled *Protecting American Savers and Retirees from DOL's Regulatory Overreach.*[151]

Investment Fees

Retirement plans pay a variety of fees and expenses, such as for plan administration and recordkeeping, services to the plan and participants, and investment expenses. Fees are a particular concern in DC plans, because small differences in fees can ultimately have a large effect on participants' account balances.[152] The complexity of 401(k) plan arrangements may provide opportunities for fees to be higher than they otherwise might be, particularly

---

[149] See Office of Rep. Ann Wagner, "Wagner Blasts Misguided, Irresponsible Fiduciary Rule," press release, October 31, 2023, https://wagner.house.gov/media-center/press-releases/wagner-blasts-misguided-irresponsible-fiduciary-rule; and Office of Rep. Bobby Scott, "Scott Applauds Proposed Rule to Strengthen America's Retirement Security," October 31, 2023, https://bobbyscott.house.gov/media-center/press-releases/scott-applauds-proposed-rule-strengthen- americas-retirement-security; and Office of Rep. Maxine Waters, "Ranking Member Maxine Waters Applauds Biden Administration's 'Retirement Security' Rule Proposal," October 31, 2023, https://democrats-financial services.house.gov/news/documentsingle.aspx?DocumentID=410916.

[150] See U.S. Congress, House Committee on Financial Services, *Examining the DOL Fiduciary Rule: Implications for Retirement Savings and Access*, January 10, 2024, https://financial services.house.gov/calendar/eventsingle.aspx?EventID=409088.

[151] See U.S. Congress, House Committee on Education and the Workforce, Subcommittee on Health, Employment, Labor, and Pensions, *Protecting American Savers and Retirees from DOL's Regulatory Overreach*, https://edworkforce.house.gov/calendar/eventsingle.aspx?EventID=410108.

[152] For example, a starting account balance of $20,000 that earned 7% in returns each year would have about $77,000 after 20 years if no fee is charged, whereas the account would have about $70,000 if a 0.5% fee is charged. The same account would have a balance of about $58,000 after 20 years if a 1.5% fee is charged (17% less than the account that charged a 0.5% fee). If a 1.5% annual fee is charged, over the course of 30 years the account holder in this example would pay more than $52,000 in fees. For more information on the fees in private sector DC plans, see EBSA, *A Look at 401(k) Fees*, September 2019, https://www.dol.gov/sites/dolgov/files/EBSA/about-ebsa/our-activities/resource-center/publications/a-look-at-401k-plan-fees.pdf; and EBSA, *Understanding Your Retirement Plan Fees*, September 2021, https://www.dol.gov/sites/dolgov/files/ EBSA/ about-ebsa/our-activities/resource-center/publications/understanding-retirement-plan-fees-and-expenses.pdf.

if plan sponsors and participants are not fully informed of the fees they pay.[153] Among the fiduciary duties of plan sponsors is a duty to ensure that the fees paid for services to the retirement plans are reasonable.

DC plan participants receive information about plan fees from several sources, including Summary Plan Descriptions (SPDs), Form 5500 filings, and benefit statements. SPDs describe how plans operate. Plan sponsors are required to automatically provide copies of these documents to plan participants upon enrollment and upon written request of plan participants. SPDs are required to disclose a summary of provisions that may result in a fee charged to a participant, the payment of which is a condition to the receipt of benefits under the plan.[154]

The Form 5500 was jointly developed by DOL, the IRS, and PBGC and is required to be submitted annually by ERISA-covered plans.[155] This annual report contains various schedules with information on the financial condition, investments, and operations of the plans. Plans with more than 100 participants are required to disclose the identity of service providers that receive direct or indirect compensation of $5,000 or greater in connection with services rendered to the plans.[156]

Plan sponsors must provide participants in DC plans with regular benefit statements. If the investments in a DC plan are participant directed (which includes most 401(k) plans), then benefit statement must be provided quarterly and contain information about the fees charged to the participant.[157]

In recent years, plan participants have brought a large number of lawsuits alleging that recordkeeping and investment management fees in their plans

---

[153] GAO, *401(k) Retirement Plans: Many Participants Do Not Understand Fee Information, but DOL Could Take Additional Steps to Help Them*, GAO-21-357, August 26, 2021, https://www.gao.gov/products/gao-21-357. Fees are not typically a concern in DB plans. Because employers are responsible for funding the plans via their contributions, they have an incentive to ensure that fees are kept to a minimum.

[154] An EBSA Field Assistance Bulletin notes that charges for hardship withdrawals, if a plan allows hardship withdrawals, might be an example of such a charge. See Field Assistance Bulletin 2003-3 issued by EBSA on May 19, 2003, at https://www.dol.gov/agencies/ebsa/employers-and-advisers/guidance/field-assistance-bulletins/2003-03.

[155] Form 5500s are available at https://www.efast.dol.gov/5500Search/.

[156] See DOL, "Annual Reporting and Disclosure," 72 *Federal Register* 64710-64857, November 16, 2007.

[157] As part of regulations related to fee disclosures issued in 2010, DOL published a model disclosure statement that plan sponsors and administrators could rely on. See https://www.dol.gov/sites/dolgov/files/ebsa/employers-and- advisers/plan-administration-and-compliance/fiduciary-responsibilities/401k-plan-fee-disclosure-tool.pdf.

were excessive.[158] This was expected to continue after a January 2022 Supreme Court of the United States ruling.[159]

Regulatory and Congressional Responses

In response to a request by Senator Patty Murray and Representative Bobby Scott, a 2021 GAO report assessed the extent to which 401(k) plan participants understood the fee information in retirement plan disclosures and suggested steps that DOL could take to improve participant understanding of fee disclosures.[160] A provision in the SECURE 2.0 Act of 2022 ("SECURE 2.0," enacted as Division T of P.L. 117-328; December 29, 2022) requires DOL to review regulations relating to disclosure requirements for participant-directed individual account plans and explore (through a public request for information) how the contents and design may be improved to better help participants understand DC plan fees.[161] The provision also requires DOL to issue a report to the House Committee on Education and the Workforce and the Senate Health, Education, Labor, and Pensions Committee with findings and legislative recommendations related to the findings.

In the 117th Congress, H.R. 7284 would have directed the Secretary of Labor to improve DC plan fee disclosures, and S. 4361 would have required DOL to study and report on retirement account disclosure requirements, including ways to improve participants' understanding of fees.

Alternative Investments in Retirement Plans

Though stocks, bonds, and mutual funds are common plan investments, pension plan fiduciaries may invest in nearly any asset class provided they adhere to fiduciary duty in the selection and monitoring of such investments. Several alternative investments, including cryptocurrency and private equity,

---

[158] See CRS Legal Sidebar LSB10636, *Supreme Court Rules on Retirement Plan Fiduciary Duty in Hughes v. Northwestern University*; and Ilana Polyak, "401(k) Lawsuits on the Rise as Participants Target Fees, Conflicts of Interest and Data Privacy," *BenefitsPro*, January 21, 2021, https://www.benefitspro.com/2021/01/21/401k-lawsuits-on- the-rise-as-participants-target-fees-conflicts-of-interest-and-data-privacy/?slreturn=20210718150301.

[159] Gregg Greenberg, "Will 2023 Be Another Banner Year for 401(k) Fee Litigation?," *InvestmentNews*, February 2, 2023, https://www.investmentnews.com/will-2023-be-another-banner-year-for-401k-fee-litigation-233242.

[160] GAO, *401(k) Retirement Plans*.

[161] A Senate Finance Committee summary of SECURE 2.0 noted that this provision builds on recommendations made in the aforementioned 2021 GAO report. See U.S. Congress, Senate Committee on Finance, *SECURE 2.0 Section-by- Section Summary*, https://www.finance.senate.gov/imo/media/doc/Secure%202.0_Section%20by%20Section%20Summary%2012-19-22%20FINAL.pdf.

have been topics of increasing congressional attention in recent years regarding their appropriateness for retirement plan participants.

Cryptocurrency

In DC plans, until recently, cryptocurrency was not available as an investment option. In 2021, FORUSALL announced that it would be the first financial services company to offer plan sponsors the option to adopt cryptocurrency as an investment for participants.[162] In April 2022, Fidelity announced its intention to allow 401(k) participants whose plan sponsors adopt it as an investment option to invest up to 20% of their account balances in Bitcoin.[163]

In DB plans, while plan sponsors may invest in cryptocurrencies, current use appears to be minimal. DOL outlined its concerns with cryptocurrencies in a March 2022 Compliance Release. The concerns included the potentially speculative nature of cryptocurrency investments, the difficulties individuals might have in evaluating whether to—or how much to—include in their investment portfolios, recordkeeping challenges, valuation concerns, and the regulatory environment.[164]

Advocates for including cryptocurrency as an investment option in retirement plans provide several reasons for why it is an appropriate investment option. They note that it is a widely used asset class outside of retirement plans. In addition, cryptocurrencies may provide diversification benefits to an investment portfolio, potentially reducing a portfolio's risk without necessarily harming the portfolio's return. Advocates also claim that younger individuals may be more likely to participate in workplace retirement plans if investment choices include cryptocurrency.[165]

Regulatory and Congressional Responses

On March 10, 2022, DOL released a Compliance Assistance Release, "401(k) Plan Investments in 'Cryptocurrencies,'" in which the department expressed "serious concerns" about plan fiduciaries' decisions to allow DC plan

---

[162] See https://www.forusall.com/press.

[163] See Fidelity, "A First-of-Its-Kind Investment Account," https://www.fidelitywork place.com/s/digitalassets.

[164] See DOL, "Compliance Assistance Release No. 2022-01: 401(k) Plan Investments in 'Cryptocurrencies,'" March 10, 2022, https://www.dol.gov/sites/dolgov/files/ebsa/employers-and-advisers/plan-administration-and-compliance/compliance-assistance-releases/2022-01.pdf.

[165] See Anne Tergesen, "Cryptocurrency Comes to Retirement Plans as Coinbase Teams Up with 401(k) Provider," *Wall Street Journal*, June 10, 2021, https://www.wsj.com/articles/coinbase-teams-up-with-401-k-provider-to-offer- crypto-11623317402.

participants to invest in cryptocurrencies.[166] The release indicated that DOL planned to conduct an investigative program aimed at plans that offer such investments and that plan fiduciaries could expect to be questioned by DOL about their decisions. Subsequently, a DOL official noted that plans that allow their participants to invest in cryptocurrency would not be automatically subjected to audits.[167]

The Financial Freedom Act of 2023 (S. 427 introduced by Senator Tommy Tuberville, and H.R. 1177, introduced by Representative Byron Donalds) would prohibit DOL regulations that require plans to consider factors beyond the risk and return relationship that would constrain or prohibit the type of investments that could be offered through a brokerage window in a DC plan.

Private Equity

Private equity funds are pooled investment vehicles that are not registered with the SEC.[168] Private equity funds are typically open to *accredited investors*, such as high-income and high-net- worth individuals, and qualified clients, such as institutional investors (which includes pension funds).

In DC plans, plan sponsors have not made private equity available as a stand-alone investment option, most likely due to characteristics of private equity, such as illiquidity and difficulty of regular valuation.

In DB plans, fiduciaries invest in private equity funds. The Pensions and Investments 1,000 Summary Report found that, as of September 30, 2021, the top 200 DB plans (both public and private sector) held $680.8 billion in private equity (out of $6.9 trillion in total assets).[169]

Regulatory and Congressional Responses

While private equity is not available as a stand-alone investment in DC plans, in June 2020, DOL issued an information letter in response to a request from Groom Law Group that clarified that a DC plan fiduciary would not violate fiduciary duty for including private equity as a component of an asset

---

[166] See DOL, "Compliance Assistance Release No. 2022-01."

[167] For more information, see CRS In Focus IF12153, *Cryptocurrency in 401(k) Retirement Plans*.

[168] See Investor.gov, "Private Equity Funds," https://www.investor.gov/introduction-investing/investing-basics/investment-products/private-investment-funds/private-equity.

[169] See Pensions and Investments, "P&I 1,000 Summary Report," https://www.pionline.com/pi1000.

allocation fund (e.g., a target-date fund), provided the fiduciary determined that it was an appropriate investment choice for the plan.[170]

In December 2021, DOL issued a Supplement Statement to the June 2020 information letter regarding private equity in DC plans.[171] The Supplement Statement cautioned plan fiduciaries from misreading the 2020 information letter as saying that private equity (as a component of an asset allocation fund in a DC plan) was appropriate for a typical 401(k) plan and stated that the letter "did not endorse or recommend such investments." DOL noted that it agreed with some stakeholders that, in the requester's original letter to DOL, "the claimed benefits of [private equity] investments reflected the perspective of the industry." DOL also cited stakeholder concerns about the ability of plan fiduciaries in a typical 401(k) plan to fulfill the obligations required to determine whether private equity was an appropriate investment for the plan.

Collective Investment Trusts in 403(b) Plans

In general, pension plans have few investment restrictions. However, 403(b) plans—which are DC plans sponsored by public educational organizations (including public primary and secondary schools, state colleges and universities, and public junior colleges), 501(c)(3) tax-exempt organizations, and certain ministers—may invest only in (1) annuity contracts provided by insurance companies and/or (2) custodial accounts invested only in SEC-registered mutual funds.[172]

In contrast, while many 401(k) plans offer mutual funds as investment options, they also often invest through collective investment trusts (CITs). CITs are pooled investment funds maintained by banks or trust companies that are available only to certain qualified retirement plans. Mutual funds and CITs differ in their regulatory structure. Mutual funds are investment trusts and are regulated by the SEC. Because CITs are held by banks, however, they are regulated by the Comptroller of the Currency.[173]

---

[170] See EBSA, "Information Letter 06-03-2020," June 3, 2020, https://www.dol.gov/agencies/ebsa/about-ebsa/our-activities/resource-center/information-letters/06-03-2020.

[171] See EBSA, "U.S. Department of Labor Supplement Statement on Private Equity in Defined Contribution Plan Designated Investment Alternatives," December 21, 2021, https://www.dol.gov/agencies/ebsa/about-ebsa/our-activities/resource-center/information-letters/06-03-2020-supplemental-statement.

[172] A third type of 403(b) arrangement, which is only available to church employees described in Title 26, Section 403(b)(9), of the *U.S. Code*, is a *retirement income account*. Retirement income accounts do not have any investment restrictions.

[173] See Office of the Comptroller of the Currency, "Collective Investment Funds," https://www.occ.treas.gov/topics/supervision-and-examination/capital-markets/asset-management/collective-investment-funds/index-collective- investment-funds.html.

Regulatory and Congressional Responses

Over the years, Congress has tried to harmonize some of the rules that cover 401(k) and 403(b) plans.[174] A provision in SECURE 2.0 (enacted as Division T of P.L. 117-328; December 29, 2022) amended the IRC to permit 403(b) custodial accounts to invest in group trusts (e.g., CITs) with other tax-preferred savings plans and IRAs. A CIT is an example of a group trust. Previously, assets of 403(b) custodial accounts could not be commingled in group trusts with assets other than those of regulated investment companies (i.e., mutual funds).

SECURE 2.0 amended the IRC but did not amend securities laws (e.g., the Securities Act of 1933, the Securities Exchange Act of 1934, and the Investment Company Act of 1940, which would be required to permit 403(b) plans to participate in CITs.

In the 118th Congress, H.R. 3063, as reported out of the House Financial Services Committee on May 24, 2023, would amend securities laws to permit 403(b) plans to invest in CITs.[175]

Qualified Professional Asset Managers

In order to facilitate transactions between DB and DC pension plans and service providers that would otherwise be prohibited by ERISA,[176] DOL issued PTE 84-14 (referred to as the QPAM exemption).[177] A QPAM is an entity independent of the plan sponsor that has discretionary authority over an investment fund (e.g., a bank, savings and loan association, insurance company, or investment advisor). The QPAM exemption permits various parties that are related to pension plans to engage in transactions involving plan assets (e.g., sale of any property, lending money, furnishing of services) if the assets are managed by QPAMs. Without this class exemption, most transactions between pension plans and a "party in interest" would be prohibited.

---

[174] For example, the SECURE 2.0 Act of 2022 (Division T of P.L. 117-328) modified the types of contributions that 403(b) participants may withdraw in hardship distributions to mirror the rules for 401(k) plan hardship distributions.

[175] The bill would also permit 403(b) plans to invest in non-registered variable annuities (referred to as *insurance separate accounts*). Insurance separate accounts are investment vehicles made available through group annuity contracts that commingle assets from multiple retirement plans. Their assets are separated from all other assets of the insurance companies.

[176] Title I of ERISA, as amended, broadly prohibits transactions between plans and "parties in interest," and Title II of ERISA, as amended, includes parallel provisions applicable to tax-qualified plans and "disqualified persons."

[177] DOL has authority to grant additional PTEs on an individual or class basis.

Regulatory and Congressional Responses

The QPAM exemption was first issued in 1984 and has twice been amended.[178] In July 2022, DOL gave notice of a proposed amendment to the QPAM exemption.[179] The comment period closed on September 26, 2022. Under current law and regulation, QPAMs may no longer qualify for the PTE if they are convicted of certain crimes. The proposed amendment would make several changes, among which include updating the list of crimes to explicitly include certain foreign crimes and adjusting the asset management and equity thresholds in the QPAM definition.

After the comment period on the proposed amendment closed on September 26, 2022, in March 2023, DOL announced it was reopening the comment period for the proposed amendment to the prohibited transaction class exemption 84-14 (the QPAM exemption).[180] The reopened comment period started on March 23, 2023, and ended on April 6, 2023.[181] As of the date of this report, DOL has not finalized the proposed amendment.

Individual Retirement Accounts (IRAs)

IRAs are tax-advantaged accounts that individuals can establish to accumulate funds for retirement.[182] Depending on the type of IRA, contributions may be made on a pretax or post-tax basis, and investment earnings are either tax-deferred or tax-free. In addition, workers can roll over savings from employer-sponsored retirement savings plans into IRAs to preserve their savings' tax advantages.

---

178 See EBSA, "Class Exemptions," https://www.dol.gov/agencies/ebsa/laws-and-regulations/rules-and-regulations/ exemptions/class.

179 See EBSA, "Proposed Amendment to Prohibited Transaction Class Exemption 84-14 (the QPAM Exemption)," 87 *Federal Register* 45204-45232, July 27, 2022, https://www.federalregister.gov/documents/2022/07/27/2022-15702/proposed-amendment-to-prohibited-transaction-class-exemption-84-14-the-qpam-exemption.

180 See EBSA, "Reopening Comment Period for the Proposed Amendment to Prohibited Transaction Class Exemption 84-14 (the QPAM Exemption)," 88 *Federal Register* 17466-17467, March 23, 2023, https://www.federalregister.gov/ documents/2023/03/23/2023-05522/reopening-comment-period-for-the-proposed-amendment-to-prohibited- transaction-class-exemption-84-14.

181 Comments are available at https://www.dol.gov/agencies/ebsa/laws-and-regulations/rules-and-regulations/public- comments/1210-ZA07.

182 For more information on IRAs, see CRS Report RL34397, Traditional and Roth Individual Retirement Accounts (IRAs): A Primer.

Traditional IRA contributions may be tax deductible depending on the IRA owner's household income and workplace pension coverage. The contributions may accrue investment earnings in an account, and these earnings can be used as a source of income in retirement. Taxes are paid on both contributions and any investment earnings when funds are distributed.

IRAs: Authority and Administration

Traditional IRAs were authorized by ERISA (P.L. 93-406). Roth IRAs were authorized by the Taxpayer Relief Act of 1997 (P.L. 105-34). One key difference between traditional and Roth IRAs is that contributions to Roth IRAs are made with after-tax funds, and qualified distributions are not included in taxable income; investment earnings accrue free of taxes. The IRS has responsibility for enforcing IRA tax laws.

An IRA must be a trust or custodial account, and the trustee must be either (1) a bank or (2) a nonbank that applies to the IRS to be considered eligible. Trustees that meet these requirements include financial institutions, credit unions, mutual fund companies, life insurance companies, and stock brokerages. Most individuals with IRAs hold them through large financial institutions (e.g., Fidelity, Vanguard).

These institutions offer an array of investment choices for IRA investors, such as mutual funds, exchange-traded funds, bonds, and publicly traded stocks. IRA investors are limited to the options offered by their financial institutions.

Some individuals save for retirement through self-directed IRAs (SDIRAs). SDIRAs are set up through IRS-approved custodians that specialize in SDIRAs. These custodians permit individuals to exercise discretion over their investment choices and invest in nearly any asset class, including cryptocurrencies; private equity; real estate; and ownership interests in limited liability corporations, partnerships, trusts, or similar entities. SDIRA owners are responsible for selecting, managing, monitoring, and retaining all investments in their accounts.

Investment Restrictions and Prohibited Transactions

Owners of IRAs or SDIRAs must adhere to IRA investment rules. In general, while IRAs have few investment restrictions, the following do apply:

- Any amounts invested in collectibles—such as artwork, rugs and antiques, metals, gems, stamps, alcoholic beverages, and most coins[183]—are treated as distributions and may be subject to income tax and a 10% penalty.[184]
- IRA owners are not permitted to invest in life insurance contracts.[185]
- IRAs (absent some meeting narrow exceptions) are not permitted to be shareholders of S corporations.[186]

Prohibited Transactions

In addition to the investment restrictions above, IRA owners, beneficiaries, and any disqualified persons—such as the IRA owners' fiduciaries and any family members—are not permitted to engage in a number of prohibited transactions.[187] These include borrowing money from an IRA, selling property to it, using it as security for a loan, and buying property for personal use (present or future) with IRA funds. An individual who engages in a prohibited transaction causes the IRA to no longer be treated as an IRA as of the first day of the year. The entire amount of the account is treated as a distribution (based on the account's value at the beginning of the year) and may be subject to tax and penalty.

DOL and the IRS have oversight responsibilities for prohibited transactions relating to IRAs.[188] IRA owners who invest in unconventional assets—typically done through SDIRAs—are more likely to engage in prohibited transactions compared to IRA owners who invest in assets offered by their financial institutions. A 2019 GAO report recommended that formalizing collaborative efforts from DOL and the IRS could strengthen oversight of prohibited transactions within IRAs.[189]

---

[183] Gold, silver, and platinum coins issued by the U.S. Treasury and gold, silver, palladium, and platinum bullion are permissible.

[184] See 26 U.S.C. §408(m).

[185] See 26 U.S.C. §408(a)(3) and 26 U.S.C. §408(e)(5).

[186] See Treasury Regulation Section 1.1361-1(h)(1)(vii).

[187] See 26 U.S.C. §4975.

[188] DOL may provide interpretive guidance and has authority to grant exemptions from prohibited transactions rules. The IRS enforces tax laws relating to IRAs (including assessing additional taxes for IRA owners who engage in prohibited transactions).

[189] See GAO, Individual Retirement Accounts: Formalizing Labor's and IRS's Collaborative Efforts Could Strengthen Oversight of Prohibited Transactions, GAO-19-495, June 2019, https://www.gao.gov/assets/gao-19-495.pdf.

Regulatory and Congressional Responses

In general, there has been little action from a regulatory or congressional standpoint regarding IRA investments. An early version of the Build Back Better Act, which later became the Inflation Reduction Act, included several provisions that would have affected IRA investments.

For example, some investments are available only to what are referred to as *accredited investors*.[190] These investments are private securities offerings, which are exempt from certain SEC requirements. Examples include hedge funds, venture capital, and private equity. Individuals can qualify as accredited investors if they meet certain income or net worth thresholds or have specified educational credentials. Section 138312 of H.R. 5376, as reported in the House on September 27, 2021, would have prohibited IRA owners from investing in securities that are available only to accredited investors.[191] This provision was not included in the version of H.R. 5376 that became law (P.L. 117-169).

---

[190] For more details on accredited investors, see CRS In Focus IF11278, *Accredited Investor Definition and Private Securities Markets*.

[191] See Section 138312 at https://www.congress.gov/117/crpt/hrpt130/CRPT-117hrpt130-pt3.pdf.

Chapter 3

Contributions to Individual Retirement Accounts (IRAs): Fact Sheet*

Elizabeth A. Myers
and John J. Topoleski

Background

Individuals can save for retirement in two types of tax-advantaged accounts: defined contribution (DC) accounts and individual retirement accounts (IRAs).[1] A DC plan is an employer-sponsored retirement plan in which contributions from a worker, the employer, or both are placed in an individual account. Individuals with wage income can also contribute to IRAs, which are privately held retirement savings accounts. Contributions—and any investment earnings—in DC accounts and IRAs can be used as a source of income in retirement. Both DC accounts and IRAs may accept rollovers. Rollovers—transfers of funds from one retirement account to another—preserve the tax advantages of retirement savings.[2] This report provides Internal Revenue Service (IRS) data on contributions to IRAs in 2020. Congress has an interest in contribution data because tax expenditures for retirement plans (estimated to be $25.0 billion for IRAs and $117.8 billion for

* This is an edited, reformatted and augmented version of Congressional Research Service Publication No. R48051, dated April 25, 2024.

[1] For further information on DC plans, see IRS, "Definitions," https://www.irs.gov/retirement-plans/plan-participant-employee/definitions. For further information on IRAs, see CRS Report RL34397, *Traditional and Roth Individual Retirement Accounts (IRAs): A Primer*.

[2] IRS, "Rollovers of Retirement Plan and IRA Distributions," https://www.irs.gov/retirement-plans/plan-participant-employee/rollovers-of-retirement-plan-and-ira-distributions.

In: Retirement Strategies: Analysis of Policies, Investments, and Security
Editor: Ryan M. Powell
ISBN: 979-8-89530-366-5

DC plans in FY2024) are one of the largest categories of revenue losses attributable to provisions in the tax code.[3]

The tax benefits of IRAs depend on whether the account is a traditional or a Roth account.[4] Contributions to a traditional IRA may be tax deductible in the year in which they are made based on income limits and depending on whether the account holder or spouse has a pension plan at his or her work.[5] Investment earnings in traditional IRAs accumulate on a tax-deferred basis.

Withdrawals from traditional IRAs (except for amounts attributed to non-deductible contributions) are included in taxable income when received. Contributions to Roth IRAs are not tax deductible in the year in which they are made. Investment earnings accumulate on a tax-free basis. Qualified distributions from a Roth account (those taken by an individual who has held the account for five years and made after death, on account of disability, or on or after attainment of age 59½) are not included in taxable income.[6]

Individuals' contributions to IRAs are subject to annual contribution limits. In 2020 (the most recent year for which contribution data from the IRS is available), an individual could contribute to his or her IRA up to the lesser of (1) his or her wage income for the year or (2) $6,000.[7] Individuals age 50 and older could make additional $1,000 catch-up contributions to their IRAs. The IRA contribution limit is adjusted annually for inflation. Beginning in tax year 2024, the $1,000 IRA catch-up contribution is adjusted for inflation.[8]

Contributions to IRAs

Table 1 provides data on contributions to traditional IRAs in 2020. Nearly 5 million taxpayers contributed to traditional IRAs, with an average contribution of $4,461. About half of individuals under age 50 (51.4%) and those age 50 to

---

[3] Department of the Treasury, *Tax Expenditures*, FY2024, https://home.treasury.gov/system/files/131/Tax-Expenditures-FY2024-update.pdf.

[4] For further information on the differences between traditional and Roth accounts, see IRS, "Topic no. 451, Individual Retirement Arrangements (IRAs)," https://www.irs.gov/taxtopics/tc451.

[5] IRS, "IRA Deduction Limits," https://www.irs.gov/retirement-plans/ira-deduction-limits.

[6] IRS, "About Publication 590-B, Distributions from Individual Retirement Arrangements (IRAs),"https://www.irs.gov/forms-pubs/about-publication-590-b.

[7] IRS, "Retirement Topics—IRA Contribution Limits," https://www.irs.gov/retirement-plans/plan-participant-employee/retirement-topics-ira-contribution-limits.

[8] IRS, "401(k) Limit Increases to $23,000 for 2024, IRA Limit Rises to $7,000," November 1, 2023, https://www.irs.gov/newsroom/401k-limit-increases-to-23000-for-2024-ira-limit-rises-to-7000.

under 70½ (50.7%) who made contributions to their traditional IRAs contributed the maximum amount ($6,000 for those under 50; $7,000 for those 50 and older in 2020).[9] Nearly 5% of taxpayers age 50 to under 70½ made catch-up contributionsof less than the maximum $1,000 amount (not shown in *Table 1*).

Table 1. Contributions totraditional IRAs tax year 2020

Age Group	*Number of Contributing Taxpayers*	*Average Contribution*	*Percentage of Contributors Making the Maximum Contribution*	*Average Non-Maximum Contribution*	*Percentage of Taxpayers Age 50 and Older Making Any Catch-Up Contribution*
All	4,961,960	$4,461	See note.	See note.	n/a
Under 35	694,818	$3,402	41.8%	$1,538	n/a
35 to under 50	1,594,588	$4,175	55.7%	$1,885	n/a
Under 50	2,289,406	$3,940	51.4%	$1,759	n/a
50 to under 65	2,108,306	$4,843	49.9%	$2,693	54.3%
65 to under 70½	562,853	$5,145	53.8%	$2,986	60.2%
50 to under 70½	2,671,159	$4,907	50.7%	$2,751	55.6%

Source: CRS analysis of Internal Revenue Service (IRS), "SOI Tax Stats—Accumulation and Distribution of Individual Retirement Arrangements (IRA)," Table 5: Taxpayers with Traditional Individual Retirement Arrangement (IRA) Contributions, by Size of Contribution and Age of Taxpayer, Tax Year 2020, https://www.irs.gov/statistics/soi-tax-stats-accumulation-and-distribution-of-individual-retirement-arrangements.

Notes: In 2020 (the latest year for which data is available), there were 130.1 million taxpayers with wage income. In 2020, the IRA contribution limit for individuals was $6,000. Individuals age 50 and older could make additional $1,000 catch-up contributions. Prior to 2020, individuals could not contribute to traditional IRAs in or after the year in which they turned 70½. IRS data for tax year 2020 does not provide data on taxpayers over age 70½. *Maximum contribution* refers only to taxpayers who contribute the exact amount of the limit. The maximum contribution for taxpayers whose earned income fell below the contribution limit is lower and was not captured in this table. In addition, the contribution limit applies to all of an individual's IRAs, so individuals who contributed the maximum amount but split contributions between traditional and Roth IRAs are not recorded in the data as having contributed the maximum amount. Because those over 50 have a different maximum contribution than those under 50 and there is no age information available for 1,395 taxpayers who contributed to traditional IRAs, CRS cannot determine the percentage of all taxpayers making the maximum contribution or the average non-maximum contribution of alltaxpayers.

Table 2 provides data on contributions to Roth IRAs in 2020. Over 9 million taxpayers contributed to Roth IRAs, with an average contribution of S3,581. Over one-third of taxpayers under 50 (34.9%) and over 40% of

[9] The $7,000 limit includes $1,000 in catch-up contributions.

taxpayers age 50 and older (41.4%) who contributed to Roth IRAs in 2020 contributed the maximum amount ($6,000 for those under 50; $7,000 for those 50 and older in 2020).[10] Between 5% and 6% of taxpayers age 50 and older made catch-up contributions of less than the maximum $1,000 amount (not shown in *Table 2*).

Table 2. Contributions to Roth IRAs tax year 2020

Age Group	*Number of Contributing Taxpayers*	*Average Contribution*	*Percentage of Contributors Making the Maximum Contribution*	*Average Non-Maximum Contribution*	*Percentage of Taxpayers Age 50 and Older Making Any Catch-Up Contribution*
All	9,210,723	$3,581	See note.	See note.	n/a
Under 35	3,233,379	$3,135	35.5%	$1,.556	n/a
35 to under 50	2,867,054	$3,200	34.2%	$1,748	n/a
Under 50	6,100,433	$3,166	34.9%	$1,647	n/a
50 to under 65	2,516,457	$4,316	40.1%	$2,517	45.9%
65 and older	588,816	$4,736	46.7%	$2,756	52.0%
50 and older	3,105,273	$4,396	41.4%	$2,558	47.0%

Source: CRS analysis of Internal Revenue Service (IRS), "SOI Tax Stats—Accumulation and Distribution of Individual Retirement Arrangements (IRA)," Table 6: Taxpayers with Roth Individual Retirement Arrangement (IRA) Contributions, by Size of Contribution and Age of Taxpayer, Tax Year 2020, https://www.irs.gov/statistics/soi-tax-stats-accumulation-and-distribution-of-individual-retirement-arrangements.

Notes: In 2020 (the latest year for which data is available), there were 130.1 million taxpayers with wage income. In 2020, the IRA contribution limit for individuals was $6,000. Individuals age 50 and older could make additional $1,000 catch-up contributions. *Maximum contribution* refers only to taxpayers who contribute the exact amount of the limit. The maximum contribution for taxpayers whose earned income fell below the contribution limit is lower and was not captured in this table. In addition, the contribution limit applies to all of an individual's IRAs, so individuals who contributed the maximum amount but split contributions between traditional and Roth IRAs are not recorded in the data as having contributed the maximum amount.

Because those over 50 have a different maximum contribution than those under 50 and there is no age information available for 5,017 taxpayers who contributed to Roth IRAs, CRS cannot determine the percentage of all taxpayers making the maximum contribution or the average non-maximum contribution of all taxpayers.

Acknowledgments

Sylvia Bryan assisted in updating this report.

[10] The $7,000 limit includes $1,000 in catch-up contributions.

Chapter 4

Ownership of Retirement Accounts in 2022: Amounts in Defined Contribution Plans and Individual Retirement Accounts*

Elizabeth A. Myers

Introduction

Households rely on a variety of income sources in retirement. In 2022, about 54% of U.S. households had savings in retirement accounts, which are defined as certain employer-sponsored, account-type pension plans, typically referred to as defined contribution (DC) plans, and individual retirement accounts (IRAs) (outlined in boxes in Figure 1). The term DC accounts is defined in this report as employer-sponsored accounts—such as 401(k), 403(b), and thrift savings accounts from current or past jobs—other current job plans from which loans or withdrawals can be made and accounts from past jobs from which the households expect to receive the account balances in the future.[1] The term retirement accounts, as defined, does not include other possible income sources in retirement, such as savings in defined benefit (DB) pension

---

* This is an edited, reformatted and augmented version of Congressional Research Service Publication No. R48143, dated July 29, 2024.

[1] This definition is derived from the definition of *retirement accounts* used by the Board of Governors of the Federal Reserve System (which also includes IRAs and Keogh plans) in its "Changes in U.S. Family Finances from 2019 to 2022" report. See https://www.federalreserve.gov/publications/october-2023-changes-in-us-family-finances-from-2019-to-2022.htm.

In: Retirement Strategies: Analysis of Policies, Investments, and Security
Editor: Ryan M. Powell
ISBN: 979-8-89530-366-5

plans[2] or payments from Social Security.[3] Most households receive Social Security payments during retirement.[4]

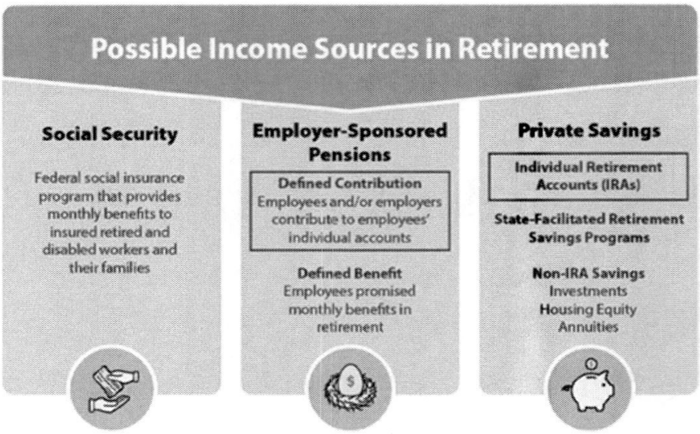

Source: CRS.

Figure 1. U.S. Retirement Income Sources.

In DC plans, workers are provided individual accounts funded by their own contributions, contributions from their employers, or both.[5] DC plans do not provide guaranteed income. The funds in the account experience investment gains and losses, and the contributions and earnings, if any, are used as a source of income in retirement. Examples of DC plans include 401(k) plans, 403(b) plans, and 457(b) plans.[6] In DB plans—which are not included in the data in this report— participants do not have individual accounts but typically receive monthly payments throughout retirement.

---

[2] Defined benefit plans are another type of employer-sponsored pension plan that typically provide workers with monthly benefits throughout retirement. DB plans are common among public sector workers.

[3] Social Security is a federal social insurance program that provides monthly benefits to insured retired or disabled workers and their eligible family members. Because Social Security has a progressive benefit structure, low earners generally receive higher replacement rates as measured by the amount of pre-retirement earnings replaced by monthly benefits. For more information on Social Security benefits, see CRS Report R42035, *Social Security Primer* and CRS Report R46658, *Social Security: Benefit Calculation.*

[4] The receipt of Social Security and DB plan benefits likely influences many households' retirement saving decisions. See CRS Report R46441, *Saving for Retirement: Household Decisionmaking and Policy Options.*

[5] For more background on pension plans, see CRS Report R47119, *Pensions and Individual Retirement Accounts (IRAs): An Overview.*

[6] For more information on different types of DC plans, see CRS Report R47152, *Private-Sector Defined Contribution Pension Plans: An Introduction.*

IRAs are tax-advantaged accounts for individuals (or married couples) to save for retirement, typically outside of the workplace.[7] Though individuals with taxable (and certain nontaxable) compensation may contribute directly to IRAs, the majority of inflows to IRAs come from rollovers, which are transfers of savings from one retirement account, such as a 401(k) account, to another retirement account, such as an IRA.[8] Most workers with DC plans roll over their savings to IRAs at job change or retirement.[9]

This report provides data on retirement account ownership among U.S. households in 2022—specifically, household ownership and account balances of DC accounts, IRAs, and DC accounts plus IRAs together—to provide a snapshot of households' retirement savings based on different socioeconomic and demographic characteristics. As Congress considers various retirement-related bills, a greater understanding of how households save for retirement—either through DC plans, IRAs, or both—could help inform discussions.

Data in this report are from the 2022 Survey of Consumer Finances (SCF). The SCF is a triennial survey conducted on behalf of the Board of Governors of the Federal Reserve that contains detailed information on U.S. household finances, such as the amount and types of assets owned, the amount and types of debt owed, and detailed demographic information on the reference person, and, if applicable, his or her spouse.[10] The SCF is designed to be nationally

---

[7] Congress has authorized two types of IRAs: traditional and Roth. Contributions to traditional IRAs may be deductible from taxable income (depending on household adjusted gross income and workplace pension coverage), and withdrawals are included in taxable income. Contributions to Roth IRAs are not tax-deductible, but qualified distributions (those made after age 59½, death, or disability from an account that is at least five years old) are tax free. An individual can move traditional IRA savings to a Roth IRA in what is referred to as a *conversion*. Congress has also authorized several types of IRA-based retirement plans that employers can offer, such as SIMPLE IRAs and SEP-IRAs.

[8] Examples of compensation include wages, salaries, tips, commissions, self-employment income, nontaxable combat pay, and alimony (which is treated as compensation for IRA purposes).

[9] Lump sum payments from DB plans may also be rolled over to IRAs. In 2020 (the latest year for which data are available), 96.4% of inflows to traditional IRAs were from rollovers, while 61.1% of Roth IRA inflows came from rollovers and conversions. (Note that conversions were higher in 2020 than in previous years.) See Investment Company Institute, Quarterly Retirement Market Data, First Quarter 2024, Tables 11 and 12, https://www.ici.org/ research/stats/retirement.

[10] The *reference person* is the single individual in a single-person household, the male in a mixed-sex couple household, or the older individual in a same-sex couple household. The SCF codebook states that no judgment about the internal organization of the household is implied by this organization of the data. More information about the SCF, including the data and codebook, is available at https://www.federalreserve.gov/econres/scfindex.htm. Because household wealth is highly concentrated, the SCF includes an oversample of relatively wealthy households.

representative of the population of U.S. households, of which there were 131.3 million in 2022.[11] Household in the SCF is defined as "the primary economic unit, which consists of an economically dominant single individual or couple (married or living as partners) in a household and all other individuals in the household who are financially interdependent with that individual or couple."

Household Ownership of Defined Contribution and Individual Retirement Accounts

Table 1 includes data on DC account ownership and balances, IRA ownership and balances, and combined ownership (DC savings and IRA savings together) among U.S. households in 2022.[12] Because many households roll over assets from DC accounts to IRAs at job change or retirement, examining DC account and IRA savings on a combined basis can provide a more complete picture of the retirement account assets available to a household during retirement.

Ownership and *balances* refer to household ownership and account balances (i.e., a household was counted as owning a DC account if the reference person or the spouse/partner indicated having one; account balances were aggregated across households).[13] Because the analysis in this report calculates medians and averages for households with these kinds of accounts, the actual median and average balance among all U.S. households would be lower.

Data in Table 1 demonstrate several points regarding household ownership of these retirement accounts in 2022 (see columns G, H, and I):

- Over half (54.3%) of households had savings in DC accounts or IRAs. Among households with these retirement accounts, the median balance was $87,000, and the average balance was $334,097.

---

[11] Estimates in this report are adjusted using population weights provided in the SCF dataset.

[12] A Keogh plan is a retirement plan for self-employed individuals. The Internal Revenue Service indicates that the term *Keogh* is seldom used because the law no longer distinguishes between corporate and other plan sponsors. The SCF combines Keogh plan assets into the IRA asset category.

[13] A household was counted as owning IRA assets if the reference person, spouse/partner, or other member in the household indicated owning IRA assets. Questions about DC account ownership were asked only of the reference person and spouse/partner.

- Ownership rates and balances (among households with accounts) increased with household income, net worth, and education level.[14] For example, 91.1% of households with household income of $150,000 or more had savings in these retirement accounts compared to 13.2% of households with income of less than $30,000.
- Ownership and account balances varied based on the race or ethnicity of the household respondent.[15] Households in which the respondents identified as Hispanic or Latino had the lowest rates of retirement account ownership (27.5%) compared to households in other racial groups—including those in which the respondent identified as White (non-Hispanic), Black/African-American (non- Hispanic), Asian, or Other/multiple race.
- Married households were more likely than single households to own these retirement accounts. Nearly two-thirds (65.6%) of married households owned these retirement accounts compared to 39.1% of single households. In addition, the median balance of married households with these retirement accounts ($113,500) was more than double that of single households with these retirement accounts ($42,000).

Table 1 illustrates the following regarding DC account ownership in 2022 (see columns A, B, and C):

- Among U.S. households, 38.0% owned DC accounts. Among households with DC accounts, the median balance was $53,000, and the average balance was $225,594.
- DC account ownership peaked when the reference person was 45-54 years old and then began to decline, likely due to households rolling over DC savings into IRAs. In addition, older households were more likely to have retirement income from DB plans compared to relatively younger households (and so might not have needed to save for retirement in DC accounts to the same extent as younger households; data not shown).[16]

---

[14] *Education level* refers to the highest education level completed by the reference person at the time of the survey.

[15] The SCF's question about race or ethnicity is asked only of the designated respondent.

[16] Over the past five decades, private sector employees have become less likely to be covered by DB pension plans and more likely to be covered by DC pension plans. See CRS In Focus

- Households in which respondents identified as Asian had the highest rates of DC account ownership (60.8%) and the highest median balance among those with accounts ($100,000) when compared to households in which respondents identified as different races or ethnicities. DC-plan-owning households in which the respondents identified as White (non-Hispanic) had the highest average balance at $260,858.

Table 1 illustrates the following regarding IRA ownership in 2022 (see columns D, E, and F):

- About 30% of households owned IRAs. Among IRA-owning households, the median balance was $87,000, and the average balance was $309,130.
- The median and average IRA balances for all IRA-owning households exceeded those of DC account owners despite IRA contribution limits being lower than DC plan contribution limits.[17] One reason for this is likely rollovers from DC accounts as workers change jobs or retire. (The average age of the reference person in an IRA-owning household was 56.0 compared to 47.2 for the reference person in a DC-account-owning household.) Another reason could be that IRA- owning households are, at the median, wealthier than non-IRA-owning households and are able to contribute more to both DC plans and IRAs. (In 2022, the median household wealth of IRA-owning households was $788,600 compared to $91,850 for non-IRA-owning households; data not shown.)
- About 63% of households with household income of $150,000 or greater owned IRAs compared to 8.8% of households with income of less than $30,000.[18]

IF12007, *A Visual Depiction of the Shift from Defined Benefit (DB) to Defined Contribution (DC) Pension Plans in the Private Sector*.

[17] In 2022, for workers under age 50, the IRA contribution limit was $6,000 compared to a $20,500 elective deferral limit for DC plans.

[18] As shown in *Table 1*, the average IRA balance for IRA-owning households with income of less than $30,000, was higher than the average IRA balance for IRA-owning households with income between $30,000, and $54,999. This appears to be because several households with little to no income had relatively large IRA balances (e.g., over $2 million), which increased the average IRA balance for this income group.

Table 1. Retirement account ownership and balances among U.S. households in 2022

Defined Contribution (DC) Accounts				Individual Retirement Accounts (IRAs)			Retirement Accounts (DC Accounts plus IRAs)[a]		
Percentage of Households with DC Accounts [A]		Median Account Balance (for Households with Accounts) [B]	Average Account Balance (for Households with Accounts) [C]	Percentage of Households with IRAs [D]	Median Account Balance (for Households with Accounts) [E]	Average Account Balance (for Households with Accounts) [F]	Percentage of Households with Retirement Accounts [G]	Median Asset Balance (for Households with Accounts) [H]	Average Asset Balance (for Households with Accounts) [I]
All Households	38.0%	$53,000	$225,594	30.1%	$87,000	$309,130	54.3%	$87,000	$334,097
Age of the Household Reference Person:[b]									
Younger than 35	42.0%	$15,000	$38,521	21.8%	$12,000	$37,752	49.6%	$18,880	$49,127
35-44	51.1%	$42,000	$112,574	28.0%	$30,000	$105,656	61.5%	$45,000	$141,517
45-54	54.8%	$90,000	$233,859	27.9%	$105,000	$238,666	62.2%	$115,000	$313,230
55-64	42.8%	$125,000	$397,696	32.4%	$167,000	$420,095	57.0%	$185,000	$537,563
65 and older	14.5%	$160,000	$500,964	40.2%	$150,000	$468,891	47.1%	$170,000	$554,422
2021 Household Income (in 2022 Dollars):									
Less than $30,000[c]	5.6%	$5,600	$58,734	8.8%	$28,000	$110,345	13.2%	$17,000	$98,254
$30,000-$54,999	22.0%	$11,500	$38,777	15.8%	$57,000	$100,984	34.4%	$20,000	$71,072
$55,000-$89,999	38.1%	$25,000	$65,026	26.6%	$51,000	$139,340	56.4%	$39,000	$109,545
$90,000-$149,999	54.3%	$50,000	$116,209	39.8%	$64,000	$175,750	75.2%	$73,000	$177,007
$150,000 or more	69.0%	$200,000	$469,546	63.1%	$199,000	$539,663	91.1%	$316,000	$729,866
Household Marital Status:									
Married	48.2%	$77,000	$273,497	38.7%	$100,000	$346,847	65.6%	$113,500	$405,381
Single	24.3%	$27,000	$96,924	20.6%	$57,000	$213,567	39.1%	$42,000	$172,598
Single female	24.1%	$27,000	$102,387	19.4%	$67,000	$200,955	38.2%	$43,000	$166,942
Single male	24.4%	$25,000	$88,120	22.5%	$50,000	$231,319	40.6%	$41,000	$181,276

	Defined Contribution (DC) Accounts			Individual Retirement Accounts (IRAs)			Retirement Accounts (DC Accounts plus IRAs)[a]		
	Percentage of Households with DC Accounts [A]	Median Account Balance (for Households with Accounts) [B]	Average Account Balance (for Households with Accounts) [C]	Percentage of Households with IRAs [D]	Median Account Balance (for Households with Accounts) [E]	Average Account Balance (for Households with Accounts) [F]	Percentage of Households with Retirement Accounts [G]	Median Asset Balance (for Households with Accounts) [H]	Average Asset Balance (for Households with Accounts) [I]
All Households	38.0%	$53,000	$225,594	30.1%	$87,000	$309,130	54.3%	$87,000	$334,097
Race or Ethnicity of the Household Respondent:[d]									
White, non-Hispanic	40.6%	$58,000	$260,858	38.6%	$100,000	$334,838	61.7%	$100,000	$380,562
Black/African-American, non-Hispanic	28.7%	$32,000	$100,885	11.4%	$22,000	$104,192	34.8%	$39,000	$117,527
Hispanic or Latino	22.7%	$44,000	$102,461	11.5%	$35,000	$85,748	27.5%	$55,600	$120,318
Asian	60.8%	$100,000	$212,068	37.4%	$80,000	$370,153	74.3%	$130,000	$359,924
Other or multiple race	37.0%	$43,000	$144,548	16.2%	$27,000	$129,836	42.8%	$40,000	$173,577
Education Level of the Household Reference Person:									
High school graduate or less	23.4%	$30,000	$89,269	13.8%	$68,000	$161,877	32.5%	$45,000	$132,845
Some college or associate's degree	36.1%	$39,000	$142,260	23.6%	$60,000	$162,748	50.5%	$53,000	$177,831
Bachelor's degree	50.6%	$70,000	$234,956	44.2%	$89,000	$305,290	71.7%	$100,000	$353,724

Table 1. (Continued)

	Defined Contribution (DC) Accounts			Individual Retirement Accounts (IRAs)			Retirement Accounts (DC Accounts plus IRAs)[a]		
	Percentage of Households with DC Accounts [A]	Median Account Balance (for Households with Accounts) [B]	Average Account Balance (for Households with Accounts) [C]	Percentage of Households with IRAs [D]	Median Account Balance (for Households with Accounts) [E]	Average Account Balance (for Households with Accounts) [F]	Percentage of Households with Retirement Accounts [G]	Median Asset Balance (for Households with Accounts) [H]	Average Asset Balance (for Households with Accounts) [I]
All Households	38.0%	$53,000	$225,594	30.1%	$87,000	$309,130	54.3%	$87,000	$334,097
Advanced degree (master's, professional, doctorate)	52.4%	$134,000	$433,865	58.9%	$150,000	$483,168	79.6%	$210,000	$643,760

Source: CRS analysis of the 2022 Survey of Consumer Finances (SCF).

Notes: Median and average account balances are calculated using the aggregated value of all accounts within an account category: A household was counted as owning a DC account if the reference person or the spouse/partner indicated having one. Account balances were aggregated across households. A household was counted as owning IRA assets if the reference person, spouse/partner, or other member in the household indicated owning IRA assets. Median account balance and average account balance are calculated for the balances of households with positive account balances. Amounts are in 2022 dollars.

[a] The term retirement accounts refers to savings in individual retirement accounts (IRAs), Keogh accounts, and certain employer-sponsored accounts—such as 401(k), 403(b), and thrift savings accounts from current or past jobs—other current job plans from which loans or withdrawals can be made, and accounts from past jobs from which the households expect to receive the account balances in the future. IRA assets include those in Keogh accounts. They do not include defined benefit (DB) pension plans or Social Security payments.

[b] In the SCF, the "reference person" is the single individual in a single-person household, the male in a mixed-sex couple, or the older individual in a same-sex couple.

[c] The average retirement account balance for retirement-account-owning households with income of less than $30,000 was higher than the average balance for retirement-account-owning households with income between $30,000, and $54,999. This appears to be because several households with little to no income had relatively large retirement account balances, which increased the average balances for this income group. This also occurs with DC and IRA balances for this income group.

[d] Race or ethnicity refers to that of the household respondent. In 80% of sampled households, the designated respondent was the reference person.

Chapter 5

403(b) Pension Plans: Overview and Legislative Developments*

Elizabeth A. Myers

Introduction

A pension is a benefit employers may offer to assist employees in preparing for retirement. Pension plans may be sponsored by private sector (nonprofit and for-profit) employers or public (governmental) employers and may be classified according to whether they are (1) defined benefit (DB) or defined contribution (DC) plans and (2) sponsored by one employer or more than one employer. In DB plans, participants (or their beneficiaries) typically receive regular, monthly benefit payments in retirement (which some refer to as a "traditional" pension). In DC plans, participants have individual accounts that can provide a source of income in retirement.

Two common type of DC plans are 401(k) plans and 403(b) plans (named for the corresponding sections of the Internal Revenue Code [IRC; Title 26 of the U.S. Code]). A 401(k) plan is a type of DC plan available to private sector employers. A 403(b) plan (which may be called a tax- sheltered annuity plan) is a type of DC plan sponsored by public educational organizations (including public primary and secondary schools, state colleges and universities, and public junior colleges), 501(c)(3) tax-exempt entities, and employers that provide retirement income accounts for ministers (e.g., churches). While many

* This is an edited, reformatted and augmented version of Congressional Research Service Publication No. IF12518, dated October 24, 2023.

In: Retirement Strategies: Analysis of Policies, Investments, and Security
Editor: Ryan M. Powell
ISBN: 979-8-89530-366-5

403(b) plans are sponsored by single employers, recent legislative changes may increase the number of those sponsored by more than one employer.

Despite distinct legislative histories, there has been a move toward harmonizing rules for 401(k) and 403(b) plans. This chapter provides background on 403(b) plans, highlights areas in which they differ from 401(k) plans, and discusses current legislative developments surrounding 403(b) plans.

403(b) Plans and Federal Pension Law

Pension plans are generally tax qualified, which means that plan sponsors and participants receive certain tax advantages provided they meet IRC requirements. Some provisions of the IRC apply to both private and public sector plans, while some apply to one or the other. Nearly all private sector pension plans are governed by the Employee Retirement Income Security Act of 1974 (ERISA; P.L. 93-406), which is enforced by the Department of the Treasury, the Department of Labor (DOL), and the Pension Benefit Guaranty Corporation (PBGC). ERISA was enacted to protect the interests of pension plan participants and beneficiaries. ERISA sets standards that private sector pension plans must follow, including with regard to participation, funding, and fiduciary responsibility (standards that govern how individuals with authority over pension plans must behave).

Whether a 403(b) plan is subject to ERISA depends on its sponsoring employer and/or the degree of employer involvement in the plan. Plans sponsored by private sector, tax-exempt 501(c)(3) entities are subject to ERISA except for those that meet a safe harbor exemption in which the employer's role is limited (see 29 C.F.R. §2510.3-2(f) and DOL's Field Assistance Bulletin 2007-02). Among other provisions, the safe harbor specifies that employers may not contribute to the plan and employee participation must be voluntary (i.e., no automatic enrollment features).

Plans sponsored by public educational organizations and churches are exempt from ERISA. However, church plans may elect ERISA coverage.

ERISA 403(b) plans submit annual Form 5500 filings with DOL, PBGC, and the Internal Revenue Service (IRS). Form 5500 includes data on the number of plan participants, financial information about the plan, and details of companies providing services to the plan. In plan year 2020 (the most recent Form 5500 data available), DOL indicated that there were 20,732 private sector 403(b) plans with 9.6 million participants. The U.S. Government

Accountability Office estimated that in 2019, ERISA 403(b) plan assets comprised 57% of all 403(b) plan assets.

Structure of 403(b) Plans

Section 403(b) of the IRC permits three categories of funding arrangements: (1) annuity contracts provided by an insurance company, (2) custodial accounts invested only in Securities and Exchange Commission–registered mutual funds, or (3) retirement income accounts for church employees described in Section 403(b)(9) of the IRC (which are treated as annuity contracts). Retirement income accounts do not have investment restrictions.

Employers have varying degrees of involvement in their 403(b) plans—ranging from minimal involvement, such as providing a list of insurance carriers to eligible employees (common in 403(b) plans sponsored by K-12 school districts), to greater involvement, such as choosing investment options and providing an employer match.

Starting in 2009, IRS regulations required that 403(b) plans—both ERISA and non-ERISA—be maintained pursuant to written plan documents (with some exceptions for certain church plans).

Features of 403(b) Plans

The following summarizes information on 403(b) plans, noting comparisons with 401(k) plans where relevant.

Enrollment. ERISA 403(b) plans may include automatic ("auto") enrollment features, in which employees are, by default, enrolled in the plan but can opt out. As a condition of the safe harbor exemption, private sector 403(b) plans that are not subject to ERISA are not permitted to auto enroll participants. In addition, some states (via state law) do not permit non-ERISA 403(b) plans to auto enroll. A provision in the SECURE 2.0 Act of 2022 ("SECURE 2.0," enacted as Division T of P.L. 117-328) required that new401(k) and 403(b) plans (with some exceptions) auto enroll newly eligible employees effective for plan years beginning after 2024. It is unclear how this provision will affect safe harbor 403(b) plans.

Contributions. Like employees in 401(k) plans, employees in 403(b) plans may make pre-tax contributions, designated Roth contributions, or after-tax (non-Roth) contributions (if permitted by the plan). Pre-tax contributions lower an individual's taxable income, but withdrawals of savings (i.e., contributions and any investment earnings) attributable to them are included in taxable income.

Designated Roth account contributions do not lower taxable income, but qualified withdrawals are not included in taxable income. After-tax (non-Roth) contributions do not lower taxable income. Withdrawals attributable to these contributions are not included in taxable income, but investment earnings attributable to them are included in taxable income. Employers may match a fixed percentage of employee contributions (such as matching contributions up to, for example, 5% of a worker's compensation).

Employers may also make nonelective contributions (those not based on an employee's contributions).

Some 403(b) plans permit employees to make additional contributions upon (1) reaching age 50 and/or (2) having at least 15 years of service with the same eligible 403(b) employer (an educational organization, hospital, home health service agency, health and welfare service agency, church, or convention or association of churches). The latter is known as the 15-year rule and is not available to 401(k) plan participants. The amount permitted to be contributed under the 15-year rule depends on an employee's contribution history and years of service. All contribution types are subject to annual limits.

The universal availability rule states that if any employee is eligible to make 403(b) elective deferrals (i.e., employee contributions), all employees must be eligible to make them. Certain employees (e.g., certain part-time employees and those making contributions to a different plan sponsored by the same employer) may be excluded.

Hardship distributions and loans. Like 401(k) plans, 403(b) plans may offer hardship distributions and loans, though specific details may vary. Hardship distributions are pre-retirement distributions for employees who face financial need. Hardship distributions are included in taxable income and subject to a 10% penalty unless an exception in Title 26, Section 72(t), of the U.S. Code applies. Loans (which can be made from the plan, known as a plan loan, or between the annuity contract issuer and the participant, known as a policy loan) permit participants to borrow from their account balances, though the mechanics differ between 403(b) plan and policy loans.

Investments. Under current law, 403(b) plans are generally limited to investing in annuities or mutual funds through custodial accounts (except for retirement income accounts for church employees). In contrast, 401(k) plans have few investment restrictions. Many 401(k) plans invest through collective investment trusts (CITs), which are pooledinvestment funds maintained by banks or trust companies that are available only to certain retirement plans (not including individual retirement accounts [IRAs], for example). CITs are regulated by the Office of the Comptroller of the Currency, an independent bureau of Treasury. CIT trustees must comply with ERISA fiduciary duty if plan assets are invested in the CIT.

Recent Legislative Developments

SECURE 2.0 (P.L. 117-328) included provisions affecting 403(b) plans:

- Section 106 amended the IRC to formalize 403(b) multiple employer plans (MEPs) and authorize 403(b) pooled employer plans (PEPs). PEPs are a type of MEP in which unrelated employers join to offer a common retirement plan. Prior to the authorization of PEPs, each employer participating in a 403(b) MEP (or "aggregation arrangement") had to demonstrate a business or organizational connection and was treated as sponsoring its own 403(b) plan under the IRC. Under Section 106, 403(b) MEPs and PEPs may file a single Form 5500 and both gain relief from the "one bad apple" rule, in which one participating employer that failed to satisfy plan qualification requirements could result in the entire plan failing them.
- Section 602 expanded the types of 403(b) contributions permitted to be withdrawn as hardship distributions to include all types. (Previously, only employee contributions without earnings were permitted to be withdrawn.) These rules will be consistent with those for 401(k) plans when the provision is effective in 2024.
- Section 128 amended the IRC to permit 403(b) custodial accounts to invest in group trusts (as described in Revenue Ruling 81-100 and subsequent rulings) with other retirement plans and IRAs. A CIT is an example of a group trust. Previously, assets of a 403(b) custodial account could not be commingled in a group trust with assets other than those of regulated investment companies (i.e., mutual funds). However, without amending relevant securities laws (e.g., the Securities Act of 1933, the Securities Exchange Act of 1934, and

the Investment Company Act of 1940), 403(b) plans are unable to invest in CITs.

In the 118th Congress, H.R. 3063, as reported out of the House Financial Services Committee on May 24, 2023, would amend securities laws to permit ERISA 403(b) plan assets to be invested with certain other retirement plan assets in CITs and in non-registered variable annuities through insurance separate accounts. Insurance separate accounts are accounts within annuity contracts typically used to hold variable annuities. Unlike general accounts, assets in separate accounts are segregated from all other assets of the insurance company.

Proponents contend that CITs and insurance separate accounts have lower fees and would assist in diversifying 403(b) participants' investment portfolios. However, some caution that CITs are less regulated than mutual funds and do not publicly disclose fee and expense information and that assets in them are not able to be rolled over to IRAs or, in many cases, to other qualified plans.

Chapter 6

U.S. Retirement Assets: Data in Brief*

John J. Topoleski
Elizabeth A. Myers
and John H. Gorman

Summary

The Federal Reserve's *Financial Accounts of the United States* provides data on the amount of retirement assets in the United States. Retirement assets are held in pension plans sponsored byemployers and in Individual Retirement Accounts (IRAs). As of December 31, 2022, a total of $37.8 trillion was held in U.S. retirement plans and accounts, of which $26.3 trillion was in employer-sponsored plans and $11.5 trillion was in IRAs. Retirement plan holdings include avariety of financial assets, including equities, securities, debt, mutual funds, claims on owed sponsor contributions, and other financial assets.

Employer-sponsored plans are classified as either defined benefit (DB) or defined contribution (DC) plans and are sponsored by private employers, the federal government, or state and local governments. In 2022, and in most years, a majority of DB holdings were held by government-sponsored plans. A majority of DC holdings were held by private employer-sponsored plans.

From 2013 to 2022, total real (inflation-adjusted) retirement assets increased by $4.4 trillion (13.3%). Total real retirement assets peaked at $44.3 trillion in 2021. The growth in IRA assets contributed most to retirement asset growth with a $2.8 trillion real increase from 2013 to 2022. DC plans sponsored by the federal government grew by the

* This is an edited, reformatted and augmented version of Congressional Research Service Publication No. R47699, dated September 20, 2023.

In: Retirement Strategies: Analysis of Policies, Investments, and Security
Editor: Ryan M. Powell
ISBN: 979-8-89530-366-5

greatest percentage rate at 43.4%. Holdings of financial assets by private sector DB, federalDB, and state and local DC plans all decreased in inflation-adjusted terms from 2013 to 2022.

The Federal Reserve's Financial Accounts of the United States reported that the total amount of U.S. retirement assets (outside of Social Security) was $37.8 trillion at the end of 2022.[1] Figure 1 shows (1) the amount of financial assets (in trillions of dollars) in pension plans sponsored by private sector employers, state and local governments, and the federal government; (2) the amount of assets in Individual Retirement Accounts (IRAs); and (3) the components of these assets. Table 1 provides more detail on the components of U.S. retirement financial assets in dollar terms. Table 2 provides historical data on inflation-adjusted end-of-year asset levels from 2013 to 2022.

In Trillions of Dollars, as of December 31, 2022

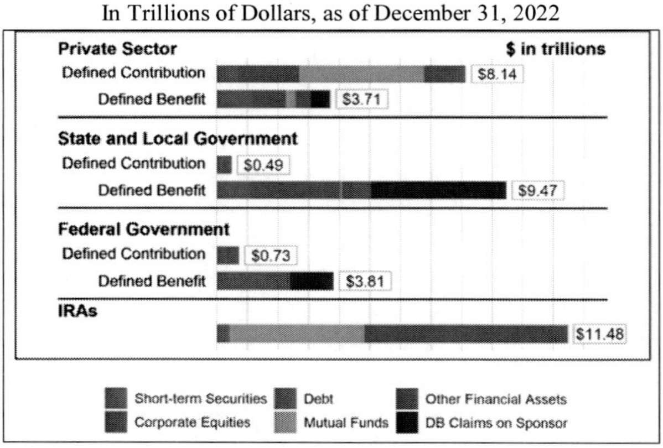

Source: Figure constructed by CRS from Board of Governors of the Federal Reserve System, Financial Accounts of the United States, https://www.federalreserve.gov/apps/fof/FOFTables.aspx. See tables L.118.b, L.118.c, L.119.b, L.119.c, L.120.b, L.120.c, and L.229.

Notes: IRAs include employer-sponsored IRAs and state-administered IRA programs. Mutual funds invest in a variety of assets, including corporate equities and debt. As a result, the total amount of corporate equities and debt held by pension plans likely exceeds the values presented in the Corporate Equities and Debt categories in the figure.

Figure 1. Total Holdings and Components of Financial Assetsin U.S. Pension Plans and Individual Retirement Accounts (IRAs).

[1] The data were downloaded on June 8, 2023, and are available at https://www.federalreserve.gov/releases/z1/default.htm.

Figure 1 shows six categories of retirement financial assets as classified by CRS: short-term securities, debt, corporate equities, mutual funds, defined benefit (DB) plans claims on sponsors, and other financial assets. Short-term securities include checkable deposits, savings deposits, money market funds, and security repurchase agreements. Debt is composed of securities such as commercial paper, U.S. Treasury securities, U.S. government agency and government-sponsored- enterprise-backed securities, foreign bonds, and corporate bonds. Corporate equities include publicly traded shares and private equity. Mutual funds pool money from investors and invest the money in securities such as stocks, bonds, and debt. DB claims on sponsors are funds owed but unpaid by plan sponsors to the plan. Unpaid funds are treated as financial assets. Other financial assets include, but are not exclusively composed of, insurance contracts and contributions receivable.

Table 1. Financial composition of U.S. pension plans and individual retirement accounts (IRAs)

In Billions of Dollars, as of December 31, 2022

Private Sector			State and Local Government		Federal Government		
	DC	DB	DC	DB	DC	DB	IRAs
Short-Term Securities	$203.3	$117.8	$2.2	$100.9	-	$0.2	$427.0
Debt	$496.4	$1,037.7	-	$1,008.2	$321.9	$2,397.4	-
Corporate Equities	$1,997.7	$1,092.0	-	$2,921.4	$403.4	$15.9	-
Mutual Funds	$4,089.7	$327.7	$198.0	$51.8	-	-	$4,398.0
Other Financial Assets	$1,352.2	$508.1	$289.0	$971.2	-	-	$6,659.0
DB Claims on Sponsor	-	$623.5	-	$4,412.1	-	$1,397.7	-
Total Financial Assets	$8,139.4	$3,706.9	$489.2	$9,465.6	$725.3	$3,811.2	$11,484.0

Source: Table constructed by CRS from Board of Governors of the Federal Reserve System, Financial Accounts of the United States, https://www.federalreserve.gov/ apps/fof/FOFTables.aspx. See tables L.118.b, L.118.c, L.119.b, L.119.c, L.120.b, L.120.c, and L.229.

Notes: IRAs include employer-sponsored IRAs and state-administered IRA programs. Mutual funds invest in a variety of assets, including corporate equities and debt. As a result, the total amount of corporate equities and debt held by pension plans likely exceeds the values presented in the Corporate Equities and Debt categories in the table.

Many employers in both the private and public sectors offer one of two types of pension plans: DB plans or defined contribution (DC) plans. Some employers offer both types. Individuals can also save for retirement outside of the workplace with IRAs.

In DB plans, participants usually receive monthly payments in retirement based on a formula that typically uses either (1) a combination of length of service, accrual rate, and average of final years' salary or (2) a flat dollar amount times the number of months or years in the plan.

In DC plans—such as 401(k) plans, 403(b) plans, 457(b) plans, and the federal government's Thrift Savings Plan (TSP)—workers and/or employers contribute a portion of their wages (up to an annual dollar limit that is adjusted annually for changes in the cost of living) to individual accounts established by the employers.[2] Employer contributions may be a match, which is equal to some or all of the worker's contribution, or a contribution made regardless of the employee's contribution. The account may accrue investment returns and can be used as a source of income in retirement.

An IRA is a privately held retirement savings account funded by individual contributions from wage income and rollovers (i.e., transfers) of DC plan savings at job change or retirement and lump sums from DB plans, typically at retirement. Most assets in IRAs are from rollovers.

About two-thirds of U.S. households had a financial stake in the U.S. retirement system in 2019 (outside of Social Security, which covers most households). An analysis of the 2019 Federal Reserve's Survey of Consumer Finances (SCF) found that among all U.S. households (which includes working and retired households) in 2019

- 63.3% had DC assets, participated in DB plans, or had IRA assets;
- 37.5% had DC assets;
- 30.2% participated in DB plans; and
- 25.4% had IRA assets.[3]

---

[2] See Internal Revenue Service, *2023 Limitations Adjusted as Provided in Section 415(d), etc.*, Notice 2022-55,https://www.irs.gov/pub/irs-drop/n-22-55.pdf.

[3] The SCF is a triennial survey of U.S. household finances conducted on behalf of the Federal Reserve. The most recent survey data available is from 2019 and is available at https://www.federalreserve.gov/econres/scfindex.htm.

Historical Retirement Asset Data

Table 2 reports the inflation-adjusted amounts in (non–Social Security) retirement assets from 2013 to 2022. The total amount of financial assets increased by 13.3% in inflation-adjusted terms from $33.4 billion in 2013 to $37.8 billion in 2022. Federal DC assets, IRAs, and private DC assets showed the largest real increases (43.4%, 32.2%, and 27.7%, respectively). The increase in assets is likely from both investment returns and increases in the number of participants. For example, the S&P 500 was 108.7% higher at the end of 2022 compared to at the end of 2013.[4]

The number of participants in private sector DC plans was 8.1% higher in 2020 (the most recent year for which data are available) compared to 2013,[5] and the number of taxpayers with IRAs was 18.8% higher in 2019 (the most recent year for which data are available) compared to 2013.[6]

Table 2. End-of-yeartotal financialassets in u.s.pension plans and individual retirementaccounts (IRAs) from 2013 to 2022

In Trillions of Dollars; Adjusted to December 2022 Dollars

Private Sector			State and Local Government		Federal Government		Individual Retirement Accounts (IRA)	Total
Year	DC	DB	DC	DB	DC	DB		
2013	$6.4	$4.3	$0.7	$8.8	$0.5	$4.0	$8.7	$33.4
2014	$6.7	$4.3	$0.6	$9.2	$0.6	$4.0	$9.2	$34.6
2015	$6.6	$4.3	$0.6	$9.6	$0.6	$4.1	$9.4	$35.0
2016	$6.9	$4.2	$0.5	$9.7	$0.6	$4.1	$9.9	$36.0
2017	$7.9	$4.2	$0.6	$9.9	$0.7	$4.1	$11.4	$38.6
2018	$7.3	$4.1	$0.5	$10.1	$0.7	$4.1	$10.8	$37.5
2019	$8.6	$4.2	$0.5	$10.1	$0.7	$4.1	$12.6	$40.9
2020	$9.7	$4.1	$0.6	$10.3	$0.8	$4.2	$14.1	$43.7
2021	$10.3	$3.9	$0.6	$9.8	$0.9	$4.0	$14.8	$44.3
2022	$8.1	$3.7	$0.5	$9.5	$0.7	$3.8	$11.5	$37.8

[4] The S&P 500 closed at 1,848.36 on December 31, 2013, and 3,839.50 on December 30, 2022. Seehttps://www.nasdaq.com/market-activity/index/spx/historical.

[5] U.S. Department of Labor, *Private Pension Plan Bulletin, Historical Tables and Graphs 1975-2020*, October 2022, https://www.dol.gov/sites/dolgov/files/EBSA/researchers/statistics/retirement-bulletins/private-pension-plan-bulletin- historical-tables-and-graphs.pdf.

[6] Internal Revenue Service, *Statistics of Income Tax Stats—Accumulation and Distribution of Individual Retirement Arrangements*, https://www.irs.gov/statistics/soi-tax-stats-accumulation-and-distribution-of-individual-retirement- arrangements.

Table 2. (Continued)

In Trillions of Dollars; Adjusted to December 2022 Dollars

Private Sector			State and Local Government		Federal Government		Individual Retirement Accounts (IRA)	Total
Year	DC	DB	DC	DB	DC	DB		
Percentage Change (2013-2022)	27.7%	-14.8%	-25.5%	7.1%	43.4%	-4.3%	32.2%	13.3%

Source: Table constructed by CRS from Board of Governors of the Federal Reserve System, Financial Accounts of the United States, https://www.federalreserve.gov/ apps/fof/FOFTables.aspx. See tables L.118.b, L.118.c, L.119.b, L.119.c, L.120.b, L.120.c, and L.229.

Notes: DC refers to defined contribution plans; DB refers to defined benefit plans. Data are from the end of the fourth quarter of each year (December 31). Data are adjusted for inflation to December 2022 dollars using the not-seasonally-adjusted December Consumer Price Index for All Urban Consumers: All Items in U.S. City Average (CPI-U) value, https://www.bls.gov/regions/mid-atlantic/data/consumerpriceindexhistorical_us_table.htm.

Chapter 7

Retirement Income Security: Issues and Policies*

Zhe Li
Paul S. Davies
and Elizabeth A. Myers

Older Americans are an economically diverse group with differing degrees of retirement preparedness. Median household income for individuals ages 65 and older (or aged individuals) was $51,906 in 2017 (CRS analysis of 2017 income data from the Health and Retirement Study linked with Social Security records). One-fifth of individuals ages 65 and older had household incomes of less than $21,840, whereas another one-fifth had household incomes of at least $110,897. Many in Congress have expressed interest in improving retirement income security for groups that are not adequately prepared for retirement.

Retirement Income Sources

Older Americans receive income from a variety of sources, including public programs such as Social Security and Supplemental Security Income (SSI); pensions (e.g., employer-sponsored defined benefit [DB] and defined contribution [DC] plans) and retirement savings (e.g., Individual Retirement Accounts or IRAs); asset income (e.g., business income, interest, dividends, and rents); and earnings. Social Security was the largest source of income among the aged in 2017, accounting for 28.0% of aggregate income. Pensions

* This is an edited, reformatted and augmented version of Congressional Research Service Publication No. IF12330, dated February 17, 2023.

In: Retirement Strategies: Analysis of Policies, Investments, and Security
Editor: Ryan M. Powell
ISBN: 979-8-89530-366-5

and retirement savings constituted 25.8% of income, and earnings accounted for 23.8%. The remainder of aggregate income included income from assets, public assistance (mainly SSI), and other sources.

The sources of income differed for aged individuals at the lower end compared to the upper end of the household income distribution (Figure 1). Social Security was the largest source of income for aged individuals with relatively low household income. The share of aggregate income from Social Security significantly decreased as household income increased. Pensions and retirement savings provided between 18% and 33% of aggregate income for aged individuals with relatively higher household income. Asset income and earnings were important for those with higher household income. Public assistance accounted for a small percentage of aggregate income for most aged individuals except for those with the lowest income.

Retirement Income Adequacy

Whether people are financially adequately prepared for retirement is the subject of debate and research. While no standard definition exists, income adequacy in retirement could mean whether income can meet basic needs (e.g., being above the poverty line) or whether income is sufficient to maintain a preretirement standard of living. SSI and other public assistance programs are designed to ensure that eligible individuals have a minimum level of resources. In contrast, Social Security and pensions, which are based on earnings, are designed to help workers amass enough resources to maintain their preretirement standard of living in retirement. Social Security benefits replace a greater share of career-average earnings for low-paid workers than for high-paid workers. Therefore, Social Security benefits generally comprise a higher share of retirement income for low earners than for high earners who have other retirement income.

For lower-income households, Social Security and SSI may account for the largest share of a household's retirement resources, in part because some low-income families are typically unable to save for retirement after meeting regular daily expenses during their working years. Because Social Security replaces a sufficient portion of their preretirement earnings, some low-income households may have less incentive to save for retirement than high-income households do. Policy changes in Social Security or SSI might better target these families to ensure they are able to meet their basic needs in retirement.

(Since 2000, the official poverty rate for aged individuals has ranged from 8.7% to 10.4%.)

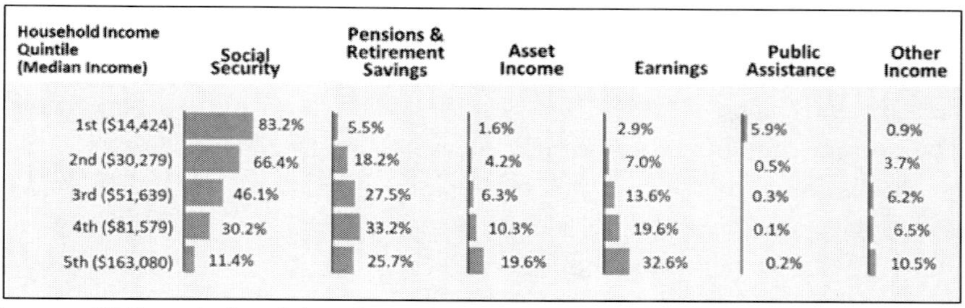

Source: CRS analysis of data from the 2018 Health and Retirement Study (HRS), reflecting income received in 2017.

Notes: Each household income quintile represents 20% of the individuals. The first quintile includes those with the lowest household income. The fifth quintile includes those with the highest household income. Household income upper limits for quintiles one through four are $21,840, $39,700, $64,295, and $110,897, respectively. (Dollar amounts shown in figure refer to medians within quintile range.) Pensions and retirement savings include DB and DC pension plans and IRAs. Asset income includes business income, interest, dividends, and rent. Other income includes veteran benefits, workers' compensation, unemployment compensation, alimony, child support, and financial assistance from outside the household. Public assistance includes SSI and other welfare income. Values have been adjusted for population weights provided by the HRS. Individual quintiles may not sum to 100% due to rounding.

Figure 1. Share of Aggregate Income from Each Source Among Individuals Ages 65 and Older, by Household Income Quintile, 2017.

Some households with the ability to save for retirement might have little or no retirement savings beyond Social Security because they do not have access to employer- sponsored pensions and do not save elsewhere (e.g., through IRAs). These households might benefit from policies designed to increase access to, participation in, or contributions to retirement plans.

Policy Considerations

Social Security. Old-Age, Survivors and Disability Insurance (OASDI, or Social Security) is a mandatory federal social insurance program that replaces income lost to a family as a result of the retirement, death, or disability of an insured worker. Insured status is earned by working in jobs covered under Social Security and subject to payroll taxes that finance Social Security benefits. Once individuals work long enough in covered jobs to be insured, they and their families become eligible for benefits based on a worker's earnings and paid without a test of economic need. In January 2023, Social Security paid approximately $112 billion to about 66 million beneficiaries. The average monthly retired worker benefit was $1,828.

Social Security income was particularly important for aged individuals with relatively lower household income. In 2017, about 62.7% of aged individuals with the lowest household incomes relied on Social Security for 90% or more of household income. Some argue that Social Securitycould be redesigned to provide more protection for vulnerable groups, such as lifetime low earners, widowed or divorced beneficiaries, and the oldest old. Reforms could include changing the minimum benefit and survivor benefit, enhancing the progressivity of the benefit formula, and increasing the cost-of-living adjustment.

The OASDI trust funds are projected to be depleted in 2035, at which point continuing program tax revenue is projected to cover approximately 80% of scheduled benefits. For the trust funds to remain solvent, an increase in revenue, a decrease in benefits, or some combination of these approaches would be needed. No consensus has emerged on how best to approach reform. Reform may involve some combination of tax increases, benefit protections for low-earners, benefit cuts for high earners or high-income individuals, general revenue transfers, or an increase in the rate of return on Social Security revenues.

Supplemental Security Income (SSI). SSI is a federal means-tested program that provides monthly cash paymentsto aged, blind, and disabled individuals (including disabled children) with low incomes and limited resources to meet basic needs such as food and shelter. The maximum SSI benefit is below the poverty level. Recipients must have countable monthly income less than the monthly federal benefit rate of $914 for individuals and $1,371 for couples in 2023. Countable resources must not exceed $2,000 for individuals and $3,000 for couples. In January 2023, SSI provided $1.3 billion to 2.4 million seniors ages 65 and older. The average monthly payment for recipients ages 65and older was $554.

In 2017, about 14% of aged individuals with the lowest household incomes received SSI, accounting for about 4% of the group's aggregate household income. Over half of aged SSI recipients also received Social Security benefits,and over one-third had no other source of income.

Recent reform options to improve the retirement income security of SSI recipients include increasing the federal benefit rates to equal the poverty guidelines, updating the resource thresholds and income exclusions and indexing them to inflation, and excluding certain retirement savingsaccounts from countable resources.

Pensions and Retirement Savings. A pension is a voluntary, tax-advantaged benefit that employers may offer to assist employees in providing for their financial security in retirement. The two types of pension plans are DB plans—in which benefits are generally funded by employers and paid according to a specified formula throughout retirement—and DC plans, such as 401(k) plans, in which employee and/or employer contributions aremade to an individual's account and used as a source of retirement income. IRAs are retirement savings accounts established outside of the workplace. Workers can *roll over* DC savings or lump sum payments from DB pensions (if available) into IRAs at job change or retirement. Income from DB plans and distributions from DC plans and IRAs can be used to finance spending in retirement. In 2017, about 59.8% of individuals ages 65 and older received household income from pensions and retirement savings, with a median amount of $18,000 (or $1,500 monthly).

Over the past five decades, private sector employers have increasingly offered DC plans instead of DB plans. Unlike DB plans, DC plans require many decisions on the part of participants (e.g., whether to participate, how much to contribute, and how to invest) and do not guarantee lifetimeincome to retirees. Some Members of Congress have expressed concern that households without access to pension plans or with limited DC plan or IRA savings may not be adequately prepared for retirement. Recently enacted legislation focused on increasing pension plan sponsorship and savings in these plans (e.g., see the Setting Every Community up for Retirement Enhancement Act of 2019 [SECURE Act; P.L. 116-94] and the SECURE 2.0 Act of 2022 [P.L. 117-328]). For example, SECURE 2.0 includeda provision aimed at promoting retirement savings among low-income households by repealing the Retirement Savings Contribution Credit and replacing it with a Saver'sMatch, effective starting in 2027.

Chapter 8

Retirement Benefits*

Social Security Administration

Social Security and Your Retirement Plan

Social Security is part of the retirement plan of almost every American worker. It's important to know how the system works and how much you'll receive from us when you retire.

This booklet explains:

- How you become eligible for Social Security benefits.
- How your earnings and age can affect your benefits.
- What you should consider in deciding when to retire.
- Why you shouldn't rely only on Social Security for all your retirement income.

This basic information about Social Security retirement benefits isn't intended to answer all questions. For specific information about your situation, you should talk with one of our representatives.

---

* This is an edited, reformatted and augmented version of Social Security Administration, Publication No. 05-10035, dated January 2024.

In: Retirement Strategies: Analysis of Policies, Investments, and Security
Editor: Ryan M. Powell
ISBN: 979-8-89530-366-5

Your Retirement Benefits

How Do You Become Eligible for Retirement Benefits?

When you work and pay Social Security taxes, you earn "credits" toward Social Security benefits. The number of credits you need to receive retirement benefits depends on when you were born. If you were born in 1929 or later, you need 40 credits (10 years of work).

If you stop working before you have enough credits to be eligible for benefits, the credits will remain on your Social Security record. If you return to work later, we will add more credits based on the amount you earn. We can't pay any retirement benefits until you have the required number of credits.

How Much Will Your Retirement Benefit Be?

We base your benefit payment on how much you earned throughout your working career. Higher lifetime earnings result in higher benefits. If there were some years you didn't work or had low earnings, your benefit amount may be lower than if you had worked steadily.

The age at which you decide to retire also affects your benefit. If you retire at age 62, the earliest possible Social Security retirement age, your benefit will be lower than if you wait. The "Early retirement" section explains this in more detail.

Get Personalized Retirement Benefit Estimates

As you make plans for your retirement, you may ask, "How much will I get from Social Security?" If you have a personal *my* Social Security account, you can get an estimate of your personal retirement benefits and see the effects of different ages to begin receiving retirement benefits. If you don't have a personal *my* Social Securityaccount, create one at *www.ssa.gov/myaccount*. To create a personal *my* Social Security account, you mustbe a U.S. citizen, at least 18 years old, and have a validemail address and Social Security number (SSN).

Full Retirement Age

If you were born in 1957 or earlier, you're already eligible for your full Social Security benefit. The full retirement age is 66 if you were born from 1943 to 1954. The full retirement age increases gradually if you were born from 1955 to 1960 until it reaches 67. For anyone born 1960 or later, full retirement benefits are payable at age 67.

The chart on the next page lists the full retirement age byyear of birth.

Age to receive full Social Security benefits	
Year of birth	*Full retirement age*
1943-1954	66
1955	66 and 2 months
1956	66 and 4 months
1957	66 and 6 months
1958	66 and 8 months
1959	66 and 10 months
1960 and later	67

Note: People born on January 1 of any year, refer to theprevious year.

Early Retirement

You can receive Social Security retirement benefits as early as age 62. However, we'll reduce your benefit if you start receiving benefits before your full retirement age. For example, if you turn age 62 in 2024, your benefit would be about 30% lower than it would be at your full retirement age of 67.

Some people will stop working before age 62. But if they do, the years with no earnings will probably mean a lower Social Security benefit when they decide to start receiving benefits.

Sometimes health problems force people to retire early. If you can't work because of health problems, consider applying for Social Security disability benefits. The disability benefit amount is the same as a full, unreduced retirement benefit. If you get Social Security disability benefits when you reach full retirement age, we convert those benefits to retirement benefits. For more information, read Disability Benefits (Publication No. 05-10029).

Delayed Retirement

You can choose to continue working beyond your full retirement age. If you do, you can increase future Social Security benefits in two ways.

Each extra year you work adds another year of earnings to your Social Security record. Higher lifetime earnings can mean higher benefits when you retire.

Also, your benefit will increase from the time you reach full retirement age, until you start to receive benefits, or until you reach age 70. We'll add 8% to your benefit for each full year you delay receiving Social Security benefits beyond full retirement age.

NOTE: You should sign up for Medicare 3 months before your 65th birthday, even if you haven't started receiving retirement benefits yet. In some circumstances, medical insurance costs more if you delay applying for it. You can find more information in the "A word about Medicare" section below.

Decide When to Start Receiving Retirement Benefits

Choosing when to start receiving retirement benefits is an important decision. No matter the age you plan to start receiving benefits, contact us in advance to learn your choices to make the best decisions. Sometimes, your choice of the month to begin receiving benefits could mean higher benefit payments for you and your family.

Social Security benefits replace a percentage of a worker's pre-retirement income. The amount of your average wages that Social Security retirement benefits replaces varies depending on your earnings and when you choose to start benefits. If you start benefits at age 67, this percentage ranges from as much as 78% for very low earners, to about 42% for medium earners, and about 28% for high earners. If you start benefits earlier than age 67, these percentages would be lower.After age 67 they'd be higher. Most financial advisers say you will need about 80% of pre-retirement income to live comfortably in retirement, which includes your Social Security benefits, investments, and other personal savings. For more information on other factors to consider as you think about when to start receiving Social Securityretirement benefits read *Your Retirement Checklist* (Publication No. 05-10377).

You can apply up to 4 months before you want your retirement benefits to start. If you're not readyto begin receiving retirement benefits, but are thinking about doing so soon, visit our website at *www.ssa.gov/benefits/retirement to learn more.*

Advance Designation

Advance Designation is available to capable adult and emancipated minor applicants and beneficiaries of Social Security, Supplemental Security Income (SSI), and Special Veterans Benefits. It allows beneficiaries to designate up to three people who could potentially serve as their representative payee in the future, if the need arises.

By selecting a representative payee in advance, you'll have peace of mind knowing that someone you trust may be appointed to manage your benefits if needed.

You can submit an Advance Designation request when you file an application for benefits, online with your personal my Social Security account, or by telephone.

Family Benefits

Benefits for Family Members

If you get Social Security retirement benefits, some members of your family may also be eligible for benefits.

Eligible members include:

- Spouses age 62 or older.
- Spouses younger than 62, if they care for a child entitled on your record who is younger than age 16 or has a qualifying disability.
- Former spouses, if they are age 62 or older (see our section "Benefits for a divorced spouse" for more information).
- Unmarried children up to age 18, or up to 19 if full-time student at an elementary or secondary school (grade 12 or below).
- Unmarried children age 18 or older with a disability that began before age 22.

If you become the parent of a child (this includes an adopted child) after you begin to get benefits, let us know. Then we'll decide if the child is eligible for benefits.

Spouse's Benefits

Spouses who never worked or have low earnings can get up to half of a retired worker's full benefits. If you're eligible for both your own retirement benefits and spouse's benefits, we always pay your own benefits first.

If your benefits as a spouse are higher than your own retirement benefit, you'll receive a combination of benefits that equal the higher spouse's benefit.

For example, a person qualifies for a retirement benefit of $1,250 and a spouse's benefit of $1,400. At full retirement age, they will get their own $1,250 retirement benefit. We also will add $150 from their spouse's benefit, for a total of $1,400. If the person takes the retirement benefit before their full retirement age, we'll reduce both amounts.

If you were born before January 2, 1954, are at least full retirement age, and are eligible for your own retirement benefits and also spouse's (or divorced spouse's) benefits, you can choose to:

- Restrict your application.
- Apply for one of the benefits.
- Delay your application for the other until a later date.

If you were born on or after January 2, 1954, and are eligible for both retirement and spouse's (or divorced spouse's) benefits, you must apply for both benefits. This is called "deemed filing." If you file for one benefit, you are "deemed" to file for the other one, too, even if you don't become eligible for it until later.

If you receive a pension based on work for which you didn't pay Social Security taxes, we may reduce your spouse's benefit. For more information see the section "Pensions from work not covered by Social Security".

If spouses receive Social Security retirement benefits before they reach full retirement age, we reduce the benefit. The amount we reduce the benefit by depends onwhen the person reaches full retirement age.

For example, if full retirement age is 67, a spouse can get 32.5% of the worker's unreduced benefit at age 62.

The benefit increases the longer you wait to receive benefits, up to the maximum of 50% at full retirement age.

Your spouse can receive full benefits, regardless of age,if taking care of a child entitled on your record. The child must be under age 16, or have a qualifying disability thatbegan before age 22.

NOTE: Your current spouse can't get spouse's benefitsuntil you file for retirement benefits.

Children's Benefits

Your dependent child may get benefits on your earnings record when you start your Social Security retirement benefits. Your child may get up to half of your full benefit.

To receive benefits, your child must be unmarried and meet one of the following requirements:

- Younger than age 18.
- 18-19 years old and a full-time student at an elementary or secondary school (no higher than grade 12).
- 18 or older and have a qualifying disability that began before age 22.

Under certain circumstances, we can also pay benefits to a stepchild, grandchild, step-grandchild, or adopted child.

NOTE: Children with disabilities whose parents have limited income and resources may be eligible for SSI. For more information, visit our website or call our toll-free number.

Maximum Family Benefits

If you have children eligible for Social Security, each will receive up to half of your full benefit. But there's a limit to how much money we can pay to you and your family.This limit varies between 150% and 180% of your own benefit payment. If the total benefits due to your spouse and children are more than this limit, we'll reduce their benefits. Your benefit won't be affected.

Benefits for A Divorced Spouse

- Your divorced spouse can receive benefits on your Social Security record if the marriage lasted at least 10 years.
- Your divorced spouse must be 62 or older and unmarried.
- The benefits they get don't affect the amount you or your current spouse can get.

Also, your former spouse can get benefits even if you haven't started to receive retirement benefits. You both must be at least 62 and divorced at least 2 years.

What You Need To Know When You're Eligible For Retirement Benefits

How Do You Sign up for Social Security?

You can apply for retirement benefits online at www.ssa.gov, call our toll-free number, or contact a local Social Security office.

Depending on your circumstances, you'll need some or all the documents listed below. Don't delay your application for benefits if you don't have all the information. If you don't have a document you need, we can help you get it.

Information and documents you'll need include:

- Your SSN.
- Your birth certificate.
- Your W-2 forms or self-employment tax return for last year.
- Your military discharge papers if you had military service.
- Your spouse's birth certificate and SSN if they're applying for benefits.
- Your children's birth certificates and SSNs, if you're applying for children's benefits.
- Proof of U.S. citizenship or lawful alien status if you (or a spouse or child applying for benefits) were not born in the United States.
- The name of your financial institution, the routing number, and your account number for direct deposit. If you don't have an account at a

financial institution, or prefer to get your benefits on a prepaid debit card, you can get a Direct Express® card. For more information, visit www.GoDirect.gov.

You must submit original documents or copies certified by the issuing office. We must see the original document(s) or copies certified by the agency that issued them.

We cannot accept expired, notarized, or photocopied documents. You can mail or bring them to us. We'll make photocopies and return your documents.

Right to Appeal

If you disagree with a decision made on your claim, you can appeal it. You can handle your own appeal with free help from us, or you can choose to have a representative help you. We can give you information about organizations that can help you find a representative. For more information about the appeals process and how to select a representative, read Your Right to Question the Decision Made on Your Claim (Publication No. 05-10058).

If You Work and Receive Benefits at the Same Time

You can continue to work and still receive retirement benefits. Your earnings in (or after) the month you reach your full retirement age won't reduce your Social Security benefits. We'll reduce your benefits, however,if your earnings exceed certain limits for the months before you reach full retirement age. (See the chart in the "*Full retirement age*" section.)

Here is how it works:

If you're younger than full retirement age, we'll deduct $1 in benefits for each $2 you earn above the annual limit.

In the year you reach your full retirement age, we'll reduce your benefits $1 for every $3 you earn over an annual limit. This reduction continues until the month you reach full retirement age. Once you reach full retirement age, you can keep working, and we won't reduce your Social Security benefit no matter how much you earn.

If, within the year, your earnings are higher or lower than you estimated, let us know as soon as possible, so we can adjust your benefits.

A Special Monthly Rule

A special rule applies to your earnings for 1 year, usually the 1st year you receive retirement benefits. Under this rule, you can get a full Social Security payment for any month you earn under a certain limit, regardless of your yearly earnings.

If you want more information on how earnings affect your retirement benefit, read How Work Affects Your Benefits (Publication No. 05-10069). This pamphlet has a list of the current annual and monthly earnings limits.

Your Benefits May Be Taxable

About 40% of people who get Social Security have to pay income taxes on their benefits. For example:

- If you file a federal tax return as an "individual," and your combined income is between $25,000 and $34,000, you may have to pay taxes on up to 50%of your Social Security benefits. If your combined income is more than $34,000, up to 85% of your SocialSecurity benefits is subject to income tax.
- If you file a joint return, you may have to pay taxes on 50% of your benefits if you and your spouse have a combined income between $32,000 and $44,000.If your combined income is more than $44,000, up to 85% of your Social Security benefits is subject toincome tax.
- If you're married and file a separate return, you'll probably pay taxes on your benefits.

At the end of each year, we'll mail you a Social Security Benefit Statement (Form SSA-1099) that shows the amount of benefits you received. Use this statement when you complete your federal income tax return to find out if you must pay taxes on your benefits.

Although you're not required to have Social Security withhold federal taxes, you may find it easier than paying quarterly estimated tax payments.

For more information, read *Tax Guide for Seniors* (IRS Publication No. 554) and *Social Security and EquivalentRailroad Retirement Benefits* (IRS Publication No. 915) at *www.irs.gov/publications*. You can also callthe Internal Revenue Service's toll-free telephone number, 1-800-829-3676.

NOTE: On the 1040 tax return, your "combined income" is the sum of your adjusted gross income plus nontaxableinterest plus half of your Social Security benefits.

Pensions from Work Not Covered by Social Security

If you get a pension from work for which you paid Social Security taxes, that pension won't affect your Social Security benefits. However, if you get a retirement or disability pension from work not covered by Social Security, we may reduce your Social Security benefit.

Work not covered by Social Security includes the federal civil service, some state or local government employment, or work in a foreign country.

Government workers who are eligible for Social Security benefits on the earnings record of a spouse, can read Government Pension Offset (Publication No. 05-10007) for more information. People who worked in another country, or government workers who are also eligible for their own Social Security benefits, can read Windfall Elimination Provision (Publication No. 05-10045).

Have Plans to Leave the United States?

If you're a U.S. citizen, you can travel to, or live in, most foreign countries without any effect on your Social Security benefits. There are, however, a few countries where we can't send Social Security payments. These countries are Azerbaijan, Belarus, Cuba, Kazakhstan, Kyrgyzstan, Moldova, North Korea, Tajikistan, Turkmenistan, and Uzbekistan. We can make exceptions, however, for certain eligible beneficiaries in countries other than Cuba and North Korea. For more information about these exceptions, contact your local Social Security office.

If you work outside the United States, different rules apply in deciding if you can receive benefits.

For more information, read Your Payments While You Are Outside The United States (Publication No. 05-10137).

A Word About Medicare

Medicare is our country's health insurance plan for people who are age 65 or older.

However, you can get Medicare at any age if:

- You've been entitled to Social Security disability benefits for 24 months.
- You've been entitled to Social Security disability benefits and have amyotrophic lateral sclerosis (Lou Gehrig's disease).
- You have End-Stage Renal Disease (permanent kidney failure that requires dialysis or a kidney transplant).

Parts of Medicare

We enroll you in Original Medicare (Part A and Part B).

- Medicare Part A (Hospital Insurance) helps cover inpatient care in hospitals, (that includes critical access hospitals), and skilled nursing facilities (not custodial or long-term care). Part A also pays for some home health care, hospice care, and inpatient care in a religious non-medical health care institution.
- Medicare Part B (Medical Insurance) helps cover medically necessary doctors' services, outpatient care, home health services, durable medical equipment, mental health services, and other medical services. Part B also covers many preventative services.
- Other parts of Medicare are run by private insurance companies that follow rules set by Medicare.
- Medicare Advantage Plan (previously known as Part C) includes benefits and services covered under Part A and Part B — prescription drugs and additional benefits such as vision, hearing, and dental — bundled together in 1 plan.
- Medicare Part D (Medicare prescription drug coverage) helps cover the cost of prescription drugs.
- Supplemental (Medigap) policies help pay Medicare out-of-pocket copayment, coinsurance, and deductible expenses.

For more information, read Medicare (Publication No. 05-10043).

When Should I Apply for Medicare?

If you're not already receiving benefits, you should contact us about three months before your 65th birthday to sign up for Medicare. You should sign up for Medicare even if you don't plan to retire at age 65 to avoid the late enrollment penalty.

If you're already receiving Social Security benefits or Railroad Retirement Board (RRB) benefits, we'll contact you a few months before you become eligible for Medicare and send you information. If you live in one of the 50 states, Washington, D.C., the Northern Mariana Islands, Guam, American Samoa, or the U.S. Virgin Islands, we'll automatically enroll you in Original Medicare (Parts A and B). However, because you must pay a premium for Part B coverage, you can choose to turn it down.

We will not automatically enroll you in a Medicare prescription drug plan (Part D). Part D is optional, and you must elect this coverage. For the latest information about Medicare, visit the website, or call the toll-free number listed below.

Medicare	Website: *Medicare.gov* Toll-free number: 1-800-MEDICARE (1-800-633-4227) TTY number: 1-877-486-2048

If you don't enroll in Part B or Part D when you're 1st eligible, you may have to pay a late enrollment penalty for as long as you have Part B or Part D coverage. Also, you may have to wait to enroll, which will delay coverage.

Residents of Puerto Rico or foreign countries won't receive Part B automatically. They must elect this benefit.

If you're 65 or older and covered under a group health plan, either from your own or your spouse's current employment, you may be eligible for a Special Enrollment Period (SEP) to sign up for Medicare Part B.

This means that you may delay enrollment in Medicare Part B without the need to wait for a general enrollment period and paying the penalty for late enrollment.

If You Have a Health Savings Account (HSA)

If you have an HSA when you sign up for Medicare, you can't contribute to your HSA once your Medicare coverage begins. If you contribute to your HSA after your Medicare coverage starts, you may have to pay a tax penalty. If you'd like to continue your contribution to your HSA, you shouldn't apply for Medicare, Social Security, or RRB benefits.

Premium-free Part A coverage begins 6 months before the date you apply for Medicare (or Social Security/RRB benefits), but no earlier than the 1st month you were eligible for Medicare.

NOTE: To avoid a tax penalty, you should stop your contribution to HSA at least 6 months before you apply for Medicare.

"Extra Help" with Medicare Prescription Drug Costs

If you have limited resources and income, you may qualify for Extra Help to pay for your prescription drugs under Medicare Part D. Our role in this program is to:

- Help you understand how you may qualify.
- Help you complete the Extra Help application.
- Process your application.

If you apply for *Extra Help*, we also will send your information to your state to start an application for the Medicare Savings Programs, unless you tell us not to.

To see if you are eligible or to apply, visit our website at *www.ssa.gov/medicare/part-d-extra-help* or contact us.

Help with Other Medicare Costs

If you have limited income and resources, your state maypay your Medicare premiums and, in some cases, other "out-of-pocket" medical expenses, such as deductibles, copayments, and coinsurance.

Only your state can decide whether you are eligible for help from the Medicare Savings Programs. For more information, contact your state medical assistance (Medicaid) office or State Health Insurance Assistance Program

(SHIP). You can look up your state telephone numbers online at *Medicare.gov/talk-to-someone or call 1-800-MEDICARE (1-800-633-4227).*

Contacting Us

There are several ways to contact us, such as online, by phone, and in person. We're here to answer your questions and to serve you. For nearly 90 years, we have helped secure today and tomorrow by providing benefits and financial protection for millions of people throughout their life's journey.

Visit Our Website

The most convenient way to conduct business with us is online at www.ssa.gov. You can accomplish a lot.

- Apply for Extra Help with Medicare prescription drug
- plan costs.
- Apply for most types of benefits.
- Start or complete your request for an original or
- replacement Social Security card.
- Find copies of our publications.
- Get answers to frequently asked questions.

When you create a personal my Social Security account, you can do even more.

Review your Social Security Statement.

- Verify your earnings.
- Get estimates of future benefits.
- Print a benefit verification letter.
- Change your direct deposit information (Social Security
- beneficiaries only).
- Get a replacement SSA-1099/1042S.
- Access to your personal my Social Security account may be limited for users outside the United States.

Call us

If you cannot use our online services, we can help you byphone when you call our National toll-free 800 Number.

We provide free interpreter services upon request.

You can call us at *1-800-772-1213* — or at our TTY number, *1-800-325-0778,* if you're deaf or hard of hearing— between 8:00 a.m. – 7:00 p.m., Monday through Friday. For quicker access to a representative, try callingearly in the day (between 8 a.m. and 10 a.m. local time)or later in the day. *We are less busy later in the week (Wednesday to Friday) and later in the month.* We also offer many automated telephone services, available24 hours a day, so you may not need to speak with a representative.

If you have documents we need to see, they must be original or copies that are certified by the issuing agency.

Chapter 9

The Department of Labor's 2024 Final Rule on Investment Advice in Private Sector Pension Plans and Individual Retirement Accounts*

Elizabeth A. Myers
and John J. Topoleski

Summary

On April 25, 2024, the Department of Labor (DOL) issued a final regulation to redefine *investment advice* within private sector pension and retirement plans, which replaced regulations issued in 1975 ("the 1975 rule"). Following the enactment of the Employee Retirement Income Security Act of 1974 (ERISA; P.L. 93-406), the 1975 rule defined *investment advice* using a five-part test. To be held to ERISA's fiduciary standard with respect to providing advice, an individual had to (1) make recommendations on investing in, purchasing, or selling securities or other property or give advice as to the value (2) on a regular basis (3) pursuant to a mutual understanding with the plan or the plan fiduciary (4) that the advice would serve as a primary basis for investment decisions and (5) would be individualized to the particular needs of the plan regarding such matters as, among other things, investment policies or strategy, overall portfolio composition, or diversification of plan investments.

Under ERISA, a person who provides investment advice is a fiduciary. Redefining the term *investment advice* could affect who is subject to this fiduciary standard. For example, under the five-part test, an individual

* This is an edited, reformatted and augmented version of Congressional Research Service Publication No. R48108, dated June 18, 2024.

In: Retirement Strategies: Analysis of Policies, Investments, and Security
Editor: Ryan M. Powell
ISBN: 979-8-89530-366-5

had to provide advice on a regular basis to be a fiduciary, which generally would not have included one-time recommendations such as an employer seeking recommendations as to which options to include in its 401(k) plan investment menu. The change in definition replaces the requirement that advice be given on a regular basis with a requirement that makes fiduciaries of financial professionals who, among other conditions, provide investment recommendations as a regular part of their business. The finalrule is accompanied by amendments to a number of prohibited transaction exemptions (PTEs). PTEs allow fiduciaries to engage in transactions that might otherwise be deemed to injure plans or plan participants (such as charging commissions for products fiduciaries recommend).

Under the 1975 rule, financial professionals who provided services to retirement investors and retirement plans and whose actions did not meet the five-part test were not fiduciaries and, thus, did not have to meet a fiduciary standard. However, their recommendations may have been subject to other standards. For example, securities brokers and dealers must meet a best interest standard, as found in the Securities and Exchange Commission's (SEC's) Regulation Best Interest. Insurance agents who sell annuities regulated by the states are subject to state standards of conduct. Most states have adopted the National Association of Insurance Commissioners (NAIC) Model Regulation. Under DOL's final rule, brokers, dealers, and insurance agents are generally considered to be fiduciaries when they provide recommendations that meet the definition of *investment advice* in certain specified contexts involving a relationship of trust and confidence between the financial professionals and retirement investors.

DOL first proposed broadening the definition of *investment advice* in October 2010. The proposed regulation generated muchcontroversy and, in September 2011, DOL announced that it would withdraw the proposed rule. DOL issued a revised proposal in April 2015 that also generated considerable controversy. DOL issued a final rule on April 8, 2016, with an effective date of June 7, 2016, and an applicability date of April 10, 2017. With the 2016 rule, DOL broadened the term's definition to capture activities that currently occur within pension and retirement plans but did not meet the 1975 definition of*investment advice*. In March 2018, the U.S. Court of Appeals for the Fifth Circuit vacated the 2016 rule. The vacatur had the effect of reinstating the five-part test. In July 2020, DOL implemented the vacatur of the 2016 rule. According to DOL, the final rule "is far narrower than the previous rulemaking" because it "specifically focuses on whether the investment recommendation can be appropriately treated as trust and confidence advice."

In October 2020, DOL issued PTE 2020-02 which, as with previous PTEs, allows fiduciaries to conduct transactions that would otherwise be prohibited. Investment advice fiduciaries who rely on PTE 2020-02 must comply with Impartial ConductStandards, which require them to provide advice that is in the best interest of retirement investors, charge no more than reasonable compensation, and make no misleading statements about investment transactions. In addition, PTE 2020-02 notedthat rollover recommendations from an employer plan to an IRA could be considered investment advice if specified conditions are met—for example, if the investment recommendation were expected to be part of an ongoing relationship. OnFebruary 13, 2023, a federal district court struck down the portion of PTE 2020-02 related to the rollover recommendations, and on June 30, 2023, a different federal district court recommended that the guidance related to rollover advice be vacated.

On November 3, 2023, DOL issued a proposed regulation that would redefine the term *investment advice* within private sector pension and retirement plans. Following the release of the 2023 proposal, DOL received more than 20,000 comments in the 60-day comment period. DOL held two days of public hearings on December 12 and December 13, 2023. On April 25, 2024, DOL issued the final regulation and amended PTEs. On May 15, 2024, resolutions were introduced in the House of Representatives and the Senate that, under the Congressional Review Act, would overturn the final rule and amended PTEs.

Overview

On April 25, 2024, the Department of Labor (DOL) adopted a final rule (2024 final rule) that updates the definition of *investment advice* within employer-sponsored private sector pension plans and individual retirement accounts (IRAs).[1] Individuals who provide recommendations thatmeet the definition of *investment advice* to plans (and their participants) that are covered by pensions law as found in Title 29 of the *U.S. Code* (often called the Labor Code) are held to a *fiduciary standard.* The fiduciary standard is a higher standard of conduct than that for individuals who provide recommendations that do not meet the definition. Individuals who are held to the fiduciary standard are required to act solely in the interests of plan participants and beneficiaries. Therefore, updating the definition of *investment advice* to include recommendationsthat are not currently considered investment advice might increase the number of individuals heldto this higher standard.

---

[1] See DOL, Employee Benefits Security Administration (EBSA), "Retirement Security Rule: Definition of an Investment Advice Fiduciary," 89 *Federal Register* 32122-32258, April 25, 2024, https://www.federalregister.gov/documents/2023/11/03/2023-23779/retirement-security-rule-definition-of-an-investment-advice-fiduciary.

Background on Pensions and IRAs

Although most workers can expect to become eligible to receive Social Security benefits after the age of 62, a number of tax-advantaged methods of preparing for retirement might also be available to them.[2] For example, their employers might sponsor pension plans, or the workers might establish and contribute to IRAs to use as sources of income in retirement.

Pension plans can be classified along several dimensions. In defined benefit (DB) plans (sometimes referred to as traditional pension plans), participants typically receive monthly payments in retirement based on a formula that uses either (1) a combination of length of service, accrual rate, and average of final years' salary or (2) a flat dollar amount times the number of months or years in the plan. Some plans offer participants the option to receive their benefits as lump-sum amounts.

In defined contribution (DC) plans, workers are provided individual accounts funded by their own contributions, contributions from their employers, or both. The funds in the account may accrue investment earnings, which can then be used as a source of income in retirement. The type of DC plan that an employer may offer depends on the type of employer (for example, the types of plans offered by public sector employers are typically different from those offered by private sector employers), as well as the employer's choices regarding plan features (for example, private sector employers have a number of types of DC plans they can offer). Examples of DC plans include profit-sharing plans, money purchase plans, 401(k) plans, 403(b) plans, and employee stock ownership plans (ESOPs).

IRAs are tax-advantaged accounts that allow individuals to save for retirement outside of employer-sponsored plans or to roll over savings from employer-sponsored plans.[3] Often individuals with savings in DC plans, or with lump-sum payments from DB plans, roll over their savings to IRAs at job change or retirement.[4]

---

[2] For more information on Social Security, see CRS Report R42035, *Social Security Primer*, and for more informationon the tax treatment of retirement savings, see U.S. Congress, Joint Committee on Taxation, *Present Law and Background Relating to the Tax Treatment of Retirement Savings*, 112th Cong., 2nd sess., JCX-32-12, April 13, 2012.

[3] For background on IRAs, see CRS Report R46635, *Individual Retirement Account (IRA) Ownership: Data and PolicyIssues*, and CRS Report RL34397, *Traditional and Roth Individual Retirement Accounts (IRAs): A Primer*.

[4] In addition, Congress has authorized several types of IRA-based retirement plans that employers can offer, such asSavings Incentive Match Plan for Employees (SIMPLE) IRAs and Simplified Employee Pension (SEP) IRAs (described below). In IRA-based plans,

Federal Law for Private Sector Pension Plans and IRAs

To protect the interests of private sector pension plan participants and beneficiaries, Congress passed the Employee Retirement Income Security Act of 1974 (ERISA; P.L. 93-406). ERISA is included in the U.S. Code in both Title 26 (the Internal Revenue Code, or IRC) and in Title 29 (often called the Labor Code). ERISA sets standards that pension plans must follow with regard to plan participation (who must be covered), minimum vesting requirements (how long a person must work for an employer to acquire a nonforfeitable right to the benefit earned), plan funding (how much must be set aside to pay for future benefits), and fiduciary duties (standards of conduct for certain individuals who have discretion over plan operations or who provide investment advice to plans or plan participants). ERISA covers only private sector pension plans and exempts pension plans established by federal, state, and local governments and by churches. The fiduciary duty requires that individuals—such as plan sponsors, administrators, and others who oversee pension plans—operate these plans prudently and in the sole interests of plan participants.

The 2024 final rule on investment advice concerns two of ERISA's four titles: Title I and Title II. Title I covers most private sector pension plans and is administered by DOL's Employee Benefits Security Administration (EBSA). Title I imposes duties and restrictions on fiduciaries with respect to Title I plans.[5] Title II specifies the requirements for plan qualifications under the IRC. While Title II is generally administered by the Department of the Treasury, the Reorganization Plan No. 4 of 1978 transferred much of Treasury's interpretive and exemptive authority over the IRC's prohibited transaction rules (including those relating to the provision of investment advice) to DOL.[6]

---

employers establish IRAs for employees at financial institutions. Employersmay also offer payroll deduction IRAs, which are available to employers who want to provide their employees a retirement savings option while limiting employer involvement. In addition, some states have established state- facilitated retirement savings programs, often IRA-based, for private sector employees.

[5] Title III assigns responsibilities for administration and enforcement to DOL and the Department of the Treasury. TitleIV of ERISA established the Pension Benefit Guaranty Corporation, an independent federal agency that insures DB pension plans covered by ERISA.

[6] See DOL, Reorganization Plan No. 4 of 1978, https://www.dol.gov/agencies/ebsa/laws-and-regulations/laws/executive-orders/4.

IRAs were first authorized by ERISA. Provisions that affect IRAs are found only in Title II of ERISA, which is codified in the IRC. Title 29 does not have any IRA provisions.[7]

Prohibited Transaction Exemptions (PTEs)

ERISA prohibits certain transactions between a plan and individuals who are fiduciaries.Fiduciaries may not

- deal with the assets of the plan in their own interests or for their own accounts;
- act in any transaction involving the plan on behalf of a party (or representing a party) whose interests are adverse to the interests of the plan or the interests of itsparticipants or beneficiaries; or
- receive any consideration for their own personal accounts from any party dealing with such plan in connection with a transaction involving the assets of the plan.

ERISA allows DOL to issue exemptions to prohibited transactions that allow an individual, a plan, or a group of individuals or plans (i.e., a class) to engage in transactions that would otherwise violate ERISA. These exemptions are referred to as prohibited transaction exemptions(PTEs).[8]

Role of DOL and the Department of the Treasury

Both DOL and Treasury oversee private sector pension plans and IRAs.[9] In general, DOL oversees the protection of pension plan participants, and the Internal Revenue Service (IRS), under the Treasury, oversees contributions to pension plans and taxes. Because IRA provisions are found only in the IRC, Treasury oversees most issues regarding IRAs. However, a 1978 executive order—subsequently ratified in P.L. 98-532—among other things, transferred

---

[7] However, DOL does oversee employer-sponsored IRA plans such as SIMPLE and SEP IRAs. SIMPLE and SEP retirement plans are designed for small businesses. More information is available at https://www.dol.gov/sites/dolgov/files/ebsa/about-ebsa/our-activities/resource-center/publications/choosing-a-retirement-solution-for-your-small- business.pdf.

[8] The procedures governing the filing and processing of PTEs are at Title 29, Sections 2570.30-2570.52, of the *Code ofFederal Regulations*.

[9] The 2024 final regulation on investment advice applies to private sector pension plans. It would not apply to the pension plans operated by state or local governments, the federal government, or churches.

regulatory authority with respect to fiduciary duty in Title II plans from the Secretary of the Treasury to the Secretary of Labor.[10]

Standards in Pension Plans

Retirement plans are complex, and employers and participants often rely on financial services professionals to assist them with their decisionmaking. For example, an employer might seek out assistance in determining what investments to offer in a 401(k) plan it has established, participants in a 401(k) plan might seek assistance in choosing their investments from among the options offered by the plan, or a worker who participates in an employer-sponsored 401(k) plan might seek assistance on whether to leave his or her 401(k) account balance in the plan or roll it over into an IRA or into another employer's DC plan upon either job change or retirement.

The way in which some financial services professionals are compensated may give rise to conflicts of interest if these professionals' recommendations result in larger commissions or otherwise benefit them. These potential conflicts could lead to the professionals making recommendations that are not in the interests of their clients. By contrast, some financial services professionals have compensation structures that do not vary based on which products clients choose. This type of compensation structure could mitigate any conflicts of interest.

Individuals who transact with pension plans may be required to meet certain standards. The standard that applies depends on the individuals' roles and the actions they are taking. For example, a financial professional providing investment advice is subject to the fiduciary standard, whereas an individual who is only executing a transaction at the direction of a plan participant would not be an investment advice fiduciary.

---

[10] See DOL, Reorganization Plan No. 4 of 1978. ERISA, as originally enacted, provided for both DOL and Treasury toissue PTEs. Reorganization Plan No. 4 of 1978 transferred much of Treasury's interpretive and exemptive authority over the IRC's prohibited transaction rules to DOL. Currently, DOL evaluates virtually all of the applications for administrative exemptions. DOL's FAQs regarding PTE 2020-02 explained how DOL enforces compliance with PTEswith regard to Title II plans (such as IRAs). See FAQ 21 of DOL, *New Fiduciary Advice Exemption: PTE 2020-02 Improving Investment Advice for Workers and Retirees Frequently Asked Questions*, April 2021, https://www.dol.gov/sites/dolgov/files/ebsa/about-ebsa/our-activities/resource-center/faqs/new-fiduciary-advice-exemption.pdf. The FAQ states, "For IRAs and other non-Title I plans, the Department has interpretive authority to determine whether the exemption conditions have been satisfied and transmits information to the IRS for enforcement of the excise tax."

Fiduciary Duty

ERISA Section 3(21)(A)[11] provides that a person is a fiduciary to the extent that the person:

- exercises any discretionary authority or control with respect to the managementof the plan or exercises any authority with respect to the management or disposition of plan assets,
- renders investment advice for a fee or other compensation with respect to anyplan asset or has any authority or responsibility to do so, or
- has any discretionary responsibility in the administration of the plan.[12]

An individual who is a Title I fiduciary is required, among other duties, to "discharge his duties with respect to a plan solely in the interest of the participants and beneficiaries."[13] ERISA identifies four standards of conduct: (1) a duty of loyalty, (2) a duty of prudence, (3) a duty to diversify investments, and (4) a duty to follow plan documents to the extent that they comply with ERISA.[14]

Investment Advice

As noted above, ERISA Section 3(21)(a) established situations in which a person qualifies as a fiduciary. One of these situations, in which an individual renders investment advice for a fee or other compensation, is the subject of the final rule that DOL published in the *Federal Register* onApril 25, 2024.[15] The rule is intended to replace a rule that was promulgated in 1975.

1975 Rule

In 1975, DOL addressed the second of the three actions that render an individual a fiduciary. DOLissued regulations that created a five-part test to determine whether an individual provided investment advice and thus was subject to the fiduciary standard.[16]

---

[11] See also IRC §4975(e)(3)(B).
[12] See ERISA §3(21)(A).
[13] See ERISA §404(a).
[14] See ERISA §404(a)(1)(A)-404(a)(1)(D).
[15] DOL, "Retirement Security Rule," 75890.
[16] DOL, "Definition of Fiduciary," 40 *Federal Register* 50840-50850, October 31, 1975, https://www.govinfo.gov/content/pkg/FR-1975-10-31/pdf/FR-1975-10-31.pdf#page=150.

To be held to the 1975 fiduciary standard with respect to his or her investment advice, an individual must (1) make recommendations on investing in, purchasing, or selling securities or other property or give advice as to the value (2) on a regular basis, (3) pursuant to a mutual understanding with the plan or plan fiduciary (4) that the advice serves as a primary basis for investment decisions and (5) is individualized to the particular needs of the plan regarding such matters as, among other things, investment policies or strategy, overall portfolio composition, or diversification of plan investments. An investment adviser is not treated as a fiduciary unless eachof the five elements of the test is satisfied for each instance of advice.

Individuals who provide investment services to retirement investors or plans may also be subject to other regulatory structures. For example, broker-dealers are subject to the Financial Industry Regulatory Authority (FINRA) regulations.[17] Individuals such as broker-dealers, who provide investment recommendations but whose actions do not meet ERISA's five-part test, may be subject to other regulatory standards, such as the Securities and Exchange Commission's (SEC's)Regulation Best Interest (Reg BI) or state securities or insurance law.[18] Investment advisers who are compensated for advising about securities investments may have to register with the SEC andconform to conduct standards in the Investment Advisers Act of 1940 (P.L. 76-768).[19]

Investment Education

Not all information that retirement investors receive meets the definition of *investment advice*. For example, providing materials of a general nature designed to encourage participants to make informed decisions in their 401(k) plans would not necessarily meet all parts of the five-part test. To assist plan sponsors to develop education materials, DOL issued guidance—Interpretive Bulletin 96-1—that provides examples of materials furnished to participants that would not, in DOL's view, be considered investment advice.[20] Such

---

[17] See FINRA, https://www.finra.org/#/.

[18] For more information on Reg BI, see CRS Report R46115, *Regulation Best Interest (Reg BI): The SEC's Rule for Broker-Dealers*, and CRS Report R47431, *Capital Markets: Overview and Selected Policy Issues in the 118th Congress*. Fixed annuities are insurance products, and individuals who sell them are subject to state insurance law. Most states follow model regulations issued by the National Association of Insurance Commissioners (NAIC). See NAIC, "Suitability in Annuity Transactions Model Regulation," 2020, https://content.naic.org/sites/default/files/model-law-275.pdf. Because variable annuities and some indexed annuities are securities, individuals who sell them may also be subject to Reg BI.

[19] See SEC, "Laws and Rules," https://www.sec.gov/investment/laws-and-rules.

[20] See DOL, "61," 29586 Federal Register 29590, July 11, 1996, https://www.govinfo.gov/content/pkg/FR-1996-06- 11/pdf/96-14093.pdf.

materials include general information about a plan; details of a plan's investment options; general financial and investment information; information that describes how investors might allocate their investments based on hypothetical characteristics; and interactive investment materials such as questionnaires, worksheets, or software that help participants understand future retirement income and needs.

Recent Regulatory Actions

In October 2010, DOL proposed (and subsequently in September 2011, announced that it would withdraw) a rule that would have expanded the definition of *fiduciary advice* that would have made more individuals and their actions subject to the fiduciary advice regulation.[21] In April 2015, DOL issued a revised proposal to broaden the definition of *investment advice*[22] and, in April 2016, issued a final rule and new and amended PTEs.[23]

Under the 2016 rule, the types of activities that would have constituted investment advice—if they were done for a fee or other compensation—were recommendations pertaining to the advisability of buying, selling, holding, or exchanging investments; how investments should have been invested after being rolled over, transferred, or distributed from an IRA; the management of investments; or IRAs, including whether, in what form, in what amount, and to what destination rollovers, distributions from IRAs, and transfers from IRAs should have been made. The rule also described certain activities that would not have constituted investment advice (e.g., marketing by platform providers, providing general investment education, and executing securities transactions).

Among the new and amended PTEs accompanying the final rule were the Best Interest Contract Exemption, the Principal Transactions Exemption, and

---

[21] See DOL, "Definition of the Term 'Fiduciary,'" 75 Federal Register 65263, October 22, 2010, https://www.federalregister.gov/documents/2010/10/22/2010-26236/definition-of-the-term-fiduciary.

[22] See DOL, "Definition of the Term 'Fiduciary;' Conflict of Interest Rule-Retirement Investment Advice," 80 Federal Register 21928, April 20, 2015, https://www.federalregister.gov/documents/2015/04/20/2015-08831/definition-of-the-term-fiduciary-conflict-of-interest-rule-retirement-investment-advice.

[23] See DOL, "Definition of the Term 'Fiduciary;' Conflict of Interest Rule-Retirement Investment Advice," 81 Federal Register 20946, April 8, 2016, https://www.federalregister.gov/documents/2016/04/08/2016-07924/definition-of-the- term-fiduciary-conflict-of-interest-rule-retirement-investment-advice/.

an amended PTE 84-24, which affects the sale of annuity products. For more information on the 2016 proposed and final rule and PTEs, see CRS Report R44884, Department of Labor's 2016 Fiduciary Rule: Background and Issues.

Actions Under the Trump Administration

In March 2017, DOL issued a Temporary Enforcement Policy that indicated it would not initiate enforcement actions against financial advisers or financial institutions that failed to satisfy the conditions of the 2016 regulation or the PTE.[24] In March 2018, the U.S. Court of Appeals for the Fifth Circuit vacated the 2016 rule.[25] The vacatur had the effect of reinstating the five-part test. In July 2020, DOL implemented the vacatur of the 2016 rule.[26]

On December 18, 2020, DOL issued PTE 2020-02, which, as with previous PTEs, allows fiduciaries to conduct transactions that are otherwise prohibited.[27] Investment advice fiduciaries who rely on PTE 2020-02 must comply with Impartial Conduct Standards, which require them to provide advice that is in the best interest of retirement investors, charge no more than reasonable compensation, and make no misleading statements about investment transactions.

In addition, PTE 2020-02 and a subsequent FAQ noted that rollover recommendations from an employer plan to an IRA[28] could be considered investment advice if specified conditions are met—for example, as FAQ 7 noted, if the investment recommendation was given as "part of an ongoing relationship or as the beginning of an intended future ongoing relationship."[29] On February 13, 2023, a federal district court issued an opinion vacating the

---

[24] See DOL, *Temporary Enforcement Policy on Fiduciary Duty Rule*, Field Assistance Bulletin 2017-01, March 10, 2017, https://www.dol.gov/sites/dolgov/files/ebsa/employers-and-advisers/guidance/field-assistance-bulletins/2017-01.pdf.

[25] See *Chamber of Commerce v. United State Department of Labor*, 885 F.3d.360 (5th Cir. 2018).

[26] See 85 *Federal Register* 40589, July 7, 2020.

[27] See DOL, "Prohibited Transaction Exemption 2020-02, Improving Investment Advice for Workers and Retirees," 85*Federal Register* 82798-82866, December 18, 2020, https://www.federalregister.gov/documents/2020/12/18/2020-27825/prohibited-transaction-exemption-2020-02-improving-investment-advice-for-workers-and-retirees.

[28] PTE 2020-02 also provided relief for an investment advice fiduciary to receive compensation for advice to roll planassets to another plan, to roll IRA assets to another IRA or to a plan, and to transfer assets from one type of account toanother.

[29] See FAQ 7 of DOL, *New Fiduciary Advice Exemption: PTE 2020-02 Improving Investment Advice for Workers andRetirees Frequently Asked Questions*.

policy referenced in FAQ 7 and remanded it to DOL for future proceedings.[30] On June 30, 2023, a magistrate judge in a different federal district court filed a report with the judge's recommendations, including that the court should vacate portions of PTE 2020-02 related to investment advice relationships in IRAs.[31]

Actions Under the Biden Administration

On November 3, 2023, DOL published in the Federal Register its "Retirement Security Rule: Definition of an Investment Advice Fiduciary," which contained proposed amendments to the definition of investment advice and related PTEs (PTE 2020-02; PTE 84-24; and PTEs 75-1, 77- 4, 80-83, 83-1, and 86-128).[32] A 60-day period for public comments followed the release of the rule (which closed on January 2, 2024). In addition, DOL held two days of public hearings on the proposals on December 12 and 13, 2023.[33] On April 25, 2024, DOL adopted the final version of the rule and amendments to PTEs.[34]

Overview of the Final Rule

The final rule consists of a revision to the definition of investment advice found in regulations and amendments to PTE 2020-02; PTE 84-24; and PTEs 75-1, 77-4, 80-83, 83-1, and 86-128.

---

[30] See Noah Zuss, "Federal Judge Strikes Down DOL Rollover Advice Guidance," *Plan Sponsor*, February 14, 2023,https://www.plansponsor.com/federal-judge-strikes-down-dol-rollover-advice-guidance/.

[31] See Findings, Conclusions, and Recommendations of the United States Magistrate Judge, Fed'n of Ams. for Consumer Choice v. U.S. Dep't of Labor, No. 3:22–CV–00243–K–BT, 2023 WL 5682411, at *27–29 (N.D. Tex. June30, 2023). The 2024 final rule included a footnote that "[a]s of the date of this final rule, the district court judge has notyet taken action regarding the magistrate judge's report and recommendations" (see 89 *Federal Register* 32127).

[32] EBSA, "Retirement Security Rule: Definition of an Investment Advice Fiduciary," 88 *Federal Register* 75890- 75979, November 3, 2023, https://www.federalregister.gov/ documents/ 2023/11/03/2023-23779/retirement-security-rule-definition-of-an-investment-advice-fiduciary.

[33] See EBSA, "Retirement Security Rule: Definition of an Investment Advice Fiduciary and Related Exemptions PublicHearing," https://www.dol.gov/agencies/ebsa/laws-and-regula tions/rules-and-regulations/public-comments/1210- AC02-hearing.

[34] See 89 *Federal Register* 32122-32258.

2024 Final Rule

ERISA 3(21)(A)(ii) states that a person is a fiduciary if the person "renders investment advice for a fee or other compensation." The final rule replaces the current five-part test with an updated definition of when recommendations would be considered investment advice. Under the updated definition, a broader range of recipients receive advice that would be required to meet fiduciary standards under ERISA.

The final rule says that a person renders investment advice if he or she makes a recommendation of any securities or investment transaction to a retirement investor. Retirement investor is defined in the final rule as a plan, plan fiduciary, plan participant or beneficiary, or IRA owner or beneficiary.[35]

The person making the recommendation additionally has to do either of the following:

- Make professional investment recommendations as a regular part of his or her business.[36] In addition, the recommendation has to be based on the needs or circumstances of the retirement investor and is to be relied upon by the retirement investor as a basis for investment decisions that are in the retirement investor's best interest.
- Acknowledge or represent that he or she is a fiduciary.[37]

In addition, a written statement that a person is not a fiduciary does not have an effect on determining fiduciary status if the statement is inconsistent with the person's actions, according tothe final rule.

A person is not a fiduciary (1) with respect to assets or investments over which the person doesnot have discretionary authority or provide investment

---

[35] In the final rule preamble, DOL noted that "communications to plan or IRA fiduciaries acting as investment advicefiduciaries will not result in the person making the communication also being considered an investment advice fiduciary." See 89 *Federal Register* 32149.

[36] The final rule added the word *professional* before *investment recommendations*. DOL noted that it added the word to"provide additional certainty that the provision would not be satisfied by the ordinary communications of a human resources employee, who is not an investment professional, in communications with plan participants." See 89 *Federal Register* 32151.

[37] The proposed rule made a person an investment advice fiduciary if the person exercised control over a retirementinvestor's assets. DOL did not include this in the final rule. For a discussion of the proposed rule, see CRS Report R48045, *The Department of Labor's Proposed Rule on Investment Advice in Private Sector Pension Plans and Individual Retirement Accounts*.

advice or (2) solely because the person executes securities transactions on the instructions of the retirement investor.

A *recommendation*, according to the final rule, is one regarding the

- advisability of acquiring, holding, disposing, or exchanging securities or other investment property as an investment strategy or how it should be invested after arollover;
- management of investments such as recommendations on investment strategies, portfolio composition, selection of persons to provide investment advice or management services, account arrangements (i.e., brokerage versus advisory), orthe voting of proxies; or
- rolling over, transferring, or distributing assets from a plan or an IRA.

The final rule makes clear that one-time instances of advice regarding the rolling over of assets from a workplace retirement plan to an IRA, "as well as recommendations to roll over, transfer, ordistribute assets from a plan or IRA," are considered fiduciary investment advice.

DOL added a paragraph to the final rule that explains that a salesperson's recommendations that do not meet the other conditions of investment advice or investment education are not investmentadvice within the meaning of the final rule.

PTE 2020-02

ERISA prohibits fiduciaries from engaging in improper transactions. These *prohibited transactions* include, for example, (1) "engaging in self-dealing and receiving compensation fromthird parties in connection with transactions" involving retirement plans and IRAs and (2) acting on behalf of their own accounts (i.e., principal transactions).[38] Fiduciaries who engage in prohibited transactions are subject to excise taxes on the amounts involved in the transactions.[39]

PTE 2020-02, which was published in the Federal Register on December 18, 2020 (under the Trump Administration), provides an exemption to these

[38] Principal transactions occur when investment advice fiduciaries sell or purchase certain investments out of their owninventories to or from plans or IRAs.

[39] See IRS, "Retirement Topics—Tax on Prohibited Transactions," https://www.irs.gov/retirement-plans/plan-participant-employee/retirement-topics-tax-on-prohibited-transactions.

prohibited transactions so that investment advice fiduciaries can receive compensation[40] and engage in principal transactions provided they follow the conditions outlined in the PTE. Without this exemption, many common transactions in retirement plans would be prohibited under ERISA, and this would disrupt the retirement marketplace.

Under the exemption, financial institutions and investment professionals[41] who provide fiduciary investment advice, as defined in the regulation, to retirement investors[42] can receive a wide variety of payments that would otherwise be prohibited. PTE 2020-02 covers investment advice (1) to hold, dispose of, or exchange securities and other investments; (2) to take a distribution from a plan or to roll over the assets to an IRA; or (3) to engage (or not engage) in other transactions such as plan-to-plan rollovers, IRA-to-IRA rollovers, or rollovers from one type of account to another type of account (e.g., commission-based accounts, fee-based accounts). The April 25, 2024, final amendment to PTE 2020-02 made changes to some, but not all, of the conditions of the exemption. Prior to the final amendment, to comply with the exemption, an investment advice fiduciary had to

- provide advice meeting the Impartial Conduct Standards, which included a best interest standard,[43] a reasonable compensation standard, and a requirement to make no misleading statements about investment transactions;
- acknowledge in writing their fiduciary status when providing investment advice, the services to be provided, and any material conflicts of interest;
- document the reasons that a rollover recommendation is in the best interest of the retirement investor;

---

[40] Compensation can include commissions, 12b-1 fees, trailing commissions, sales loads, mark-ups and mark-downs,and revenue sharing payments from investment providers or third parties. Fees known as 12b-1 fees are annual marketing or distribution fees. See SEC, "Distribution [and/or Service] 12b-1 Fees," https://www.investor.gov/ introduction-investing/investing-basics/glossary/distribution-andor-service-12b-1-fees.

[41] *Financial institutions* refers to SEC- and state-registered investment advisers, broker-dealers, banks, and insurance companies. *Investment professionals* refers to the individual employees, agents, and representatives who work for thesefinancial institutions.

[42] *Retirement investors* includes retirement plan participants and beneficiaries, IRA owners, and plan and IRAfiduciaries.

[43] In PTE 2020-02, DOL notes that the best interest standard is broadly aligned with the SEC's Reg BI and the standardincluded in NAIC's Suitability in Annuity Transactions Model Regulation.

- adopt policies and procedures designed to ensure compliance with the Impartial Conduct Standards; and
- conduct a retrospective review of compliance.

The exemption also allowed a financial institution to engage in transactions in which the institution purchases or sells certain investments from its own account and receives a mark-up or mark-down or similar payment on the transaction, referred to as a principal transaction.[44]

The exemption specified that financial institutions and investment professionals were ineligible to rely on the PTE if, within the previous 10 years, they were convicted of certain crimes related to their provision of investment advice, or they engaged in systemic or intentional violation of the exemption's conditions or provided materially misleading information to DOL.

Final Amendment to PTE 2020-02

The 2024 final rule was accompanied by amendments to several PTEs, including PTE 2020-02.[45] The amendment is effective September 23, 2024.

DOL stated that the amendment would cover more transactions and revise "some of the exemption's conditions to emphasize the core standards underlying the exemption."[46] The amendment makes several changes, including those described below.

Changes to the Exemption's Scope

The amendment expands the exemption to cover investment advice provided by

---

[44] A principal transaction may be a *riskless principal transaction* (in which a financial institution purchases or sells thesame investment product for the financial institution's own account to offset the transaction with a retirement investor)or a covered principal transaction (which is non-riskless and limited to specific investment products).

[45] See EBSA, "Amendment to Prohibited Transaction Exemption 2020-02," 89 *Federal Register* 32260-32299, April 25, 2024, https://www.federalregister.gov/documents/2024/04/25/2024-08066/amendment-to-prohibited-transaction-exemption-2020-02. The proposed amendment stated that DOL "notes that more parties may need to rely on an amended PTE 2020-02, because of the Department's proposed amendment to the definition of 'fiduciary investment advice.' If the new rule is adopted, parties that have not been fiduciaries under the five-part test may become fiduciariesin the future." See EBSA, "Proposed Amendment to Prohibited Transaction Exemption 2020-02," 88 *Federal Register* 75979-76003, November 3, 2023, https://www.federalregister.gov/documents/2023/11/03/2023-23780/proposed- amendment-to-prohibited-transaction-exemption-2020-02.

[46] See 89 *Federal Register* 32261.

- pooled plan providers (PPP), which DOL says would allow pooled employer plans (PEPs, which were authorized in the Setting Every Community Up for Retirement Enhancement Act of 2019 [SECURE Act; enacted as Division O of P.L. 116-94]) to receive investment advice in the same manner as other retirement plans;[47] and
- financial institutions that provide advice through computer models ("robo advice").

Compared to the proposed amendment, the final amendment further expands the exemption's scope to include recommendations of any investment products, regardless of whether the productis sold on a principal or agency basis. As part of this expansion, financial institutions, investment professionals, and their affiliates and related entities can receive reasonable compensation (including commissions, fees, mark-ups, mark-downs, and other payments) that would otherwisebe prohibited. The original PTE 2020-02 and proposed amendment granted limited relief for "covered principal transactions" and "riskless principal transactions." DOL noted that the expansion in scope responds to concerns that the proposed amendment "did not sufficiently clarify whether recommendations involving insurance and annuity products were covered transactions."[48]

In addition, the final amendment adds nonbank health savings account (HSA) trustees andcustodians to the definition of *financial institutions* with respect to HSAs.[49]

Changes to Impartial Conduct Standards

In the final amendment, DOL retains the substance of PTE 2020-02's requirement to act in theretirement investor's "Best Interest," but replaces the term *Best Interest* with its two separate components: the Care Obligation[50] and the Loyalty Obligation.[51] DOL states that the final amendment refers to each

[47] While the proposed amendment would have created a separate category for PPPs, the final amendment clarifies thatthey can rely on PTE 2020-02 when the PPP is selected by an independent fiduciary.

[48] See 89 *Federal Register* 32263.

[49] For more information on HSAs, see CRS Report R45277, *Health Savings Accounts (HSAs)*.

[50] To meet the Care Obligation, "advice must reflect the care, skill, prudence, and diligence under the circumstances then prevailing that a prudent person acting in a like capacity and familiar with such matters would use in the conductof an enterprise of a like character and with like aims, based on the investment objectives, risk tolerance, financial circumstances, and needs of the Retirement Investor." See 89 *Federal Register* 32266.

[51] To meet the Loyalty Obligation, "the Financial Institution and Investment Professional must not place the financialor other interests of the Investment Professional, Financial Institution

obligation separately but that they are unchanged in substance from the previous version of PTE 2020-02 and the proposed amendment.

Changes to Disclosures

In the pre-transaction disclosure to retirement investors, the amendment:

- clarifies the fiduciary acknowledgment requirement;
- requires a financial institution to include a written statement of the Care Obligation and Loyalty Obligation owed by the investment professional and financial institution to the retirement investor;
- requires the financial institution to disclose in writing all material facts relating to the scope and terms of the relationship with the retirement investor, including (1) material costs and fees that apply to the retirement investor's transactions, holdings, and accounts; (2) the type and scope of services provided to the retirement investor, including any material limitations on the recommendations that may be made to them; and (3) all material facts related to conflicts of interest that are associated with the recommendation; and
- revises the language to clarify that the disclosure must be provided at or before the time a covered transaction occurs.[52]

DOL stated that it based the final amendment's disclosure obligation on the SEC's Reg BI disclosure obligations to ensure that retirement investors receive critical information while reducing compliance burdens for financial institutions.

In the rollover disclosure, the amendment requires financial institutions and investment professionals to consider and document the bases for recommending that a retirement investor engage in a rollover from a Title I plan or how a plan participant or beneficiary should invest post-rollover assets currently held in a Title I plan. Factors to be considered include, but are not limited to, alternatives to a rollover, associated fees and expenses, whether an employer or other party pays for some of all of a plan's administrative

---

or any Affiliate, Related Entity, or other part ahead of the interests of the Retirement Investor or subordinate the Retirement Investor's interests to those of the Investment Professional, Financial Institution or any Affiliate, Related Entity." See 89 *Federal Register* 32266.

[52] The proposed amendment would have required financial institutions to inform retirement investors of their right to obtain specific information regarding costs, fees, and compensation and how they can receive this information free ofcharge.

expenses, and the different levels of services available under the plan and the recommended investment or account. This documentation must be provided to the retirement investor.

The final amendment's disclosure requirement applies only to rollover recommendations from Title I plans and would no longer require disclosures regarding advice for IRA-to-IRA rollovers or rollovers from one type of account to another. In the final amendment, DOL clarified the language that the disclosure applies only to advice to engage in a rollover recommendation to a plan participant or beneficiary as to the post-rollover investment of assets currently held in a Title I plan.[53]

In the final amendment, DOL revised the disclosure requirements to more closely track other regulators' disclosure requirements with respect to investment advice.[54]

Changes to Policies and Procedures

The amendment provides more guidance for financial institutions and investment professionals when implementing policies and procedures to comply with the Impartial Conduct Standards. It also requires that the policies and procedures mitigate conflicts of interest. Financial institutions "may not use quotas, appraisals, performance or personnel actions, bonuses, contests, special awards, differential compensation, or other similar actions or incentives that are intended, or that a reasonable person would conclude are likely, to encourage Investment Professionals to make recommendations that are not in Retirement Investors' Best Interest."[55] In addition, the amendment states that financial institutions must not "offer incentive vacations, or even paid tripsto educational conferences, if the desirability of the destination is based on sales volume and satisfaction of sales quotas."[56]

The amendment requires financial institutions to provide their policies and procedures to DOLwithin 30 business days of request.[57]

---

[53] The proposed amendment's disclosure requirement would have extended to plan-to-plan, plan-to-IRA, IRA-to-plan, and IRA-to-IRA rollovers, as well as rollovers from one type of account to another (e.g., commission-based account toa fee-based account).

[54] In the proposed amendment, DOL sought comment on whether it should require financial institutions to maintain public websites containing various disclosures. In the final amendment, DOL did not include a website disclosure requirement.

[55] See 88 Federal Register 75987.

[56] See 88 Federal Register 75987.

[57] The proposed amendment's time requirement was 10 business days.

Changes to Retrospective Review

The amendment requires financial institutions, as part of their retrospective reviews, to report nonexempt prohibited transactions associated with fiduciary investment advice and pay any resulting excise taxes.[58]

Changes to Circumstances Under Which a Financial Institution or Investment Professional Becomes Ineligible to Rely on the Exemption

The amendment sets forth a list of specific crimes (including foreign crimes) that could cause ineligibility to rely on the exemption for 10 years. The final amendment excludes foreign convictions that occur within foreign jurisdictions that are included on the Department of Commerce's list of "foreign adversaries."[59] In addition, financial institutions and investment professionals become ineligible to rely on the exemption if there is a final judgment or court-approved settlement in a federal or state criminal or civil court proceeding brought by specifiedagencies, regulators, or state attorneys general.[60]

A financial institution or investment professional convicted of a felony crime by a U.S. federal orstate court of competent jurisdiction would not have an opportunity to be heard by DOL. The final amendment stated that a financial institution or investment professional will become ineligible after it has been determined in a final judgment or court-approved settlement that improper conduct (as defined in the regulation) has occurred.[61] The final amendment limits the provision to the "controlled group."[62]

The regulation changes the "winding down" time period before ineligibility from a variety of timeperiods to a one-year transition period after

[58] The final rule adds failure to do so to the list of behaviors that could make a financial institution ineligible to rely onthe PTE for 10 years.

[59] The list is available at 15 C.F.R. §7.4. The proposed amendment did not include an exception for certain foreignjurisdictions.

[60] See 89 *Federal Register* 32297 for the list of specified agencies, regulators, and state attorneys general.

[61] The proposed amendment had stated that following receipt of the petition, DOL would provide the financial institution or investment professional with an opportunity for a hearing and then issue a written determination regarding the financial institution or investment professional's ability to rely on the PTE.

[62] The proposed amendment would have expanded ineligibility to include financial institutions that are affiliates, ratherthan the more limited definition of *controlled group*, which refers to two or more corporations connected through stockownership by related persons. See CCH Answer Connect, "Definition of Controlled Group," https://answercon nect.cch.com/topic/b233b6867d5a1000b7950050568869390a/definition-of-controlled-group.

the date of the conviction, DOL's written determination regarding a foreign conviction, or DOL's written ineligibility notice regarding othermisconduct.[63]

Additional Changes from the Proposed Amendment to PTE 2020-02

Compared to the proposed amendment, DOL provides new streamlined exemption provisions for financial institutions that give fiduciary advice in connection with a Request for Proposal (RFP) to provide investment management services as a particular type of investment manager as defined in Section 3(38) of ERISA.[64]

Unlike the proposed amendment, which would have expanded recordkeeping requirements for financial institutions following covered transactions, the final amendment keeps the existing recordkeeping requirements in PTE 2020-02 in place.

In addition, in response to comments that the proposal lacked sufficient time for financial institutions to comply with the amended PTE, DOL added a section that provides for a one-year phase-in period beginning September 23, 2024.

PTE 84-24

Prior to the final amended version, PTE 84-24 covered transactions in connection with the purchase of insurance and annuity products and other investment securities that would otherwise be prohibited by ERISA.[65] Insurance companies offer three common types of annuities: fixed annuities, indexed annuities, and variable annuities. A fixed annuity provides the investor with specified payouts in the decumulation phase. An indexed annuity provides the investor with payouts that are based on the performance of a market index, such as the S&P 500. A variable annuity is invested in options chosen by the investor (typically mutual funds), and payouts arebased on the performance of the underlying investments.[66]

---

[63] The proposed amendment included a six-month time period.

[64] For more on ERISA section 3(38) investment managers, see Morgan Stanley, "Understanding Your Fiduciary Liability: 3(21) vs. 3(38) Services," https://advisor.morganstanley.com/compass-point-wealth-management/documents/field/c/co/compass-point-wealth-management/understanding-fiduciary-liability-3-21-v-3-38.pdf.

[65] PTE 84-24 was originally granted in 1977 (as PTE 77-9) and has since been amended several times. See 42 *FederalRegister* 32395 (June 24, 1977) and 49 *Federal Register* 13208 (April 3, 1984).

[66] For more discussion of the different types of annuity products, see 88 *Federal Register* 75928.

Insurance companies that sell fixed annuities likely did not have to make use of PTEs for fiduciary investment advice, because their activities typically did not meet the definitions in the previous five-part test.[67] When DOL finalized PTE 2020-02 on December 18, 2020, it indicated that insurance companies could rely on either the finalized PTE 2020-02 or PTE 84-24 as it existed at the time. Generally, insurance agents are one of two types: (1) *A captive agent* works for and sells the products of a single insurance company, and (2) an *independent agent* does not work for a particular insurance company and sells the products of more than one insurance company. Under the 2024 definition of *investment advice*, many actions by insurance agents—whether captive or independent—to retirement plans or investors are likely considered *investment advice*.

One of the compliance challenges regarding the selling of insurance products to retirement plansand retirement investors is that an insurance company may not have much authority or control over independent agents. This could be problematic if insurance companies were fiduciaries regarding their products sold by independent agents.

Amendment to PTE 84-24

DOL's amendment to PTE 84-24 limits the exemption to independent agents, who are required tomake fiduciary acknowledgements.[68] Insurance companies are generally not fiduciaries when independent agents sell their products. However, insurance companies would be required to supervise the selling of their products by independent agents.

PTE 84-24, as modified by the amendment, is available to independent agents who sell annuitiesfrom two or more insurers to retirement plans and retirement investors. It is not available to agents who also sell annuities regulated by the SEC (such as variable annuities) or other noninsurance products. These agents have to rely on PTE 2020-02.

---

[67] They may have to rely on other PTEs based on their interactions with retirement plans and retirement investors.

[68] See EBSA, "Amendment to Prohibited Transaction Exemption 84-24," 89 *Federal Register* 32302-32344, April 25, 2024, https://www.federalregister.gov/documents/ 2024/04/ 25/2024-08067/amendment-to-prohibited-transaction-exemption-84-24. The final amend ment allows an employee of an insurance company that has no financial interest in the transaction to rely on the PTE. The proposal would have completely excluded employees of an insurance company, whether or not the company had a financial interest in the transaction. See EBSA, "Proposed Amendment to ProhibitedTransaction Exemption 84-24," 88 *Federal Register* 76004-76032, November 3, 2023, https://www. federal register.gov/documents/2023/11/03/2023-23781/proposed-amendment-to-prohibited-transaction-exemption-84-24.

Insurance agents who rely on PTE 84-24, as modified by the amendment, are required to meet certain conditions similar to those in PTE 2020-02, including adhering to Impartial Conduct Standards, limiting the types of compensation agents can receive, maintaining proper records, andproviding disclosures to IRA owners. Insurance companies are required to establish, maintain, enforce, and retrospectively review policies and procedures to ensure agents' compliance with theImpartial Conduct Standards and other conditions of the amendment to PTE 84-24, though the amendment specifically notes that an insurer is not required to supervise an agent's recommendations of products other than the annuities offered by the insurer. Similar to the amendment to PTE 2020-02, independent agents and insurers could lose their eligibility to rely on PTE 84-24 for convictions of felony financial crimes by U.S. federal or state courts or by foreigncourts.[69]

Changes from the Proposed Amendment to the Final Amendment to PTE 84-24

The changes to PTE 84-24 from the proposed amendment to the final amendment include thefollowing:

- Providing a less restrictive definition of *compensation* that could be the basis ofusing the PTE.[70]
- Allowing statutory employees of insurance companies to use the exemption,provided the insurance company has no financial interest in the transaction.
- Making changes to the best interest standard and Impartial Conduct Standards similar to the changes made in PTE 2020-02 (such as separating the Care Obligation and the Loyalty Obligation).
- Requiring disclosures involving only rollovers from Title 1 plans into insuranceproducts.
- Allowing insurance companies to rely on sampling to conduct their retrospectivereviews.
- Making changes to the eligibility provisions similar to the changes made in PTE 2020-02 (such as using the term *controlled group* rather than *affiliates*, removing DOL's discretion to determine ineligibility,

---

[69] The crimes include, for example, those that involve employee benefit plans, financial fraud, or securities violations.See 88 *Federal Register* 76029.

[70] The proposed amendment limited covered compensation to mutual fund commission or an insurance salescommission, whereas the final rule adopted the phrase *sales commissions*.

and exempting conviction by “foreignadversaries” as a cause to lose eligibility to rely upon the exemption).

- Providing narrower recording requirements.
- Adding in a one-year phase in period.

PTEs 75-1, 77-4, 80-83, 83-1, and 86-128

The 2024 final rule was accompanied by amendments to PTEs 75-1, 77-4, 80-83, 83-1, and 86- 128 (collectively referred to as the *Mass Amendment*).[71] These PTEs provided relief to investmentadvice fiduciaries for the following investment advice transactions:

- PTE 75-1 provided an exemption for broker-dealers, reporting dealers, and banksto engage in certain classes of transactions with plans and IRAs.[72]
- PTE 77-4 provided relief for a plan or IRA’s purchase or sale of open-end investment company shares[73] (i.e., mutual fund shares) where the investmentadviser for the investment company is also a fiduciary to the plan or IRA.[74]
- PTE 80-83 provided relief for a fiduciary causing a plan or IRA to purchase a security when the proceeds of the securities issuance may

---

[71] See EBSA, “Amendment to Prohibited Transaction Exemptions 75-1, 77-4, 80-83, 83-1, and 86-128,” 89 Federal Register 32347, April 25, 2024, https://www. federal register.gov/documents/2024/04/25/2024-08068/amendment-to-prohibited-transaction-exemptions-75-1-77-4-80-83-83-1-and-86-128, For the proposed amendment, see EBSA, “Proposed Amendment to Prohibited Transaction Exemption 75-1, 77-4, 80-83, 83-1, and 86-128,” 88 *Federal Register* 76032-76045, November 3, 2023, https://www.fede ralregister.gov/documents/2023/11/03/2023-23782/proposed-amendment-to-prohibited-transaction-exemptions-75-1-77-4-80-83-83-1-and-86-128.

[72] “Exemptions from Prohibitions Respecting Certain Classes of Transactions Involving Employee Benefit Plans andCertain Broker-Dealers, Reporting Dealers and Banks,” 40 *Federal Register* 50845, October 31, 1975, as amended at71 *Federal Register* 5883, February 3, 2006.

[73] See SEC, “Mutual Funds,” https://www.investor.gov/introduction-investing/investing-basics/glossary/mutual-funds.

[74] “Class Exemption for Certain Transactions Between Investment Companies and Employee Benefit Plans,” 42 *Federal Register* 18732, April 8, 1977.

be used by the issuer toretire or reduce indebtedness to the fiduciary or an affiliate.[75]

- PTE 83-1 provided relief for the sale of certificates in an initial issuance of certificates by the sponsor of a mortgage pool to a plan or IRA when the sponsor,trustee, or insurer of the mortgage pool is a fiduciary with respect to the plan or IRA assets investment in such certificates.[76]
- PTE 86-128 provided an exemption for certain types of fiduciaries to use theirauthority to cause a plan or IRA to pay a fee to the fiduciary, or its affiliate, foreffecting or executing securities transactions as an agent for the plan.[77]

Amendments to PTEs 75-1, 77-4, 80-83, 83-1, and 86-128

The amendments to PTEs 75-1, 77-4, 80-83, 83-1, and 86-128 remove the relief in the exemptions for the receipt of compensation as a result of the provision of investment advice and require that these investment advice fiduciaries instead rely on the relief provided in the amendedPTE 2020-02 or PTE 84-24.[78] DOL's stated goal for this change is to provide for a single standardof care that would apply to all fiduciary investment advice.

The amendments also include administrative amendments, such as revoking certain parts of someof the PTEs and adding disclosure requirements for some transactions. The amendment is effective September 23, 2024.

Changes from the Proposed Amendments to the Final Amendments to PTEs 75-1,77-4, 80-83, 83-1, and 86-128

In response to concerns that certain parties would no longer be able to rely on the PTEs affected by the Mass Amendment or the relief provided in PTE 2020-02, DOL said that it broadened the scope of PTE 2020-02 instead of making changes to the Mass Amendment. DOL also revised the final Mass

---

[75] "Class Exemption for Certain Transactions Involving Purchase of Securities Where Issuer May Use Proceeds to Reduce or Retire Indebtedness to Parties in Interest," 45 *Federal Register* 73189, November 4, 1980, as amended at 67*Federal Register* 9483, March 1, 2002.

[76] "Class Exemption for Certain Transactions Involving Mortgage Pool Investment Trusts," 48 *Federal Register* 895,January 7, 1984, as amended at 67 *Federal Register* 9483, March 1, 2002.

[77] "Class Exemption for Securities Transactions Involving Employee Benefit Plans and Broker-Dealers," 51 *FederalRegister* 41686, November 18, 1986, as amended at 67 *Federal Register* 64137, October 17, 2002.

[78] For PTE 75-1, the proposed amendment would remove the exemptive relief for Parts III and IV.

Amendment to clarify that only "the receipt of compensation as a result of the provision of investment advice within the meaning of ERISA section 3(21)(A)(ii) or Code section 4975(e)(3)(B) and regulations thereunder" is excluded from the amended PTEs. In addition, DOL did not finalize revocations of certain parts of some of the PTEs.

DOL's Rationale for the Rule

DOL's rationale for updating the current definition of *investment advice* includes the following: inadequacy of the current five-part test, gaps in the current rule, a desire for a uniform standard ofadvice, and expectations held by retirement investors.

DOL stated that it "drafted this rule to be responsive to the Fifth Circuit's decision in Chamber,which emphasized relationships of trust and confidence," noting that "fiduciary status attaches only if compensated recommendations are made in certain specified contexts, each of which describes circumstances in which the retirement investor can reasonably place their trust and confidence in the advice provider."[79]

For evidence of the harm under the 1975 rule, the proposal pointed to discussions in the 2016 final rule's Regulatory Impact Analysis (RIA), which it said provided evidence that retirement investors, who may have inadequate financial literacy, are harmed by financial professionals' conflicts of interest. DOL said that a review of the data "suggests that IRA holders receiving conflicted investment advice can expect their investments to underperform by an average of 50 to100 basis points per year over the next 20 years … [which] could cost IRA investors between $95billion and $189 billion over the next 10 years."[80]

Some of the rationale is based on the changes to the private sector pension system since the 1975rule was issued. In 1975, most workers who had retirement plans at work were in DB plans (70.8% of the 38.4 million active private sector plan participants). While DC plans existed, Congress had not yet authorized 401(k) plans, which have since become the predominant type

[79] See 89 Federal Register 32176.

[80] For example, see DOL, Regulating Advice Markets: Definition of the Term "Fiduciary" Conflicts of Interest— Retirement Investment Advice Regulatory Impact Analysis for Final Rule and Exemptions, April 2016, p. 9, https://www.dol.gov/sites/dolgov/files/ebsa/laws-and-regulations/rules-and-regulations/completed-rulemaking/1210- AB32-2/ria.pdf.

of retirement plan.[81] By 1984, a majority of active private sector plan participants were in DC plans,and in 2021 (the most recent year for which data is available), 88.3% of participants were in DC plans.[82]

DOL's Concerns Regarding the Adequacy of the Five-Part Test

DOL noted in the preamble to the final regulation that "the 1975 regulation's five-part test is underinclusive in assigning fiduciary status as it fails to capture many circumstances in which aninvestor would reasonably expect that they can place their trust and confidence in the advice provider."[83] Examples of situations in which not all recommendations met each part of the five- part test included

- *Regular basis prong.* One of DOL's concerns is that under the 1975 rule, one- time recommendations generally did not meet the *regular basis* prong of the five- part test. For example, an individual considering rolling over DC plan assets or an IRA might contact a financial professional. The financial professional's recommendation might not have been considered investment advice if it was provided once but not on a regular basis. The final rule addresses this scenario by making fiduciaries of financial professionals who provide professional investment recommendations as a regular part of their business, among other conditions, regardless of whether the retirement investor receives the recommendations one time or as part of an ongoing relationship.
- *Mutual understanding prong.* DOL said that firms may have lines in their contracts that disclaim that they are fiduciaries (and therefore the mutual understanding prong does not apply) or that tell investors

---

[81] The Revenue Act of 1978 (P.L. 95-600) authorized 401(k) plans, which started to become more widespread after theIRS issued regulations in 1981. See IRS, "Cash or Deferred Arrangements Under Employee Plans," 46 Federal Register 55544-55549, November 10, 1981, https://www.govinfo.gov/content/pkg/FR-1981-11-10/pdf/FR-1981-11-10.pdf#page=50.

[82] See CRS In Focus IF12007, A Visual Depiction of the Shift from Defined Benefit (DB) to Defined Contribution (DC) Pension Plans in the Private Sector, and EBSA, Private Pension Plan Bulletin Historical Tables and Graphs 1975- 2021, September 2023, Table E7, https://www.dol.gov/sites/dolgov/files/ebsa/researchers/statistics/retirement-bulletins/private-pension-plan-bulletin-historical-tables-and-graphs.pdf.

[83] See 89 Federal Register 32136.

to get other opinions (thereby avoiding the primary basis prong). The final rule relies on the circumstances surrounding the recommendation—including how investment professionals hold themselves out to retirement investors and describe the services offered—and replaces "primary basis" with "may be relied upon by theretirement investor as a basis for investment decisions that are in the retirement investor's best interest." A written statement that a person is not a fiduciary doesnot have an effect on determining fiduciary status if the statement is inconsistentwith the person's actions.

- *Primary basis prong.* DOL noted that some financial professionals skirted this prong by telling clients to not rely solely on their recommendations and to seek other opinions. By doing so, the recommendations would not have met this prongof the five-part test.

Rollover Recommendations

The updated definition of *investment advice* includes recommendations on rollovers. DOL stated that the decisions to take a benefit distribution or engage in a rollover are among the most important financial decisions that a plan participant or IRA owner can make. DOL noted that when retirement assets are held within ERISA plans, plan sponsors have the fiduciary duty to facilitate sound investment options, whereas retirement assets held in IRAs "often operate under conflicts of interest" by investment advice providers. Furthermore, an investment advice provider may have incentives to recommend rollovers from a workplace plan to an IRA held by his or her financial institution. PTE 2020-02 noted that when recommending a rollover, a firm "can generally expect to earn transaction-based compensation such as commissions or an ongoing advisory fee, from the IRA, but may or may not earn compensation if the assets remain in the Title I plan."[84]

Current Regulatory Gaps

The rule addresses what DOL calls gaps in the current regulatory structure. For example, Reg BI covers recommendations of securities to retail investors.

---

[84] See 85 Federal Register 82802.

Anti-*Shechita* Prosecutions in the Anglo-American World, 1855–1913

"A major attack on Jewish freedoms..."

Reg BI does not apply to (1) recommendations of non-securities (such as commodities, fixed indexed annuities, and real estate) to retail investors[85] and (2) recommendations to plan sponsors (because they are not retail investors). By updating the definition of investment advice, the rule covers these two situations.

DOL "expects that participants, in general, will benefit from the stronger, uniform standards imposed by the amendments to the rule and PTEs."[86] For example, under the previous rule, recommendations from broker-dealers might have been subject to Reg BI, whereas recommendations from insurance agents might have been subject to state regulations. These are generally covered recommendations under the final rule.

The sales of insurance products are generally regulated at the state level.[87] Most states have adopted the Suitability in Annuity Transactions Model Regulation #275, developed by the National Association of Insurance Commissioners (NAIC), which sets standards for the recommendation of annuity products. In the final rule, DOL noted what it considered to be potential issues with the NAIC model regulation—for instance, that the term material conflict of interest does not include cash compensation or noncash compensation and that it does not cover transactions involving ERISA plans.[88]

Congressional Responses to the Proposed and Final Rule

The following sections describe the congressional responses to the proposed and the final rule, asof the date of this report.

As of the date of this report, congressional responses to the final rule include the introduction of resolutions of disapproval under the Congressional Review Act and press releases and statements from several Members of Congress.

---

[85] Other types of annuities, such as variable annuities, are considered securities and subject to Reg BI.

[86] See 89 *Federal Register* 32198.

[87] The final rule states that "while all annuity products are subject to State regulation, variable annuities and some indexed annuities are considered securities, and therefore are also subject to SEC and FINRA regulations." See 89*Federal Register* 32188.

[88] See NAIC, "Suitability in Annuity Transactions Model Regulation." See also NAIC, "Additional Proposed Conflictof Interest FAQ Question and Answer," https://content.naic.org/sites/default/files/call_materials/Conflict%20of%20Interest%20FAQ%20Proposed%20Q%26A%20clean.pdf. See 89 *Federal Register* 32192.

Legislation

In the 118th Congress, H.J.Res. 140, H.J.Res. 141, H.J.Res. 142, and H.J.Res. 143 (introduced on May 15, 2024, by Representative Rick Allen) and S.J.Res. 79 (introduced on May 15, 2024, by Senator Ted Budd) would overturn the final rule and associated PTEs under the Congressional Review Act.[89]

Press Releases and Statements

Some Members of Congress objected to the proposed and final rule, indicating that they felt itwould limit retirement savers' investment options and access to investment advice.[90] Some Members of Congress supported the final rule,

---

[89] For more information on the Congressional Review Act, see CRS Report R43992, *The Congressional Review Act(CRA): Frequently Asked Questions.*

[90] See, for example, the following opposing the final rule: House Committee on Education and the Workforce, "Chair Foxx Statement on Final Fiduciary Rule," press release, April 23, 2024, https://edworkforce.house.gov/news/ documentsingle.aspx?DocumentID=410481; Office of Rep. Ann Wagner, "Wagner Slams Department of Labor Fiduciary Rule, Vows to Protect Retail Investors," press release, April 23, 2024, https://wagner.house.gov/media-center/press-releases/wagner-slams-department-labor-fiduciary-rule-vows-protect-retail; Office of Rep. Rick W. Allen, "Allen Statement on Biden's Overreaching Fiduciary Rule," press release, April 23, 2024, https://allen.house.gov/news/ documentsingle.aspx? DocumentID=6241; and Senate Committee on Health, Education, Labor and Pensions, "Ranking Member Cassidy, Budd Slam DOL's New Fiduciary Rule Threatening Americans' Access to Retirement Savings," press release, April 23, 2024, https://www.help.senate.gov/ranking/newsroom/press/ranking-member-cassidy-budd-slam-dols-new-fiduciary-rule-threatening-americans-access-to-retirement-savings. See, for example, the following opposing the proposed rule: letter from Reps. Foxx, Good, Walberg, Grothman, Stefanik, Allen, Banks, Smucker, McClain, Bean, and Houchin to Acting Secretary Su, December 21, 2023, https://edworkforce. house.gov/uploadedfiles/.21.23_final_comment_ltr_house_committee_on_education_and_the_workforce.pdf; letter from multiple Members of Congress to Acting Secretary Su and Assistant Secretary Gomez, January 8, 2024, https://si-interactive.s3.amazonaws. com/prod/planadviser-com/wp-content/uploads/2024/01/08165414/2024.1.8_Bipartisan_Hill_DScott_DOL_Retirement_Security_Proposed_Rule_Comment_Letter-FINAL-SIGNED.pdf; letter from Reps. Williams, Meuser, Alford, and Bean to Acting Secretary Su, December 7, 2023, https://smallbusiness. house.gov/uploadedfiles/12.07.2023_-_letter_to_dol_re_rfa_fiduciary_rule.pdf; letter from Sens. Marshall, Barrasso, Braun, Collins, Cornyn, Ernst, Grassley, Hagerty, Hyde-Smith, Rounds, and Thune to Acting Secretary Su, December 18, 2023, https://www.marshall.senate.gov/wp-content/uploads/Letter-to-DOL-Fiduciary-Rule-12.18.23.pdf; and Office of Rep. Ann Wagner, "Wagner Blasts Misguided, Irresponsible Fiduciary Rule," press release, October 31, 2023, https://wagner.house.gov/media-center/press-releases/wagner-blasts-misguided-irresponsible-fiduciary-rule.

saying that conflicted investment advice harms retirement savers because they either pay unnecessary fees or are directed to inappropriate investments.[91]

Hearings on the Proposed Rule

Congressional hearings held included

- a hearing from the House Financial Services committee on January 10, 2024, entitled *Examining the DOL Fiduciary Rule: Implications for Retirement Savingsand Access*;[92]
- a hearing from the Health, Employment, Labor, and Pensions subcommittee ofthe House Education and Workforce Committee on February 15, 2024, entitled*Protecting American Savers and Retirees from DOL's Regulatory Overreach*.[93]

---

[91] See, for example, the following supporting the final rule: Office of Sen. Elizabeth Warren, "Warren Reveals Insurer's Use of Hidden Kickbacks, Slams 15 Largest Annuity Companies for Opposition to New Retirement Security Rule," press release, April 30, 2024, https://www.warren.senate.gov/newsroom/press-releases/warren-reveals-insurers- use-of-hidden-kickbacks-slams-15-largest-annuity-companies-for-opposition-to-new-retirement-security-rule; and statement, Joint Economic Committee Democrats, "ICYMI: The Biden Administration Just Took Massive Steps to Protect Workers and the Climate," May 8, 2024, https://www.jec.senate.gov/public/index.cfm/democrats/2024/5/icymi-the-biden-administration-just-took-massive-steps-to-protect-workers-and-the-climate. See, for example, the following supporting the proposed rule: letter from Sen. Sanders and Rep. Scott to Acting Secretary Su, January 2, 2024, https://democrats-edworkforce.house.gov/imo/media/doc/ scott_sanders_comment_letter_to_dol_re_retirement_security_rule.pdf; Office of Rep. Bobby Scott, "Scott Applauds Proposed Rule to Strengthen America's Retirement Security," press release, October 31, 2023, https://bobbyscott.house.gov/media-center/press-releases/scott-applauds-proposed-rule-strengthen-americas-retirement-secu rity; and Office of Rep. Maxine Waters, "Ranking Member Maxine Waters Applauds Biden Administration's 'Retirement Security' Rule Proposal," press release, October 31, 2023, https://democrats-financialservices.house.gov/news/documentsingle.aspx?Docu mentID=410916.

[92] See Financial Services, Subcommittee on Capital Markets, *Examining the DOL Fiduciary Rule: Implications forRetirement Savings and Access*, https://financialservices.house.gov/calendar/eventsingle.aspx?EventID=409088.

[93] See U.S. Congress, House Committee on Education and the Workforce, Subcommittee on Health, Employment,Labor, and Pensions, *Protecting American Savers and Retirees from DOL's Regulatory Overreach*, https://edworkforce.house.gov/calendar/eventsingle.aspx?EventID=410108.

Stakeholder Comments on the Proposed Rule

The 2023 proposed rule received over 20,000 comments.[94] Stakeholders had varying opinions, ranging from requests to withdraw the proposal to suggesting changes to endorsing the proposal. This section includes a discussion of some stakeholder viewpoints regarding aspects of the proposal and the extent to which DOL addressed them in the final rule.[95]

Updated Definition of Investment Advice

Some stakeholders believe that the proposal's definition of *investment advice* is "overly broad."[96] The proposal's updated definition would capture interactions between financial professionals andretirement investors that some stakeholders think are not fiduciary investment advice. For example, some stakeholders stated that a fiduciary advice relationship is one built on trust and confidence, which would not be expected to be present for many of the interactions that would becaptured by the proposal, such as a one-time instance of a recommendation (for example, whethera retirement investor should roll over 401(k) assets into an IRA).[97] Some stakeholders referenced the Fifth Circuit's reasoning that vacated the 2016 rule, indicating they think it applies to parts of the current proposal. For example, one comment letter noted that "the Proposed Rule's interpretation of investment advice fiduciary again lacks any requirement of a special relationshipof 'trust and confidence.'"[98]

---

[94] This report provides a brief overview of selected comment letters, not a comprehensive summary of each letter. Many of the letters address a variety of aspects of the proposed rule, and summarizing all of them is beyond the scopeof this report.

[95] CRS identified topics that were discussed across many different letters and/or mentioned during DOL's two days of public hearings on the proposed rule. CRS incorporated a range of viewpoints from different stakeholders regarding each topic. More thorough discussions of DOL's responses to the comments are in the discussions of the final rule andeach of the amended PTEs.

[96] See, for example, comment letter from the American Investment Council at https://www.dol.gov/sites/dolgov/files/ebsa/laws-and-regulations/rules-and-regulations/public-comments/1210-AC02/00362.pdf.

[97] See, for example, comment letter from T. Rowe Price at https://www.dol.gov/sites/dolgov/files/ebsa/laws-and-regulations/rules-and-regulations/public-comments/1210-AC02/00363.pdf.

[98] See, for example, comment letter from the National Association of Insurance and Financial Advisors at https://www.dol.gov/sites/dolgov/files/ebsa/laws-and-regulations/rules-and-regulations/public-comments/1210-ZA33/ 00018.pdf.

Other stakeholders support the updated definition of *investment advice*, noting that they believe that financial professionals hold themselves out as acting in positions of trust by, as one commentletter noted, "the use by advisers of titles used to engender a sense of trust and confidence amongclients."[99] Another comment letter noted that "any reasonable investor would view these relationships as trusted advice relationships and expect to receive retirement investment advice that is in their best interest."[100]

Other stakeholders supported the updated definition of *investment advice* because recommendations to plan sponsors are *not* covered by Reg BI and the NAIC model regulation.[101]One comment letter noted that this could be of particular concern for small employers who might not have the same level of financial sophistication or knowledge as large employers have. The comment letter noted that "under the current federal and state regulatory framework, small business owners establishing a retirement plan for their employees are often provided zero regulatory protection with respect to the advice given to them regarding plan investment options."[102] Other stakeholders noted the benefits to retirement investors as a result of the rule. For example, Morningstar analysis indicated that retirement investors would save $55 billion infees over the next 10 years and, when rolling over into fixed annuity products, would realize significant savings.[103]

Some stakeholders argue that the existing regulatory framework for brokers/dealers and insurance professionals adequately protect retirement investors. For example, NAIC indicated that it "fundamentally disagree[d]" with "the Administration's characterization of state consumer protections around annuity sales as 'inadequate' and providing 'misaligned incentives.'"[104]

---

[99] See comment letter from Better Markets at https://www.dol.gov/sites/dolgov/files/ebsa/laws-and-regulations/rules-and-regulations/public-comments/1210-AC02/00374.pdf.

[100] See, for example, comment letter from the Consumer Federation of America at https://www.dol.gov/sites/dolgov/files/ebsa/laws-and-regulations/rules-and-regulations/public-comments/1210-AC02/00336.pdf.

[101] Reg BI applies only to retail customers, which plan sponsor are not. See SEC, "Frequently Asked Questions on Regulation Best Interest," https://www.sec.gov/tm/faq-regulation-best-interest. The NAIC model regulation does notapply to contracts used to fund ERISA plans. See NAIC, "Suitability in Annuity Transactions Model Regulation."

[102] See comment from the American Retirement Association at https://www.dol.gov/sites/dolgov/files/EBSA/laws-and-regulations/rules-and-regulations/public-comments/1210-ZA32/00068.pdf.

[103] See comment letter from Morningstar at https://www.dol.gov/sites/dolgov/files/ebsa/laws-and-regulations/rules-and-regulations/public-comments/1210-AC02/00290.pdf.

[104] See comment letter from NAIC at https://www.dol.gov/sites/dolgov/files/ebsa/laws-and-regulations/rules-and-regulations/public-comments/1210-AC02/00165.pdf.

In the final rule, DOL said that the final rule is not overly broad and "is far narrower than the previous rulemaking," because it "specifically focuses on whether the investment recommendation can be appropriately treated as trust and confidence advice."[105] In addition, DOLindicated that it drafted the rule "to be responsive to the Fifth Circuit's decision in Chamber, which emphasized relationships of trust and confidence."[106] Additionally, DOL noted that the focus of the final rule is on "defining those circumstances in which the retirement investor has a reasonable expectation that the recommendation reflects a professional or expert judgment offered on their behalf and in their interest."[107]

DOL noted that it had concerns that the NAIC model regulation "is not as protective as either theDepartment's approach under ERISA or the SEC's approach under Regulation Best Interest."[108] DOL noted that the definition of *material conflicts of interest* in the NAIC model regulation "excludes all 'cash compensation' and 'non-cash compensation'" and that "NAIC also expressly disclaimed that its standard creates fiduciary obligations."[109]

Investment Advice Relationships for IRAs

The proposed rule made clear that recommendations of any securities or investment transactions to IRA owners or beneficiaries would be fiduciary investment advice. Some stakeholders disagree with DOL's position that ERISA's fiduciary standards should apply to advice to IRA owners through the PTEs. One comment letter stated, "The fact that the prohibited transaction rules in Sec. 4975 of the Code apply to IRAs do not confer on the Department the authority to regulate the conduct of financial professionals making recommendations to IRAs."[110]

In the final rule, DOL stated it "has clear authority to promulgate the regulatory definition of a fiduciary under both Title I and Title II of ERISA, and the Department has taken care in this finalrule to honor the text and purposes of Title I and Title II of ERISA."[111]

---

[105] See 89 *Federal Register* 23141.
[106] See 89 *Federal Register* 32176.
[107] See 89 *Federal Register* 32137.
[108] See 89 *Federal Register* 32136.
[109] See 89 *Federal Register* 32137.
[110] See comment letter from Allianz Life Insurance Company of North America at https://www.regulations.gov/comment/EBSA-2023-0014-0428.
[111] See 89 Federal Register 32136.

"Hire Me" Conversations

Some stakeholders have expressed concerns that interactions where financial professionals bid for client services (what are referred to as "hire me" conversations) could be considered fiduciary advice. While DOL said it "does not intend to suggest, however, that a person could become a fiduciary merely by engaging in the normal activity of marketing themselves as a potential fiduciary to be selected by a plan fiduciary or IRA owner," one comment letter noted that, "like other market participants, banks found the 'hire me' exception difficult to employ when the 2016 Rule was in effect, due to uncertainty regarding its parameters."[112]

In the final rule, DOL did not provide any additional provisions related to "hire me" conversations. However, it did note that people can tout their own services and provide information about their services that would not be *investment advice*. DOL also noted that to the extent that "'hire me' communications include covered investment recommendations, those recommendations are evaluated separately under the provisions of the final rule."[113]

Call Centers

Some stakeholders have expressed concerns that resources that investors regularly engage with, such as call centers, could be considered sources of fiduciary advice. One comment letter noted that call center representatives "would need to follow tightly controlled scripts.... The true impactof the Proposal would be reducing these interactions to an exercise of sharing factual, bare minimum and one-dimensional information resulting in the retirement investor being left to eitherfend for themselves or take on additional cost to hire an investment advice provider for further assistance."[114]

In the final rule, DOL did not specifically address call center activities, though it noted that theactivities of call center personnel as described by some

---

[112] See page 75906 of the proposed rule and comment from American Bankers Association, p. 15, at https://www.dol.gov/sites/dolgov/files/ebsa/laws-and-regulations/rules-and-regulations/public-comments/1210-AC02/ 00296.pdf.

[113] See 89 Federal Register 32164.

[114] See comment letter from John L. Carter, president and chief operating officer of Nationwide Financial Services, at https://www.dol.gov/sites/dolgov/files/ebsa/laws-and-regulations/rules-and-regulations/public-comments/1210-AC02/ 00292.pdf.

commentators are covered by a DOL interpretive bulletin on investment education (IB 96-1) as discussed in the preamble to the finalrule. DOL also noted that "unless call center personnel provide an acknowledgment of ERISA Title I or Title II fiduciary status with respect to the recommendation, they can provide investment-related information that is not based on the particular needs or individual circumstances of the retirement investor without ERISA fiduciary status attaching."[115]

Lifetime Income

Some policymakers have a long-standing interest in ensuring that individuals receive regular income throughout their retirement—what is referred to as lifetime income. The decline in the number of private sector employers offering DB plans has raised concerns about participants possibly outliving their DC retirement assets. Purchasing annuities, either within participants' DBplans or in IRAs after rolling over DC assets, is the primary means by which individuals can ensure regular income throughout retirement. Some insurance companies have noted that as a result of changes they foresee to the annuity marketplace, the proposal would make "it more difficult and expensive for plans to offer lifetime income" and that "efforts that would restrict or nearly eliminate the use of such products in defined contribution plans are contrary to Congressional intent."[116]

In the final rule, DOL noted that it is "especially concerned about the proper regulation of fixed annuities" and that "uniquely among regulators, [DOL] can impose uniform standards for the provision of investment advice to Retirement Investors."[117] DOL also indicated that while many retirement investors will benefit from the final rule, DOL "expects Retirement Investors investingin annuities to see the greatest benefits."[118]

---

[115] See 89 Federal Register 32168.

[116] See comment letter from Mindset at https://www.dol.gov/sites/dolgov/files/ebsa/laws-and-regulations/rules-and-regulations/public-comments/1210-AC02/00366.pdf.

[117] See 89 *Federal Register* 32193-32194.

[118] See 89 *Federal Register* 32196.

Changes to Ineligibility to Rely on PTE 2020-02

Some stakeholders disagree with DOL's proposed changes to the ineligibility provisions, whichwould be expanded to include conviction of an affiliate rather than a "controlled group" and set forth a list of specific crimes (including foreign crimes) that could make the financial institution or investment professional ineligible to rely on the exemption for 10 years. One comment letter noted that "a conviction of an affiliate does not reflect in any way on the policies, procedures, orcompliance of the affiliated investment advisory firm."[119] Another noted that the proposed expansion of the definition of *controlled group* to include affiliates "can lead to the anomalous result of a fiduciary's ineligibility resulting from the criminal conduct of a foreign affiliate that has no contact or relationship with the fiduciary and which may be engaged in activities that are wholly unrelated to the investment management of retirement assets (e.g., foreign real estate brokerage, human resources support)."[120]

In the final amendment, after consideration of comments, DOL returned to the use of the term *controlled group* for purposes of determining ineligibility under PTE 2020-02.[121] In addition, thefinal amendment excludes foreign convictions that occur within foreign jurisdictions that are included on the Department of Commerce's list of "foreign adversaries."[122]

Compliance Concerns

The proposed amendment to PTE 2020-02 included additional disclosures and modifications to existing disclosures. Some stakeholders expressed concern with the compliance costs that would be associated with these changes to disclosures. The proposed amendment to PTE 2020-02 included time and cost estimations for the changes included in the proposal, but one comment letter noted that "these exemption changes would impose significant costs on the

---

[119] See, for example, comment letter from the Securities Industry and Financial Markets Association (SIFMA) andSIFMA Asset Management Group at https://www.regulations.gov/comment/EBSA-2023-0014-0377.

[120] See, for example, comment letter from the American Bankers Association at https://www.regulations.gov/comment/EBSA-2023-0014-0345.

[121] See 89 *Federal Register* 32281. PTE 84-24 has similar ineligibility provisions for independent agents and insurers.

[122] The list is available at 15 C.F.R. §7.4. The proposed amendment did not include an exception for certain foreignjurisdictions.

retirement industry that far exceed the Department's estimates, with no clear evaluation of the need for changes and no demonstrable benefit to investors,"[123] and that "many small entities are likely to face significant compliance costs associated with the proposed rule."[124] Some stated that the proposed changes to amended PTE 2020-02 would make it harder for service providers to complyand that "their natural reaction will be to either cease providing information, advice, and investment products to retirement investors or redouble their efforts to avoid classification as investment advice fiduciaries."[125]

In the final amendment, DOL modified some of the disclosure requirements from those includedin the proposed amendment. For example, DOL stated that it based the final amendment's disclosure obligations on the SEC's Reg BI disclosure obligations, and the final amendment is intended to keep retirement investors informed while reducing compliance burdens.[126] In addition, DOL narrowed the rollover disclosure requirement so that it applies only to recommendations to rollovers from Title I plans.[127]

Changes to Incentives

Some stakeholders do not agree with DOL's proposed prohibition of certain types of compensation, such as paid trips to educational conferences, noting that DOL's "restrictive approach to the types of compensation that Investment Professionals are entitled to is at direct odds with Regulation BI and FINRA."[128] Others describe the prohibition of the various types of compensation as "completely arbitrary" and "speculative, subjective and capable of being violated in every single employee's compensation setting."[129]

---

[123] See comment letter from the Investment Company Institute at https://www.regulations.gov/comment/EBSA-2023-0014-0444.

[124] See comment letter from the U.S. Small Business Administration Office of Advocacy at https://www.regulations.gov/comment/EBSA-2023-0014-0355.

[125] See comment letter from Cetera Financial Group at https://www.regulations.gov/comment/EBSA-2023-0014-0422.

[126] See 29 Federal Register 32272.

[127] See 29 Federal Register 32273.

[128] See comment letter from the Financial Services Institute at https://www.regulations.gov/comment/EBSA-2023- 0014-0391.

[129] See, for example, comment letters from SIFMA at https://www.regulations.gov/ comment/EBSA-2023-0014-0377 and Davis and Harman LLP at https://www. regulations.gov/comment/EBSA-2023-0014-0138.

Other stakeholders support the proposed changes, noting that "these types of incentives would encourage investment professionals to violate their best interest obligation."[130]

In the final amendment, DOL stated that it "neither bans differential compensation, nor prohibits educational meetings." It also stated that financial institutions must "take special care to ensure" that their compensation systems are not likely to result in recommendations that do not meet the Care Obligation or Loyalty Obligation.[131] With regard to educational conferences, DOL stated that "the conferences must be structured in a manner that ensures they are not likely to lead Investment Professionals to make recommendations that do not meet the exemption's Care Obligation or Loyalty Obligation."[132]

Efficiency Changes Resulting from Proposed Amendments to PTEs 75-1, 77-4, 80-83, 83-1, and 86-128

Some stakeholders disagree with the proposed change to remove existing exemptive relief for certain transactions covered by PTEs 75-1, 77-4, 80-83, 83-1, and 86-128 (so that amended PTE 2020-02 would be used instead). One comment letter noted that "the efficiencies associated with the current more tailored exemptions the Department proposes to amend would be lost, resulting in higher costs and fewer benefits to investors."[133]

In the final amendments, DOL stated that it believed that a common set of protective standards for a wide range of advice transactions as provided in PTE 2020-02 and PTE 84-24 promotes efficiency and clarity.[134]

Investment Education

Some interactions with retirement plan participants and plan sponsors, such as communications ofa general nature, do not meet the definition of *investment*

---

[130] See comment letter from the Consumer Federation of America at https://www.regula tions. gov/comment/EBSA-2023-0014-0385.

[131] See 89 Federal Register 32274.

[132] See 89 Federal Register 32275.

[133] See comment letter from the Investment Company Institute at https://www.regulations. gov/comment/EBSA-2023-0014-0444.

[134] See 89 *Federal Register* 32349.

advice. For example, communications that describe the features of a participant's 401(k) plan are considered investment education.

DOL's Interpretive Bulletin 96-1 (IB 96-1) describes the circumstances under which communications are considered investment education and therefore would not constitute investment advice.[135] While DOL stated that it "believes that the IB 96-1 would continue to provide accurate guidance under the proposed regulation," some stakeholders have expressed concerns that about whether "routine interactions and investment education would newly triggerfiduciary status" and that "further clarity is needed."[136]

In the final rule, DOL added a paragraph that it says "provides confirmation that sales pitches andinvestment education can occur without ERISA fiduciary status attaching."[137]

---

[135] See DOL, "Interpretive Bulletin 96-1; Participant Investment Education," 61 *Federal Register* 29586-29590, June 11, 1996, https://www.govinfo.gov/content/pkg/FR-1996-06-11/pdf/96-14093.pdf. The categories in IB 96-1 are plan information, general financial and investment information, asset allocation models, and interactive investment materials.

[136] See 88 *Federal Register* 75911 and comment letter from the ERISA Industry Committee.

[137] See 89 *Federal Register* 32154.

Chapter 10

Conflict of Interest in Investment Advice Within Retirement Plans: An Overview*

John J. Topoleski and Elizabeth A. Myers

Introduction

A pension is a voluntary benefit offered by employers to assist employees in preparing for retirement. Pension plans can be classified along several dimensions, such as whether the plan is a defined benefit (DB) plan (sometimes called a traditional pension) or a defined contribution (DC) plan (like a 401(k) plan), whether the plan sponsor is a private sector or public sector employer, and whether the plan is sponsored by one employer or more than one employer.

Federal pensions laws and regulations govern many aspects of pension plans, such as setting standards for individuals who provide recommendations to private sector plans and plan participants. The Department of Labor (DOL) issued regulations in 1975 that defined investment advice using a five-part test, and in 2016, DOL expanded the definition of investment advice so that more such individuals were subject to a higher standard of conduct. A U.S. court of appeals vacated the rule in 2018, meaning that the five-part test was reinstated. DOL guidance and regulations apply only to private sector plans and do not apply to public sector plans.

---

* This is an edited, reformatted and augmented version of Congressional Research Service Publication No. IF12492, dated September 15, 2023.

In: Retirement Strategies: Analysis of Policies, Investments, and Security
Editor: Ryan M. Powell
ISBN: 979-8-89530-366-5

In September 2023, DOL submitted a proposed rule for review to the Office of Management and Budget (OMB) that DOL said would more appropriately define when recommendations constituted investment advice.

Recommendations Within Pension Plans

Retirement plans are complex, and individuals often rely on financial-services professionals to assist with decisionmaking. For example, an employer might seek out assistance in determining what investments to offer in a 401(k) plan it has established, participants in 401(k) plans might seek assistance in choosing their investments from among the options offered by the plans, or workers who participate in employer-sponsored 401(k) plans might seek assistance on whether to leave their 401(k) account balance in the plan or roll it over into an Individual Retirement Account (IRA) or into another employer's DC plan either upon job change or at retirement.

The compensation structure of some financial-services professionals may give rise to conflicts of interest, particularly if these professionals' recommendations result in larger commissions or otherwise benefit them. These potential conflicts could lead to recommendations that are not in the interests of their clients. By contrast, some financial-services professionals have compensation structures that do not vary based on which products clients choose. This type of compensation structure could mitigate some conflicts of interest. Individuals who provide recommendations to pension plans are required to meet standards of conduct that depend on the individuals' roles and the actions they are taking.

Federal Pensions Law

To protect the interests of private sector pension plan participants and beneficiaries, Congress enacted the Employee Retirement Income Security Act of 1974 (ERISA; P.L. 93-406). ERISA is included in the U.S. Code in both Title 26 (the Internal Revenue Code) and in Title 29 (often called the Labor Code). ERISA contains fiduciary standards, which require that individuals who make decisions for private sector pension plans and their participants (referred to as fiduciaries) adhere to specified standards of conduct.

Prohibited Transaction Exemptions (PTEs)

ERISA also prohibits fiduciaries from engaging in transactions deemed likely to injure pension plans, referred to as *prohibited transactions.* ERISA bars certain transactions between a plan and persons connected to a plan (referred to as a *party in interest*) and between a plan and a plan fiduciary. To facilitate transactions between pension plans and service providers that would otherwise be prohibited by ERISA, a number of *Prohibited Transaction Exemptions (PTEs)* exist, either in statute or as issued by DOL.

Current Investment Advice Regulations

Following the enactment of ERISA, DOL issued regulations in 1975 that created a five-part test to determine whether an individual provided investment advice and thus was subject to the fiduciary standard (see 29 C.F.R.§2510.3-21). In addition, DOL issued a PTE to ensure that fiduciaries could continue to engage in practices that would otherwise be prohibited (such as brokers receiving commissions for products they recommend).

To be held to the 1975 fiduciary standard with respect to his or her recommendations, an individual must (1) make recommendations on investing in, purchasing, or selling securities or other property or give advice as to the value (2) on a regular basis, (3) pursuant to a mutual understanding that the advice (4) would serve as a primary basis for investment decisions and (5) would be individualized to the particular needs of the plan regarding such matters as, among other things, investment policies or strategy, overall portfolio composition, or diversification of plan investments. An individual is not treated as a fiduciary unless each of the five elements of the test is satisfied.

Individuals who provide investment services to retirement investors or plans may also be subject to other regulatory structures. For example, broker-dealers who provide investment recommendations but whose actions do not meet ERISA's five-part test are subject to Securities and Exchange Commission's (SEC's) Regulation Best Interest (Reg BI), which requires that brokers and dealers act in the best interest of their clients. For more information, see CRS Report R47431, *Capital Markets: Overview and Selected Policy Issues in the 118th Congress.*

Recent Regulatory Actions

In October 2010, DOL proposed, and subsequently withdrew in September 2011, an expansion of the definition of *fiduciary advice* that would have made more individuals and their actions subject to the fiduciary advice regulation. In April 2015, DOL issued a revised proposal to broaden the definition of *investment advice* and, in April 2016, issued a final rule and new and amended PTEs.

Under the 2016 rule, the types of activities that would constitute investment advice, if they are done for a fee or other compensation, are recommendations pertaining to the advisability of buying, selling, holding, or exchanging investments; how investments should be invested after being rolled over, transferred, or distributed from an IRA; the management of investments; or IRAs, including whether, in what form, in what amount, and to what destination rollovers, distributions from IRAs, and transfers from IRAs should be made. The rule also described certain activities that did *not* constitute investment advice (e.g., marketing by platform providers, providing general investment education, and executing securities transactions).

Among the new and amended PTEs accompanying the final rule were the Best Interest Contract Exemption, Principal Transactions Exemption, and an amended PTE 84-24, which affects the sale of annuity products. For more information on the 2016 proposed and final rule and PTEs, see CRS Report R44884, *Department of Labor's 2016 Fiduciary Rule: Background and Issues*.

Actions Under the Trump Administration

In March 2017, DOL issued a Temporary Enforcement Policy that indicated it would not initiate enforcement actions against financial advisers or financial institutions that failed to satisfy the conditions of the 2016 regulation or PTE (see Field Assistance Bulletin 2017-01). In March 2018, a U.S. District Court ruled that the 2016 rule was improperly promulgated and in March 2018, a U.S. court of appeals vacated the 2016 rule. This meant that the five-part test was reinstated (see 85 Federal Register 40589-40594, July 20, 2020).

In October 2020, DOL issued PTE 2020-02 which, as with previous PTEs, allows fiduciaries to conduct transactions which are otherwise prohibited. Investment advice fiduciaries who rely on PTE 2020-02 must comply with

Impartial Conduct Standards, which require them to provide advice that is in the best interest of the retirement investor, charge no more than reasonable compensation, and make no misleading statements about investment transactions.

In addition, PTE 2020-02 noted that rollover recommendations from an employer plan to an IRA could be considered investment advice if specified conditions are met—for example, if the investment recommendation were expected to be part of an ongoing relationship. On February 13, 2023, a federal district court struck down the portion of PTE 2020-02 related to the rollover recommendations, and on June 30, 2023, a different federal district court recommended that the guidance related to rollover advice be vacated.

Actions Under the Biden Administration

Since spring 2021, DOL has indicated its intent to release a proposed rule that it said would more appropriately define when a person providing investment advice would be a fiduciary. In September 2023, DOL submitted a proposed rule for review to OMB that DOL said would more appropriately define when recommendations constituted investment advice.

Proponents of a new rule cite the changing retirement landscape since 1975, when most individuals in retirement plans had DB plans compared to the DC plans that are common today. In DC plans, participants have more responsibilities regarding plan contributions, investments, and withdrawals and may need more assistance from financial services professional regarding their choices.

Responses to Notice of Proposed Rule in the 118th Congress

In an August 2023 letter to DOL, Senator Bill Cassidy and Representative Virginia Foxx wrote that they opposed a rule that would revise the definition of fiduciary under ERISA, noting that shifting interpretations "created confusion in the marketplace and unwarranted compliance expenses."

Chapter 11

Americans' Investment Options in Capital Markets for Retirement*

Eva Su

One of the main ways Americans prepare for retirement is to invest in various financial assets. Their investment options include investing directly in stocks, bonds, and investment funds through individual brokerage accounts and investing indirectly through pension funds that invest on behalf of employees. This In Focus examines certain investment options related to retirement preparedness and provides CRS resources on investment management and regulation. CRS does not take a position on the relative merits of particular investments and does not offer or endorse specific investment advice.

Direct and Indirect Investments

According to the Federal Reserve's 2022 Survey of Consumer Finances, close to all American families own some form of financial assets, such as bank accounts, certificates of deposit, stocks, bonds, investment funds, cash value life insurance, retirement accounts, savings bonds, and other financial assets. This In Focus covers investments in capital markets and securities, such as stocks, bonds, mutual funds, exchange-traded funds (ETFs), and digital assets. The investments in these types of instruments could be direct—meaning held in accounts and controlled generally without restriction by the individuals themselves (e.g., in individual brokerage accounts)—or indirect—meaning

* This is an edited, reformatted and augmented version of Congressional Research Service Publication No. IF12674, dated May 24, 2024.

In: Retirement Strategies: Analysis of Policies, Investments, and Security
Editor: Ryan M. Powell
ISBN: 979-8-89530-366-5

through a claim to a pension fund that invests on behalf of individuals or certain retirement accounts with access restrictions and investment options selected by plan sponsors, such as 401(k) plans. While defined contribution retirement plans, including 401(k) plans, normally provide some investment choices for individual decisionmaking, pension funds generally have their fund sponsors act as institutional investors in selecting investment instruments and conducting transactions on behalf of plan participants.

An investment's classification in securities regulations as public or private plays a significant role in how accessible an investment is for direct ownership. Federal securities regulation requires offers and sales of securities, such as stocks and bonds, to be either registered with the Securities and Exchange Commission (SEC) or undertaken pursuant to specific exemptions. Registered offerings, often called public offerings, are available to all types of investors. By contrast, securities offerings that are exempt from certain registration requirements are referred to as private offerings and are generally available only to accredited investors—institutions or individual investors who meet certain net worth, income, or technical expertise thresholds. Thus, while non-accredited individual investors can take direct ownership of public securities, they can generally gain only indirect exposure to private securities markets through certain institutional investors, such as pension funds.

Investment Options

Americans' investment options in capital markets and securities that would generally be available both directly or indirectly include the following instruments if they are publicly traded pursuant to related SEC regulatory requirements: (a) stocks, also called equities or shares, referring to ownership of a firm; (b) bonds, also called fixed income or debt securities, referring to the debt of a firm or a government entity (e.g., corporate bonds and U.S. Treasury securities); (c) mutual funds, also called open- ended funds, referring to a type of public fund that provides continual offering of shares and daily redemptions; (d) closed-end funds, which are publicly traded investment funds that sell a limited number of shares rather than continually offering them; (e) exchange-traded funds, which are investment funds that combine features of both mutual funds and closed-end funds, allowing investors to pool their money into funds with continual share offerings that can also trade on exchanges like a stock; and (f) digital assets, such as cryptocurrencies, referring to digital representations of value.

Investments that are generally available only indirectly to non-accredited investors through institutional investors such as pension funds and certain insurance products include (a) private equity, referring to pooled investment vehicles that typically concentrate on investments not offered to the public, such as ownership stakes in privately held companies; (b) private credit, including direct lending, referring to lending undertaken by nonbank financial institutions and made to small and medium-size private companies that are not publicly traded; (c) venture capital, referring to startup financing for early stage, high- potential firms, such as high-tech startups; and (d) hedge funds, referring to asset management vehicles that generally pool accredited investors' money and invest it on their behalf for a fee and are often identified by their complex investment strategies relative to other conventional funds. See "CRS Resources on Investments" section for more details on the investment options mentioned above.

Investment Risks and Returns

The various investment instruments contain different levels of risks and returns. In well-functioning capital markets, the higher the risks, the higher the expected returns for investors. Typical investment risks include the safety of assets, possibilities of issuer defaults, market volatility, interest rate fluctuation, and liquidity (i.e., how readily and quickly investors could get their money back without affecting the price). For example, Figure 1 illustrates medium-term historical returns for multiple public and private market investments using data consolidated by an asset manager.

Risk versus return considerations apply to retirement investment in particular ways because of the long-term nature of a retirement timeline. Even small differences in returns can lead to large differences in accumulated assets over the long run. In addition, volatility over short time periods is less important when retirement assets are not going to be liquidated for many years or even decades.

Arguably, then, retirement investment would be more attracted to high-return investment options. However, some of the higher-return investment opportunities available are private investments. That means that (1) if individuals could gain access directly to certain private investments, it may help their retirement readiness, but they may also face higher risks; and (2) pension fund sponsors may gravitate to the higher-risk, higher-volatility, higher-return options. For example, CalPERS, the largest U.S. public pension plan with around $500 billion in assets under management, announced in March 2024 that it plans to increase its total private market allocation from 33% of plan assets to 40% to"maximize returns from the highest performing asset classes."

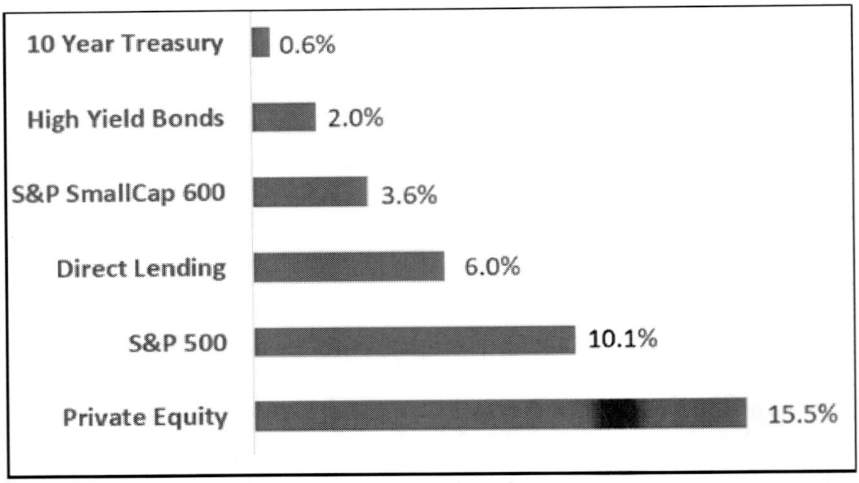

Source: CRS using data from Kohlberg Kravis Roberts.

Figure 1. Annualized Returns of Different Investments During the Past Five Years Ending December 5, 2023.

Policy Issues Concerning Investments

To prepare for retirement, Americans could save more or seek better investment returns. Policy considerations from an investment and capital markets regulation perspective (regulation of retirement savings account operations is beyond the scope of this In Focus) include

Investors' Access to Potentially Higher-Return Investment Opportunities

While broadened investment options, such as increased access to private equity, may provide higher returns and diversification benefits, it also comes with potential risk exposure and financial risk management challenges.

Financial Stability Concerns

With the increased investment flow into the less-transparent private securities markets, the markets' increased size and complexity have drawn financial stability concerns. Relative to the more transparent public securities markets, private markets pose more challenges for market-wide risk assessments and systemic risk monitoring.

Financial Education and Financial Literacy

As complex investment options become available to individual investors, increased financial education may be necessary to enable sophisticated investment decisionmaking.

Availability of Regulated Financial Advice Intermediaries

Given the challenges facing financial education, increased access to investment intermediaries who could help individuals to navigate complex investment decisions (e.g., SEC-regulated investment advisers and broker-dealers) may benefit those individuals' retirement savings outcome.

Financial Readiness for Retirement

Retirement readiness does not have a standardized measure. Each family or individual may perceive their savings goals and retirement financial needs differently. Surveys from investment management firms (e.g., Fidelity, Goldman Sachs, and Northwestern Mutual) uniformly convey the existence of retirement savings gaps. Investment options and asset allocation could affect retirement preparedness. See CRS Reports R46617 and R47341, coordinated by Zhe Li, for more on income for older Americans.

CRS Resources on Investments

CRS has multiple product series to address investment regulation and investment instruments.

Investment Regulation Overview

CRS In Focus IF11062, Introduction to Financial Services: Capital Markets
CRS In Focus IF11714, Introduction to Financial Services: The Securities and Exchange Commission (SEC)
CRS Report R45957, Capital Markets: Asset Management and Related Policy Issues
CRS Report R47431, Capital Markets: Overview and Selected Policy Issues in the 118th Congress
CRS Report R45221, Capital Markets, Securities Offerings, and Related Policy Issues
CRS In Focus IF11278, Accredited Investor Definition and Private Securities Markets
CRS In Focus IF10747, Private Securities Offerings: Background and Legislation

Investment Instruments

CRS Report R47309, Money Market Mutual Funds: Policy Concerns and Reform Options
CRS Report R45318, Exchange-Traded Funds (ETFs): Issues for Congress
CRS Report R47053, Private Equity and Capital Markets Policy
CRS In Focus IF12642, Private Credit: Trends and Policy Issues
CRS In Focus IF12511, Hedge Funds: Background and Policy Issues
CRS In Focus IF12412, Venture Capital Operations and Regulation
CRS Report R46208, Digital Assets and SEC Regulation

Index

G

H

I

T

U

V

W

Y